# ADVANCE PRAISE FOR *UNSCREWED*

"This book should be required reading in schools across the US. Honest, sometimes painful, and brimming with empathy. It couldn't have come at a better time. Jaclyn draws you in to a world of possibility. I am hopeful reading her writing. There is so much work to do to change the systems in which we live, and Jaclyn gives us practical, applicable ways of doing it."
— Tatiana Maslany, Emmy-winning star of *Orphan Black*

"*Unscrewed* is not just a book you should read, it's a book you'll love to read. Jaclyn Friedman's writing sings, and makes thinking about necessary and important issues a real pleasure. I can't wait to read it again."
— Jessica Valenti, author of the *New York Times*–bestselling *Sex Object*

"In this visionary and necessary book, Jaclyn Friedman cuts through the hypocrisy, mixed messages, and confusion about sex, women, and power. *Unscrewed* is firmly pro-pleasure, but also bitingly critical of the same old sexism dressed up in the language of 'empowerment'— it's power, Friedman argues, that matters, and she neatly eviscerates the formal and informal barriers that keep women from accessing it. Required reading for anyone who cares not just about women and sex but about building a better society, *Unscrewed* will leave you with just one question: Can Jaclyn lead the new sexual revolution and unscrew us all?"
— Jill Filipovic, author of *The H-Spot*

"There are so many things to love about *Unscrewed*. What I love most is that I feel smarter, more powerful, and far less crazy after reading this book. From the very first page, I realized that 'It isn't just me. Other women struggle with how to have the hot empowered sex feminists are always raving about.' I wish I'd had this book when I was twenty. I'm so glad to have it now, to read, to teach to my students, and to share with my homegirls. Jaclyn doesn't just lay out all the problems with contemporary discourses on sex. She also shows us the way forward by profiling some of the pathbreaking feminist badasses that are leading the way. It goes without saying that Jaclyn herself is one of these bad-asses. Every chapter reminds us in tangible ways that these problems can be solved. We can get this right. There is hope. And the very first step is to get and read *Unscrewed*."

— Brittney Cooper, Crunk Feminist Collective cofounder and author of *Eloquent Rage*

"Gender equality has enough superficial solutions, and *Unscrewed* is a precise rebuke to the notion that signifying progress is enough. Jaclyn Friedman's book reminds men that it is our job to end misogyny and rape culture, and tells women not to expect anything less."

— Jamil Smith, journalist and essayist

"As our society has become increasingly obsessed with the paradoxical pursuit of simultaneously controlling and liberating women sexually, there is no better expert than Jaclyn Friedman to help us dissect the complicated and surreal world we are currently living in. Sexuality has always been a tough and complicated topic for women but Jaclyn somehow always manages to make it fun and easy to talk about. You will find yourself nodding in agreement and whispering 'yas' over and over as she captures the essence of every thought and feeling you've always had, but never shared. Jaclyn Friedman is the quintessential modern sex expert, at once understanding and empathetic yet honest and raw."

— Elizabeth Plank, senior producer and correspondent, Vox Media

Women, Sex, Power,
and How to Stop

# UNSCREWED

Letting the System
Screw Us All

## JACLYN FRIEDMAN

SEAL PRESS

Seal Press
Hachette Book Group
1290 Avenue of the Americas
New York, NY 10104
www.sealpress.com

Printed in the United States of America
First Edition: November 2017

Published by Seal Press, an imprint of Perseus Books, LLC, a subsidiary of Hachette Book Group, Inc.

The publisher is not responsible for websites (or their content) that are not owned by the publisher.

*Print book interior design by Jeff Williams*

Library of Congress Cataloging-in-Publication Data

Names: Friedman, Jaclyn, author.
Title: Unscrewed : women, sex, power, and how to stop letting the system screw us all / Jaclyn Friedman.
Description: Berkeley : Seal Press, 2017.
Identifiers: LCCN 2017023481| ISBN 9781580056410 (hardback) | ISBN 9781580056427 (ebook)
Subjects: LCSH: Feminism—United States. | Women—Sexual behavior—United States. | Sexism—United States. | Sex role—United States. | BISAC: SOCIAL SCIENCE / Women's Studies. | SOCIAL SCIENCE / Feminism & Feminist Theory.
Classification: LCC HQ1426 .F8475 2017 | DDC 305.420973—dc23
LC record available at https://lccn.loc.gov/2017023481

LSC-C

10  9  8  7  6  5  4  3  2  1

*In her hips, there's revolutions.*
— BIKINI KILL

# CONTENTS

## INTRODUCTION

# WE THE FAUXPOWERED

YOU MAY HAVE thought that we already had a sexual revolution. You may have heard that women are free to go wild now, that we can do what we want with our bodies. You may have even heard that we're in charge now when it comes to sex, and that it's men who have to cater to us.

But most women don't quite feel it. Like Leigh Anne Arthur, a South Carolina high school teacher who sent her husband a nude photo of herself for Valentine's Day. A few weeks later, a student snuck into Arthur's desk while she was out of the room between classes. The student opened Arthur's cell phone, found the naked selfie, and distributed it to all of his classmates. Arthur lost her job. In doing so, she joined a long line of female teachers fired for what they did with their private sex lives on their own time.

Getting fired for being sexual would have been preferable to what happened to Janese Talton-Jackson. In the wee hours of a Friday morning in 2016, Charles McKinney made a pass at her in a Pittsburgh bar. She declined his attentions. He followed her to her car and shot her dead.

If you're a woman, you know this story in your body. You know what that flinch of fear feels like when a man turns his sexual attention on you. You know that churning feeling in your gut urging you to let him down easy. Or the bile you swallow when you decide it might be safer not to say no at all.

1

At conferences, colleges, and over friends' coffee tables, I'm struck by a common agony in what women tell me about their sex lives. They want to know—and because I'm a national expert on women's sexuality, they think I can answer—*why don't I feel free?* They're bombarded with messages telling them that every choice they make makes them more powerful, and yet they're constantly looking over their shoulders, guarding against a laundry list of possible consequences, measuring their sex lives against what they know or imagine about others', and using that comparison to find themselves wanting. That's true whether they're college freshmen or young graduates, stay-at-home moms or power professionals.

It's not always a job at stake, or the fear of a man with a gun. Take, for instance, my friend Louise, a twentysomething media professional and outspoken feminist, who confessed to me that she has compulsively clicked on every celebrity sex tape and nude photo leak published in the last decade—even the skeezy, immoral, stolen stuff, like Jennifer Lawrence's photos. She clicks not because this type of porn gets her off, but because she can't get a handle on her "reptilian curiosity" about famous women's sex lives. "I want to know how girls that gorgeous and fun do relationships," she wrote to me, too sheepish to admit it out loud. (For what it's worth, Louise, I barely managed to avoid clicking on Lawrence's photos myself, for similar reasons.)

Other women have expressed more poignant distress. I remember one college student, in particular, who came to one of my talks years ago—let's call her Claire. Claire lit up when I said that I didn't identify with the "sex-positive" movement, despite dedicating my career to improving the way we fuck. It's been too long for me to reliably quote her directly, but her meaning left a permanent mark. She said that she didn't feel welcome at sex-positive events because sex hadn't been positive for her. What she needed more than cheerleading about butt plugs and lube—that is, the standard fare of many college sex talks—was a place where she could be real about her sexual pain and struggles. When discussing sex, she felt just as much a freak among liberals as among conservatives.

Women like Louise and Claire strike me as like Neo at the beginning of *The Matrix* (just the first movie, before things got terrible). They've got this little splinter in their minds telling them something is wrong with their sex lives. Their doubts won't go away and are driving them crazy. Most of the books on the shelf are telling them this is somehow their fault, that they'll feel better if they gather more self-confidence, more techniques and tips, more experience. But even most of us who've read all the books and tried all (or at least most of) the tips are still plagued by insecurity.

Individual solutions don't heal our sex lives because the biggest problems we're facing aren't individual. They're systemic. We don't need a pill to make us want sex more—we need a world where straight men aren't almost 50 percent more likely to have an orgasm with a partner than straight women are.[1] We need universal access to quality sex education. We need a media ecosystem shimmering with portrayals of three-dimensional women who get to be sexual on their own terms. We need rape to be rare and swiftly punished. We need a new cultural definition of masculinity. We need a government that recognizes our autonomy over our own bodies.

We're living in a particular moment that I like to call the era of *fauxpowerment*, a time when shiny pictures of individual women wielding some symbol of sexual power are used to distract us from the still mostly retrograde and misogynist status quo. "Empowerment" is an unstable illusion requiring constant upkeep. We look externally for cues on how to behave sexually because we're not yet free to trust our own instincts—or, sometimes, even to hear them.

Fauxpowerment is the Matrix. It's all around us, whether we're looking right, toward abstinence-only sex ed programs and anti-choice politicians, or left, to rah-rah sex cheerleading and raunchy pop culture. It's Kenneth Branagh selling his Cinderella reboot as "modern" because Cinderella says the word *courage* a lot, even though she's just as passive as the classic animated version. It's Anastasia Steele in *Fifty Shades of Grey*, portrayed as "choosing her choice" while she's stalked and abused by a controlling billionaire.

Fauxpowerment is Meghan Trainor's hit song "Dear Future Husband." A sample lyric: "After every fight / Just apologize / And maybe then I'll let you try and rock my body right." That's fauxpowerment in a nutshell: sexism with bright colors and a funky beat. It's like that mythical nail polish J-Law's *American Hustle* character, Rosalyn, is on the hunt for—the one that smells like flowers, but with garbage. Our current sexual culture is built on the rotten foundations of a gutted, aging, unfinished sexual revolution, but it's got a bright, candy-colored coat of paint slapped on top. From a distance, it looks like a cheery and fun place to hang out. Once we're a little closer, we can see how treacherous it is, but most of us climb on board anyway, because we don't see any other option.

Advertisements do some of fauxpowerment's most enthusiastic cheerleading these days, especially when they feature "real women." *Don't worry*, these campaigns tell us: *even if you don't look like a model, you too can be ogled.* More surprising are the respected, even wonky feminists contributing fauxpowered messages to the zeitgeist. Naomi Wolf recently wrote a whole book, *Vagina: A New Biography*, about how every straight woman needs deep, slow regular G-spot stimulation—ideally with a penis—to be truly self-actualized.

Fauxpowerment is why women are confused about sex. Fauxpowerment is why we're unsatisfied. It's the reason why we feel that disconnect between the sexuality we experience and the one pop culture tells us we're experiencing, why few of us are as secure in our sex lives as we think we're supposed to be. Every day, we're being sold an idea of empowerment and pushed away from the actual power to support it. Telling us to value ourselves more is not the answer. We need to create a culture in which we have more actual value.

The question, of course, is how to go about doing that. Breaking free of fauxpowerment is not easy, even when it looks that way and even if we're trying really, really hard. That Matrix analogy is no joke: it's hard to see a system clearly when we're trapped in it. But that's just what I plan to do in the pages that follow—expose the way cultural forces like economics, government, technology, and the law are perpetuating the culture of women's sexual fauxpowerment and explore how we can unscrew ourselves from this system one step at a time.

Along the way, you will meet a merry band of pioneers: sexual revolutionaries striking out in new directions, blazing imaginative trails in an effort to overthrow the misogynist messages that have shaped all of our pasts and to make it easier for each of us to figure out what we want from our sexual futures. None of these people are prophets, but each of them is asking crucial questions and providing part of the solution, too.

These stories are case studies of what's in the way of possible. They show us that there's no single strategy to get unscrewed, that a wild array of approaches is necessary for transforming such a complex web of systems. Most of all, they serve as invitation and example—we're all caught in this mess together, and we're all going to have to pitch in to free ourselves.

Some of these pioneers are leaders in their fields or visionary full-time activists. Some are ordinary citizens whose attempts to muddle through the morass of our sexual culture are instructive in how much they reveal about what we're all up against.

Take Isabelle Cass (not her real name), for example. I met Cass years ago when she was a radical cheerleader, showing up at feminist events in saucy outfits with her squad. If she's a little bit of a hippie—she's currently building a career as a midwife, and her bedroom is adorned with a moon calendar and a magpie wing gifted to her by a lover—then she's a hippie with a critical, feminist worldview who can do a perfect smoky eye while talking about her sex life.

The first time we met, I was instantly charmed by her cool-girl ease and her radical politics. I was more than a little jealous of the confidence with which she seemed to inhabit her body. But that was just me yielding to the siren call of fauxpowerment: the idea that if I could be a little more like some shiny ideal, I could be truly happy in my body and in my bed.

What I didn't know was that, at the same time Cass was cheekily shaking her pompons at political rallies, she was making a living having sex with strangers for money, and not because she liked that work.

Escorting was not a good experience for Cass. Raised in a Pentecostal household, she already held profound shame about her body and her sexuality. Escorting only exacerbated that dynamic. "It can be hard to say no in general, in sexual situations," she told me. "And a million times more so is [that] true at work, because it's not just a fear of 'will this person like me,' it's also like it's your livelihood and it's your pay- check. [Clients] can hold shit over your head. What you're doing is ille- gal, and they know where your apartment is that you work out of, and they could report you in a second with no consequence to them ever."

Nevertheless, Cass had run out of borrowing power a semester shy of her college degree and was drowning in debt, with no diploma to show for it. For a long time, escorting was the only way she could find to feed herself.

While I was blaming myself for failing to live up to the glossy sur- face she was projecting (Maybe if I could just lose twenty pounds? Maybe if I bought whatever eyeliner she's using?), Cass was struggling hard to create some kind of feeling of control over her sexuality and wondering, like Louise and Claire and most every woman, why she couldn't seem to get truly free. The details of her story might seem extreme when compared with most women's lives, but the themes all rhyme. It's just that fauxpowerment so often pits us against each other that we fail to notice.

Cass and I recently met up so I could help her prepare for a one-afternoon stint as an "alternative" art model, a day that turned into an object lesson in how little power is afforded to even the women held up as symbols of sexual empowerment. Founded in Brooklyn and now boasting chapters in over a hundred cities around the world, Dr. Sketchy's Anti-Art School is an art event that replaces the class- room with bars and booze and life drawing of burlesque and other underground performers, almost all of whom are women. The idea behind the venue is cool: open life drawing to people who don't have access to art school. Introduce visual artists to performance artists, fostering cross-arts collaboration. Celebrate the female form in all its widely varied glory. It sounds like the epitome of bohemian sex posi- tivity. But it turned out there was little more respect here for the body and experience of the model than there is at your average seedy strip joint by the highway.

The gig started out okay. Turnout wasn't near what Cass had been promised; maybe nine people showed up instead of the anticipated dozens, which matters when you're getting paid in tips and a cut of the door. But the artists who were there were respectful and friendly. It was after her second costume change that things turned sour. She was looking into the middle distance, wearing next-to-nothing while leaning one hand on a stool and balancing in heels on the tiny wooden platform in the back of the room, when her face went hard.

"Eyes to the ground, gentlemen," she said to a group of men who had just arrived, with the cool seriousness of someone who is used to being obeyed. "Drink or don't, but don't stare."

Our host fluttered to her side, making soft noises of disapproval. Cass had none of it. "You don't need to shush me," she snapped without breaking her pose. We all fell silent while some aggro dude-rock rang raucously from the bar's speakers.

Dr. Sketchy's held its first session in 2005, the same year Brad left Jennifer for Angelina. *Girls Gone Wild* and *Desperate Housewives* were at their peak. It could easily have been called the Year of the Bad Girl. The culture howled that being sexually transgressive was the fast pass to power for women. Meanwhile, the federal government was spending over a hundred million dollars on abstinence-only education,[2] while countless untested rape kits piled in cities across the country, abandoned for lack of funding and police departments' mistrust of rape victims, among other reasons.[3]

Some of those kits have since been tested, mostly thanks to public pressure and private fund-raising. But a lot has gone downhill. In the last decade state legislatures imposed hundreds of obstacles to abortion access. Our federal government has been taken over by men who rape and beat the women in their lives, whose general attitudes toward women are essentially indistinguishable from those of men's rights activists.[4] The head of Health and Human Services openly supports the right of companies to fire women simply for using birth control. But somehow we're supposed to be "empowered" by starlets competing to wear the least clothing possible on high-fashion red carpets. I've got nothing against people who show their underwear in public; I've done it myself more than once. But it's a poor substitute for actual power.

Just ask Cass. The men who walked in weren't there to draw her. They were just a few dudebros who wandered in for a drink and saw a hot chick onstage in her underwear. That changed everything for Cass, who had agreed to figure model for paying artists, not give a free show to some random guys off the street. Yet there were no modesty screens anywhere. No one was posted at the door to provide context and guidelines to people as they came in. Dr. Sketchy's has been operating at this venue for eight years but didn't bother to warn Cass that this might happen.

The hosts of Dr. Sketchy's made a mistake so common it's hard to even blame them for it: confusing a woman's willingness to be publicly sexual with her invincibility. I could even believe it's an honest mistake; after all, it really does take a powerful bravery to appear unapologetically sexual while female. Just ask any girl who's shared a private naked selfie with a guy who goes on to distribute it widely. But confusing the courage to risk such outcomes with the possession of some bulletproof magic is, in practice, cruel. Strong women are not superheroes, nor should we be required to be. We still possess a complex humanity, complete with vulnerabilities, limits, and straight-up personal preferences. We're also not always as powerful as we look.

The easy signifiers of sexual empowerment that pass for liberation these days—the kind of alt-pinup aesthetic that Dr. Sketchy's trades in, the endless parade of female pop stars selling sexual transgression, the *Act Like a Lady, Think Like a Man* school of "how to trick a man into marrying you" relationship advice—are not cutting it. Shifting uncomfortably there on that stage, Cass needs what we all need: a better range of economic and creative options so she has more choices in how to pay off her student loans, an empathetic community, and a culture that recognizes her as a full human being with the right to do as she pleases with her body. Not just another venue for her to be ogled.

Fauxpowerment is a quintessentially American trap. It proposes to solve a structural societal problem—that women like Cass aren't viewed as full human beings with as much inherent value and sexual autonomy as men have—with an individualistic solution: just claim your sexuality, ladies! The freakier you get, the freer you'll be. But we can't pretend our way to sexual liberation. A woman saying and doing what she wants is not free if she gets punished for it. And a woman who doesn't feel free enough to know what she wants, a woman who is just saying and doing what she thinks she should want, isn't free either.

I don't mean to suggest that fauxpowerment is an actual conspiracy: the evil forces of patriarchy trying to hypnotize the masses with see-through dresses and power anthems. It's more complicated than that. When Beyoncé famously sang "If you liked it then you should've put a ring on it," I doubt she thought she was reinforcing the idea that women are property for whom the best outcome is to find someone to own them forever. E. L. James wrote *Fifty Shades of Grey* because it was the sexual fantasy she most wanted to read, not because she wanted to give real, actual men an excuse to non-consensually tie up their real, actual girlfriends or stalk and assault women. That's still what happened. Intentions aren't magic. But they are important to understand if we want to shift the frame from fauxpowerment to power.

Most fauxpowerment is perpetrated at the intersection of wish fulfillment and a failure of imagination. I have no doubt that the hosts at Dr. Sketchy's imagine that they're providing a "safe space" for women with "alternative" sexual identities to get the recognition and adoration they deserve. But the organizers have clearly failed to imagine what the experience might be like for the women they claim to be celebrating.

"I just feel really gross and slimy," Cass told me the morning after she modeled there. "You know that moment in the morning when you don't remember something, and then you do? I just feel so silly and small for putting myself in a position where I did something fairly harmful and didn't even get paid hardly at all."

Cass agreed to model at Dr. Sketchy's for the same reason she got into sex work. She needed the money. That's not to say that she didn't expect it to be better than seeing a private client. Several times she mentioned to me that she had only ever been to this (actually very straight) venue once for an LGBT event, so she had mistaken it for a gay bar. She thought she was walking into a community she identified with, a context that she knew.

It's not hard to imagine how that would have made a difference. One of the main differences between fauxpowerment and real sexual power is whether, when we make sexual decisions, we have the support of a broader community. There's a big difference between playacting freedom and being actually free. All kinds of people and institutions, from media, government, and churches to our parents, friends, the host of an art happening, and even some random dudes walking into a bar on a Sunday afternoon, they all have a say-so in how sexually free we are, whether we admit it or not.

That's why fauxpowerment sells so well. Few of us know where to start the glacial work of changing the culture. In the meantime, we're desperate for something to make us feel better about the world and our position in it, something easy and soothing that can help us through the moment.

## Why We Can't Be Complacent

Living in a fauxpowered world is frustrating, to say the least. But the stakes are actually much higher than frustration. When women are encouraged to just "free ourselves" in a world that hasn't caught up, it can get dangerous.

Just ask Shaunna Lane, a twenty-three-year-old from Essex, England, who was struggling with hating her body when a model friend suggested she do a private nude shoot to boost her confidence. It worked in the short term: she felt so good about how she looked in the photos that she even shared them with her boyfriend. It's when her boyfriend became her ex that things turned. She got flooded with Facebook messages from men she'd never met, some containing bold propositions, others threatening to rape her. It turned out that those "empowering" photos had been posted to a "revenge porn" site, complete with her name and social media accounts. Even after she paid a $400 extortion to have the photos removed from that site—a common practice on these sites, which make their money off such fees—they continued to circulate, popping up on the Facebook accounts of acquaintances and showing up when you searched her name on Google. Lane was terrified and too humiliated to even leave her apartment.[5]

Fauxpowerment doesn't protect women from the very real consequences of sexual oppression. I'm far from the first person to point this out. In 2015, feminist thinker Leora Tanenbaum published *I Am Not a Slut*, an entire book detailing the ways women and girls are punished for being perceived as "sluts," even as they try to claim the identity positively for themselves. Although her research is on point and her intentions are pure, she ultimately concludes that claiming slut as an identity is too dangerous and should be abandoned as a practice. She falls prey to the same individual-based solutions that hobble the fauxpowerment advocates and the handwringing concern-trolls of the Internet.

Tanenbaum is right that identifying as a slut is a dangerous proposition for many women, even when they choose it for themselves. I may have control over what I mean when I call myself a slut, but I can't control how others will use that identity against me. I don't just mean the extreme examples like Lane's (who certainly didn't claim the moniker, but still had it publicly attached to her name) or the constant deployment of *slut* in blaming women when someone else rapes them. Tanenbaum rightly identifies that the everyday shaming power of the word is enough to discourage young women from taking important steps like getting birth control and managing sexually transmitted infection prevention. But responding to that danger by limiting what girls and women can call ourselves is playing the same game as all the people who would tell women just to never take naked pictures if we don't want to be shamed on the Internet. Telling us to narrow our sexual lives to avoid misogynist violence and shame means accepting that misogynist violence and shame are inevitable. They aren't.

Advising us to color inside the lines of sexual oppression also paints a dangerous line between the "smart" girls who don't make choices about their sexuality likely to draw negative attention and the "foolish" ones who heedlessly do. It's an understandable impulse. If there are rules we can follow, we feel in control of whether or not we'll be targeted. But it's a trap for two reasons. First, any framework that splits women into a "smart about sex" camp and a "foolish" one is a virgin/whore dichotomy in sheep's clothing. Monitoring some arbitrary line between the good girls and the bad ones gives quarter to those who will use those categories to blame and target women, no matter how pure our intentions. Policing women's sexual choices also expends critical energy we could be using to make a better world for everyone. (Just because it's corny doesn't mean it isn't true.)

Still, warning girls to be "smart" might be worth the risk if it actually kept anyone safe. But "good" girls who aren't doing anything sexual in public are harmed by fauxpowerment all the time. In a case currently wending through the courts, one fifteen-year-old girl on Long Island is suing her school district after her Spanish teacher raped her. The district has successfully petitioned the court for access to her entire private Facebook history because it alleges her postings disprove her claims of emotional damage. The evidence? Pictures of her drinking with friends and happily embracing her boyfriend.

Let me spell that out for you: the argument is that individual moments in which a teen girl appeared happy prove that she suffered no emotional damage after her Spanish teacher raped her. Meanwhile, men on street corners everywhere holler at women to "smile," and Katy Perry exhorts those who feel like they're "already buried deep" to just "own the night like the Fourth of July." But if you try to live up to that fauxpowerful anthem while female, pictures of you owning the night can be used to argue your rape wasn't that big of a deal.

It's time to stop accepting the rules and start changing them. It's time to make a world where women feel free to say no to anal or yes to a threesome and, most importantly, to discover and explore what they genuinely want, free of threats, shame, and violence. But that's going to take some doing.

Among other things, it's going to take getting comfortable with what it means for women to have actual power. And it's not necessarily going to be so sexy, especially not at first. Over burgers and drinks after Dr. Sketchy's, Cass told me that the one thing she really loved about the experience was seeing the art it produced. "You can kind of see the progression [in the artists' sketches]," she mused, "of me feeling kind of awkward at first and then getting a little comfortable and then getting pissed. I really like the blue one that makes me look super harsh. That's how I felt."

I get it, at least a little. Seeing my anger and pain validated by the culture around me has been at least as empowering an experience as seeing some aspect of my sexuality celebrated. In the darkest days after I was sexually assaulted in college, one of the few things that made me feel powerful was a song, "Me and a Gun," a haunting first-person account of being raped in a parking lot, performed by Tori Amos. I played it over and over and over. It was all at once a repudiation of shame, an affirmation that I wasn't alone, and a suggestion of how I might proceed from here. Real female sexual power means there's room in the culture for all of our sexual experiences—not just the pretty ones.

"Me and a Gun" was inspired by the rape scene in *Thelma and Louise*, a film that rejects both fauxpowerment and acquiescence to the status quo. In it, the titular pair set off on a weekend road trip but soon become fugitive outlaws when Louise shoots a man she finds raping Thelma in the parking lot of a roadside bar. There are no you-go-girl messages here, just a clear-eyed look at the costs and benefits of seizing your power from a system that doesn't want you to have it. Thelma and Louise know that real sexual power for women requires real personal cost and real social upheaval. But they also know that the price they've been paying for staying screwed is even higher than that.

The pioneers I profile in this book know it, too, which is why they're not settling for fauxpowerment. They're devoting (and sometimes risking) their lives to challenge the Hollywood bosses, free our government from the grip of the Religious Right, and dismantle and rebuild modern masculinity—whatever it takes to build a world where women don't have to drive off a cliff to be truly free.

I can't wait to introduce you to them.

**CHAPTER ONE**

# THIS IS NOT MY BEAUTIFUL HOUSE

S ETTING OUT TO write this book, I knew I had to do one thing first: drive out to Mount Holyoke College, where longtime activist Loretta Ross was at the time in residence as a writing fellow. I'm tempted to call Ross the Forrest Gump of the modern women's movement, except that she didn't just happen to be there for so many key events—she made them happen. And she started right around the time when women were supposedly freed by the sexual revolution.

Loretta Ross had no choice but to join the counterculture. Born Black and poor, the sixth child of eight, to a conservative mother and Army staff sergeant father, Ross was raped by a stranger at age eleven, then sexually abused by an older cousin when she was fourteen years old. ("That kind of made a feminist out of me," she told the women's documentary project Makers, in the understatement of the century.) The second violation resulted in a pregnancy in 1969, and when the San Antonio school district tried to bar her from reenrolling after she decided to keep the baby, she and her family successfully sued to insist on her right to finish her education.

After terminating an unintended pregnancy in her early twenties, she decided to get the Dalkon Shield inserted, because it was said to be safer than taking the Pill and didn't require her to adhere to a rigid daily routine. The Dalkon Shield, an early intrauterine device, had a string hanging from it to help the doctor remove it when the time came. But that string also turned out to act like a wick, drawing bacteria from the vagina up through the cervix and into the uterus. Ross started getting fevers and went to a doctor, who misdiagnosed her with a rare venereal disease. By the time the cause of her illness was correctly diagnosed, her fallopian tubes had ruptured and she required a hysterectomy. Ross became one of the first women to sue the makers of the Dalkon Shield, opening the door to a massive class action lawsuit that forced the IUD off the market and spurred the Food and Drug Administration to require testing and approval of all medical devices (a standard that, unbelievably, had not previously been mandated).

A few years later, a friend she'd met through housing rights activism convinced her to visit the DC Rape Crisis Center, the first such project in the country. Ross was skeptical going in, but once she got there, she was hooked. "All of a sudden, I was able to put it all into context. That I wasn't alone. I wasn't the only young girl who experienced this. Who couldn't get an abortion. Who ended up raising the child of her rapist. These were things that were very important to find out." She started volunteering at the center in 1978 and by 1979 was its executive director. And from there, her feminist career really took off.

There's no bad reason to talk with Loretta Ross. Somehow both regal and profane, she's always sharp, good company. But I'm starting with her here because she's spent her lifetime trying to make real the false promises of the sexual revolution. After all, none of Ross's rebellions would have been required if the sixties sexual revolution had really freed women. And the myth that it has is one of the basic premises of fauxpowerment. We've already had a revolution, the thinking goes, so if we don't feel liberated, there must be something wrong with us personally, individually, something only the fauxpowerment peddler can help us with. If we're to defeat the myth of fauxpowerment once and for all, it helps to know how it was constructed and what's worked so far to leverage it into real power for women.

For sure, some things are better for women on the sex front now than they were before the 1960s. It's now legal for queer women to dance with (and even marry!) each other. Having access to the Pill is certainly much better than not having it, and birth control technology has improved significantly in the intervening decades. But we still find ourselves careening like pinballs between the expectations that our virtue lies in keeping our legs closed and that our value lies in our willingness to open them. The last sexual revolution may have changed some of the rules about which kinds of behavior were permissible for which kinds of women, but it didn't change the fact that there are still rules that treat women's sexuality as a volatile but precious resource that needs to be properly managed. It's a pernicious enough attitude that Canadian scientists were compelled to do a longitudinal study to prove that vaccinating middle school girls against human papillomavirus doesn't cause them to become more promiscuous because so many parents were reluctant to allow the cancer-preventing shots for fear they would turn their daughters slutty. That is, they would rather their daughters have cancer than sex.[1] So, where did the last revolution go so wrong? Understanding where it got lost, and what's happened since, is the only way to find our way to real sexual freedom.

Like most revolutions, the sexual revolution simmered for a long time before it boiled over in the 1960s. And, like most revolutions, it wasn't caused by just one thing. Ask any historian, and you'll get multiple explanations for its genesis: trends toward urbanization in the first half of the twentieth century, women entering the workforce in greater and greater numbers, the exposure of World War II soldiers to European sexual mores, and so on.

Here's what most of them agree on: premarital sex was on the rise decades before the birth control pill was introduced and that number would have been even higher if people weren't getting married so young, at an average age of twenty for women and twenty-two for men. As cultural historian Stephanie Coontz put it, "When it came to sexual intercourse, young people were not taught how to 'say no,' they were simply handed wedding rings."[2]

What really changed in the 1960s was that more people started admitting that this was happening, and that it might in fact be okay. That's in part thanks to the legalization of the Pill in 1960, which by nature required a mass conversation about the fact that women like to have sex for pleasure. It certainly was a hit. By the mid-1960s, the Pill had become the most popular form of birth control in the entire country, with 6.5 million users.

But it wasn't just the Pill shaking things up. The civil rights movement, gay and lesbian liberation fights, the Kennedy assassination, the rise of hippie culture, even the British Invasion all contributed to a chaotic cultural moment in which the future felt profoundly uncertain, young people reigned, and challenging authority was the thing to do. Hedonism became conflated with liberation, planting the seeds of fauxpowerment for decades to come.

Still, there's no denying it: the late sixties were great for sex in many ways. Masters and Johnson published their landmark study, demolishing then-dominant ideas about women's limited sexual capacity. Syphilis was finally under control, HPV hadn't been discovered yet, and HIV didn't exist. Many men's colleges were going coed. More women entering the workforce meant fewer women dependent on marriage for financial security.

But as the saying goes, freedom isn't free. And neither, as it turned out, was "free love." At least not for everyone. The Pill was only really available to middle-class (mostly white) married women; shame and a range of state laws kept it controlled by private-practice doctors, who could prescribe or deny it to their patients according to their own biases. That meant poorer single women, often women of color, were the most likely to suffer the gruesome consequences of botched illegal abortions or to be saddled with unwanted motherhood.

Even for women with access to contraception, the sixties revolution promised more than it delivered. When the taboo started to lift from women having sex outside of marriage, women still didn't have enough cultural power and individual know-how to demand a sex life that would be good for them. "With every man knowing you were armed with the pill," remembers British journalist Virginia Ironside in a 2011 essay, "pregnancy was no longer a reason to say 'no' to sex. And men exploited this mercilessly. Now, for them, 'no' always meant 'yes.' . . . Often it seemed easier and, believe it or not, more polite, to sleep with a man than to chuck him out of your flat. . . . [Men] continued to satisfy their own needs and never for a moment considered whether the women they were having sex with found it pleasurable or satisfying. Most of us girls, at least those on the London rock scene as I was, didn't have a clue as to what sex could be like when it was good."[3]

It's no accident, then, that at the same time the sexual revolution was brewing, the women's movement was taking new shape as well. The year 1966 saw the founding of the National Organization for Women (NOW), and 1969, appropriately enough, brought us NARAL (then the National Association for the Repeal of Abortion Laws, now the National Abortion Rights Action League). The next year, the very first edition of *Our Bodies, Ourselves* rolled off the presses and onto the streets.

This new wave of feminists echoed Ironside's critique. Writer, activist, and cultural critic Ellen Willis called out how "male [sexual] libertarians intensified women's sexual anxieties by equating repression with the desire for love and commitment, and exalting sex without emotion or attachment as the ideal" while simultaneously "women who took too literally their supposed right to sexual freedom and pleasure were regularly put down as 'easy,' 'aggressive,' or 'promiscuous.'"[4] Alix Kates Shulman put it more bluntly: "Women are discovering," she wrote in her classic essay "Organs and Orgasms," "that it is not they who have individual sex problems; it is society that has one great big political problem."[5]

But feminism had political problems, too. An early issue of *Ms.* magazine treated homosexuality like a disease, echoing the sentiments of NOW founder Betty Friedan, who was so concerned that having lesbians in the movement would discredit the whole operation that she famously called them "the Lavender Menace" and blocked the Daughters of Bilitis, an early lesbian rights advocacy organization, from sponsoring the First Congress to Unite Women in 1969. Friedan's stance so angered lesbian feminist Rita Mae Brown (future author of the landmark coming-out novel *Rubyfruit Jungle* as well as two dozen delightful mysteries she "coauthored" with her cat) that she resigned her staff position at NOW and got to work becoming the Lavender Menace Friedan feared. By the Second Congress to Unite Women, held in New York City in May 1970, Brown and her compatriots pulled off what the gay liberation movement of the time called a "zap," a highly coordinated and fully disruptive piece of political theater.

Karla Jay, one of the participants, remembers it this way:

> Just as the first speaker came to the microphone, Jesse Falstein, a GLF [Gay Liberation Front] member, and Michela [Griffo] switched off the lights and pulled the plug on the mike. . . . I was planted in the middle of the audience, and I could hear my coconspirators running down both aisles. Some were laughing, while others were emitting rebel yells. When Michela and Jesse flipped the lights back on, both aisles were lined with seventeen lesbians wearing their Lavender Menace T-shirts and holding the placards we had made. Some invited the audience to join them. I stood up and yelled, "Yes, yes, sisters! I'm tired of being in the closet because of the women's movement." Much to the horror of the audience, I unbuttoned the long-sleeved red blouse I was wearing and ripped it off. Underneath, I was wearing a Lavender Menace T-shirt. There were hoots of laughter as I joined the others in the aisles. Then Rita [Mae Brown] yelled to members of the audience, "Who wants to join us?"[6]

The stunt made room for discussion of homophobia and lesbian rights at the congress and beyond. It was a turning point for the acceptance of lesbians in the feminist movement.

While Friedan and co. were focused on the "threat" of lesbians, a real threat to feminist sexual liberation slipped in, bearing checks and wearing a smoking jacket. In the early seventies, Hugh Hefner, the captain of the thriving Playboy empire, saw an opportunity for increased respectability in the women's movement. Already years into writing monthly essays he said would constitute "the Emancipation Proclamation of the sexual revolution," he started pouring significant money and resources into the fight for abortion rights and full birth control legalization. He hired lawyers to write amicus briefs in support of the two abortion rights cases that would essentially combine to become *Roe v. Wade*. He hosted a fund-raiser for the Equal Rights Amendment at the Playboy Mansion. And as he wrapped himself in feminism, he also managed to wrap himself around it, coopting and branding the movement to liberate women's bodies and selling it back to men at a markup.

In a 2007 interview, Hefner told *Esquire*, "I was a feminist before there was such a thing as feminism" and claimed "women were the major beneficiary of the sexual revolution. It permitted them to be natural sexual beings, as men are." Of course, the construction of "natural" female sexuality has changed considerably throughout the centuries. Hefner didn't mean, for example, that women should be feared and revered for our insatiable sexual appetites and profound fecundity, as was considered natural in medieval times. (The myth of the violently unquenchable "vagina dentata" was particularly popular in this era.) In the Playboy universe, men decide what's "natural" for a woman when it comes to sex.

Hef explained his ideal to an Italian journalist in 1967: "She is a young, healthy, simple girl—the girl next door . . . we are not interested in the mysterious, difficult woman, the femme fatale, who wears elegant underwear, with lace, and she is sad, and somehow mentally filthy." That is, women who had full lives and their own thoughts and needs and boundaries, women who were not ashamed to pursue their own sexual gratification—women who behaved much like the men Playboy sought as its customers—were mentally filthy and therefore "unnatural." Only naive and pliant "simple" girls—girls who could be easily controlled by the Playboy man—need apply. And it's no wonder why. When a then-unknown writer named Gloria Steinem went undercover at the New York Playboy Club, she found widespread wage theft and sexual harassment, even dictates of whom a "bunny" could date and whom she couldn't. Would a "mysterious, difficult woman" accept those terms of employment? Moreover, would such a woman put up with men who assume she's sexually available to them at all times but who care precious little about her satisfaction?

But pay no attention to the actual human women behind the curtain. Even as *Playboy*'s standard for docility got more draconian (in the 1950s, the average *Playboy* centerfold weighed about 9 percent less than the average US woman; by 1978, she was 16 percent smaller), it came to dominate our cultural ideas of what was sexy in a woman and what was smart for a man. Wrapping *Playboy* up in feminist rhetoric made it respectable enough for the likes of Truman Capote, Lenny Bruce, John Updike, and even Supreme Court Justice William O. Douglas to publish in it. Hefner raised fauxpowerment to an art form. He sold an idea of sexual revolution that visually centered on women but in fact left men squarely in control. And we're still paying for it. In 2015, when the magazine announced it would no longer run fully nude pictorials (a move it reversed less than two years later), the UK's *Telegraph* declared, "*Playboy* has always been boldly progressive."[7] The proof? A link to a slideshow of magazine covers. Some of the women weren't even white!

Of course, most people at the time didn't have a key to a Playboy Club, and most of them weren't feminist activists either. Still, these ideas trickled down. My parents were twenty-three and twenty-six during the Summer of Love. They had no time for revolution: they were working-class newlyweds just trying to make ends meet. They had me in 1971, only weeks before the Supreme Court began hearing arguments in *Roe v. Wade*. But it was Hefner's worldview that won out in our household. I was given my exceedingly rare (for the time) name after my father saw it was the name of a woman modeling a bikini in a local newspaper. A few years later, Jaclyn Smith hit the big time as one of Charlie's Angels.

The Angels are a perfect representation of the way the sexual revolution was commodified, stripped of its transformative power, and sold back to us as entertainment. The Angels felt modern but posed no actual threat to the status quo. They were smart, sure. They could fight and fire a gun. But they were sex bombs, too. They could bring down the bad guy and give him a boner. In case the purpose of the show was too subtle, one episode even features a barely disguised Playboy Club (this one features women dressed as cats, not bunnies), in which the "Feline Girls" are being picked off by a serial killer, a plot device plainly devised to get Farrah Fawcett's "Jill" to don the costume and play kitty.

Self-assured, capable women who weren't available for men to sexually consume would have been too much like those "man-hating" feminists Betty Friedan wanted to avoid being mistaken for. And sexy ladies without the gloss of power would have, at the time, seemed retrograde. But put the two together, and you got "modern" women who weren't threatening to men. And if feminists complained (and they did, calling *Charlie's Angels* "Jiggle TV"), they could be dismissed as uptight and anti-sex.

The trouble is, some of them were exactly that. As the seventies wore on, and the only parts of the sexual revolution that seemed to stick were the ones that served men's interests, feminists fractured over what it all meant and how to respond. The extreme was occupied by separatists, who believed that the only way to be free of patriarchy was to cut off all contact with men. But while separatism remained a fringe pursuit, more of the feminist movement coalesced around an anti-pornography agenda.

So-called radical feminists like Andrea Dworkin, Catharine MacKinnon, and Susan Brownmiller argued that pornography was inherently harmful to women and should be prohibited. They also opposed the practices of BDSM (bondage and discipline, dominance and submission, and sadism and masochism) and viewed sex work as inherently victimizing and degrading to anyone who does it.

It was an appealing proposition in its simplicity. The mainstreaming of pornography was, after all, primarily by and for men. It featured women as consumable, passive objects of desire at best, and as humiliated objects of sexualized violence at worst. At a time when Loretta Ross and her colleagues were building up the anti-rape movement and scoring some early wins in criminalizing marital rape, the radical feminist arguments about sex felt bold and strong.

But their blanket opposition to porn also stigmatized and alienated women who were themselves turned on by it as well as women who worked in it. The across-the-board anti-porn stance also erased the fact that, though some porn, like some novels, some movies, some of any kind of media, is misogynist, some porn is made by and for women, centering women's desire. By making all frank depictions of sex the enemy, instead of focusing on addressing the misogyny in porn, the radical feminists came to symbolize an anti-sex stance that was popular with few. And their belief that censorship of porn would be good for women proved naive, because the power to censor always belongs to the most powerful. (In fact, when MacKinnon and Dworkin finally prevailed in getting the 1992 Canadian legislation banning all "degrading or dehumanizing" erotic materials passed, the law was primarily used to crack down on depictions of feminist and LGBT sex, including books by Oscar Wilde, Audre Lorde, Langston Hughes, and Dworkin herself.)

In response, a "pro-sex" wing of feminism began to coalesce, and Ellen Willis was the one to give it its name. In her 1982 essay "Toward a Feminist Sexual Revolution," Willis chastised mainstream feminists for arguing that "sexual coercion [was] a more important problem for women than sexual repression" and making the "uncritical assumption that men find predatory, solipsistic sexual relations satisfying and inherently preferable to sex with affection and mutuality." That's not to say, of course, that sexual coercion wasn't a significant problem or that toxic ideas about masculinity weren't poisoning sexuality for most women. (Both dynamics are sadly still a problem today.) But Willis and others argued convincingly that positioning women as universal sexual victims and men as sexual predators was a wild oversimplification that stripped women of agency, men of humanity, and all of us of a chance to articulate the kind of sex lives we want to create.

The increasing radicalism of the anti-porn feminists galvanized pro-sex feminists like Willis, Joan Nestle, Dorothy Allison, Amber Hollibaugh, and Cherrie Moraga, and the two groups clashed more publicly in print and in person, most especially at a now-infamous 1982 conference on feminism and sexuality held at Barnard College. These skirmishes came to be known as the Feminist Sex Wars, a legendary rift largely considered to have helped crash the Second Wave surge.

But that's the easy answer: *women, they're so catty, they undermined their own revolution.* In reality, much larger forces were at play. After two decades of massive social upheaval, Reagan rode to power on a surge of counter-countercultural backlash, a nostalgia for the way things never really were. His victory, reliant as it was on the nascent Moral Majority, legitimized evangelical Christians as a political force. Then AIDS arrived, and as it spread it carried with it a terror of homosexuality, promiscuity, and all unconstrained sexual desire. Welcome to the age of abstinence-only education.

The path to "just say no" sex ed (which, let me be plain, is scientifically proven[8] not to delay sexual activity and only puts young people at greater risk for STI [sexually transmitted infection] transmission and pregnancy) started auspiciously enough, with a push to make contraception available to teen girls. It may seem hard to believe now, but for most of US history, the federal government believed birth control to be a private matter, far outside its purview. That started to change in the 1960s, when as part of his War on Poverty President Johnson quietly routed funds to community-based programs to help them provide family planning services to more low-income women. Congress did him one better in 1970, implementing Title X of the Public Health Services Act, which made voluntary family planning services readily available to "all persons desiring such services."

Just as Congress was getting into the birth control business, a new specter was rising from the mist of the public imagination: the pregnant teen. The past decade had generated four related trends: an increase in birth control usage among adults, a spike in teen sexual activity, handwringing among older citizens about the sexual revolution, and a growing (and often racist) concern about global population growth, especially what lawmakers and pundits saw as the "excess fertility" of young Black women here at home. By the mid-1970s, those strands intertwined to create a monster mirage: the teen pregnancy "epidemic."

At the time, adolescent pregnancies were at a twenty-year low. But widespread adoption of birth control had caused adult pregnancies to fall off even more precipitously than teen rates so that the gap between the rate of teen pregnancies and the rate among the general population had widened. And though the epidemic was imaginary, the impact of it was not: in 1977, the Supreme Court ruled against a New York state law that prohibited people younger than sixteen years old from accessing contraception. In the ruling, the Court explicitly afforded teens "the right of privacy in connections with decisions affecting procreation." In other words, teens' sex lives were legally their own business. The sexual revolution had reached the highest court in the land.

But it didn't last long. Reagan and his newly activated evangelical base seized on federal family planning programs, claiming that they promoted promiscuity (they don't and never did). Instead, the administration asserted, young women had to be taught that it wasn't unplanned pregnancy that threatened their future but the premarital sex that made pregnancy possible in the first place. Abstinence activists claimed that birth control could leave young women sterile (by the early eighties, this was flat-out false), that girls who had sex before marriage would fail to bond properly with their husbands (also a lie), and that girls were far more likely than the boys they might get frisky with to be plagued with guilt afterward (perhaps true, but culturally constructed by these very arguments). The one thing they did agree about with family planning advocates was that the federal government had a role to play in the sex lives of young women. In 1981, Senators Hatch and Denton successfully passed AFLA, the Adolescent Family Life Act, which granted funds to states for demonstration and research projects promoting abstinence.

Reagan and his allies rolled back the imperfect revolutions of the 1960s in every way that the government could control. Gay rights were off the table—the president said the movement was "asking for recognition and acceptance of an alternative lifestyle which I do not believe society can condone, nor can I." He didn't speak of AIDS in public for the first five years of his administration, and in private he and his top aides actively refused to take any action to address the crisis, allowing tens of thousands to suffer and die on his watch. Abortion was protected by the Court, but Reagan still tried to amend the Constitution to make all abortion illegal except when necessary to save the life of the mother. Sex was something for heterosexual married people to do quietly at home, and that was that.

But even Reagan's political charisma wasn't strong enough to put the genie back in the bottle altogether. While he and his pals were trying to take the country backward, Sheena Easton was imploring you to come inside her Sugar Walls, Cyndi Lauper rubbed one out in "She Bop," Salt-N-Pepa ordered you to Push It, *Dirty Dancing* humanized abortion and framed teen girls' sexual exploration as an act of political rebellion, and Madonna humped a veil on the stage of the MTV Awards while belting about her lack of virginity. It's no accident that each of these ladypower juggernauts drew from Black or gay culture (or their intersection). As more and more straight white folks shed their hippie aspirations to join the Reagan revolution in exchange for cultural respectability, those not invited to the party created their own countercultural celebrations of outsiderness.

Not that feminism was dead, no matter what the headlines said. But between the sex wars, the rise of the Reagan era, and major setbacks like the passage of the Hyde Amendment (which prohibits federal dollars from being spent on abortion care) and the defeat of the Equal Rights Amendment, it was in a more fractured state than ever. Some (mostly white) feminist leaders sought to find common ground with the new political majority. In an attempt to placate right-leaning voters, NARAL started arguing for abortion rights on the grounds that the government had no business telling people what to do—as opposed to insisting that the state has an affirmative right to ensure that all women can access abortion—an argument that abandoned the poor women, mostly women of color, who had been effectively shut out of abortion rights by the Hyde Amendment.[9] That shift didn't go unnoticed by Loretta Ross, who spent much of the eighties at NOW simultaneously fighting to make the organization a more welcoming place for women of color and working to get women of color to focus some of their political energy on reproductive rights. As part of her work on the latter, she attended and helped organize delegations of US women of color to attend a series of United Nations meetings on women, health, and related issues.

As global population control became the narrow focus of these meetings, Ross and her colleagues pushed back, demanding instead genuine support for developing nations. "What studies have revealed over and over and over again, is that when a woman is convinced that the children she has will grow beyond five years of age, she will have fewer of them," Ross explains. "If she's offered an opportunity for education, she will have fewer children. If she's offered employment opportunities, she will have fewer children. . . . When you try to talk about family planning or contraception or abortion outside of the context of what's happening to that country as a whole, to those communities as a whole, then you're really erring on the side of supporting population control. You're not talking about women's true empowerment."[10]

Frustrated with the international conversation and alarmed at the increasing likelihood that the Clinton administration's proposal for universal health care wouldn't cover abortion or other key parts of reproductive care, Ross and some members of the delegation joined other Black feminist activists at a conference sponsored by the Illinois Pro-Choice Alliance and the Ms. Foundation for Women, with the intention of crafting a public statement. In the process, they started a movement and coined a name for it: "reproductive justice." It locates a woman's reproductive freedoms and everything that influences them—from access to a full range of health care options to the economic means to raise children if they choose, safety from violence, freedom from forced or coerced sterilization, and more—not just as a matter of privacy but as a human right, and the defense of that right as an issue of justice.[11]

But I'm getting ahead of myself. Three years before Ross and her colleagues defined reproductive justice, the first President Bush nominated Clarence Thomas to the Supreme Court to fill the seat vacated by retiring civil rights legend Thurgood Marshall. Thomas was a canny pick for Bush, enabling the president to nominate a Black man to fill Marshall's seat while also shifting the court to the right. Thomas's confirmation was opposed by NOW and the NAACP thanks to his conservative stances on issues like abortion and affirmative action, but it was a woman from his past who would throw the real wrench in his coronation.

Anita Hill had worked for—and been sexually harassed by—Thomas years earlier, when both were at the Equal Employment Opportunity Commission. So, when she saw that the green-for-the-bench Thomas's nomination hinged on his character, she privately reached out to the FBI to share what she knew. When the FBI's investigation into her statement was leaked to the press, all hell broke loose.

Has there ever been a more naked evaluation of the value of female sexual agency than the Hill hearings? The image itself galvanized the nation: a lone Black woman facing a phalanx of white male senators and insisting that a man's refusal to respect a woman's sexual boundaries be considered as part of his character. Instead, they maligned hers, painting her as delusional, scheming, spurned, whatever it took to ignore her testimony. Thomas was confirmed by a 52–48 vote.

But the world changed anyhow. Sexual harassment reports to the EEOC doubled in the years following Hill's testimony. For some of us, the revelation that sexual harassment had a name and did not have to be borne came too late for legal action, but we still found ourselves liberated by Hill's clarity and bravery. I had been targeted by the owner of a small auction company I worked for one summer, just a couple of years before the Thomas hearings, but never heard the words "sexual harassment" until Hill uttered them on television. Until then, I had just assumed I had sent him the wrong signals and that that miserable summer was by my own design. I followed the Thomas-Hill story obsessively, astonished to discover not only that I was just one of countless women who had been the recipient of a boss's lecherous and terrorizing advances but also that there was at least one woman who was willing to stand up in front of Congress and the world and declare those working conditions unacceptable.

I was far from the only one listening. "It did result in what was a huge spate of organizing by African American women," recalls Loretta Ross. "There was this huge signature ad campaign, . . . 'African American Women in Defense of Ourselves,' where we raised thousands of dollars, like overnight, to get this ad in the *New York Times* . . . in defense of Anita Hill. And it raised the consciousness in the African American community about sexual harassment, something we'd been talking about for close to twenty years, but it took a celebrated case like this to really generate a discussion about boundaries and sexual harassment at the workplace."[12]

Hill's impact extended even beyond the workplace. It galvanized women back into a collective mind-set, reinvigorating and reinventing the feminist project. It inspired Rebecca Walker, daughter of Alice, to join with her friend Shannon Liss to found the Third Wave Direct Action Corporation, one of the earliest efforts to organize a new generation of feminist activism.

Out west, a loose group of female punk musicians, already fed up with misogyny in the punk scene, were inspired to broaden their political ambitions by Hill's testimony and treatment. Riot Grrrl was born. With lyrics like "In her hips, there's revolutions," Riot Grrrl confrontationally equated sexual agency with political freedom. Bikini Kill, widely considered the band at the heart of Riot Grrrl, produced a fanzine called *Girl Power*, which expanded on their lyrics, telling raw, angry, first-person stories about rape and abuse, rejecting male objectification and dominance, and generally encouraging girls and women to take up all the space and make all the trouble they want in the music scene and in their lives in general, to hell with anyone who didn't like it.

But if that slogan sounds familiar, it's likely for another reason. In 1994, as Riot Grrrl was gaining cultural power as the soundtrack to the Third Wave of feminism, another musical revolution was brewing in a UK lab. They were called the Spice Girls. They were safe; the most they ever demanded of men was probably "If you want to be my lover, you gotta get with my friends." They were conventionally pretty and nearly all white, but for Scary Spice (of course). Their glitter-pink slogan, emblazoned on everything from the ubiquitous nineties baby tees they helped to popularize to ersatz Barbies of the band members: Girl Power. Only this version didn't signify a call to upset patriarchy. Instead, the Spice Girls brand of Girl Power was about looking cool, feeling confident, and being loyal to your friends. Individual "empowerment," not cultural power.

In some ways, this was the same maneuver Hugh Hefner pulled all those decades ago, latching on to a political movement on the rise, stripping it of any power to change the culture, and selling it to a mainstream audience for a profit. But the Spice Girls were innovators in at least one respect: they (or their management team, headed by future *American Idol* creator Simon Fuller) recognized that fauxpowered women weren't just a fantasy to sell to men. They could sell fauxpowerment directly to women.

And sell they did. By the late nineties, they had licensing deals with hundreds of brands and products, from Polaroid to Pepsi to Play-Station. Bikini Kill broke up for good in 1997. The next year, the Spice Girls earned $49 million, setting a record for the highest-ever annual earnings by an all-female group.

The Girl Power market was open for business and was soon flooded with media content vying for a slice of that lucrative pie. But what "girl power" meant varied wildly. On *Sex and the City*, it meant fierce female friendships were more important than men, and women's sexual pleasure and adventure were paramount. It also meant a very specific kind of white, heterosexual consumerism and romanticized an emotionally withholding asshole as Carrie's One True Love. *Buffy the Vampire Slayer* countered with an ass-kicking heroine who subverted the trope of the sexy blonde teenager and let men into her Scooby Gang but found that having sex with them was mostly dangerous and destructive. Destiny's Child modeled what it could look like to call the shots in your sexual relationships with your posse by your side, while the Pussycat Dolls saw no reason to promote friendship at all, instead promoting female competition over men, with lyrics like "Don't cha wish your girlfriend was hot like me? / Don't cha wish your girlfriend was a freak like me?"

Men wielded power over each of these projects in one way or another. Though the book that inspired *Sex and the City* was written by Candace Bushnell, it was Darren Star who created the show for HBO. Buffy, of course, was the breakout passion project of Joss Whedon. No one would accuse Beyoncé Knowles of being controlled by anybody these days, but it was her father, Matthew, who first pushed her into show business and managed her career until after Destiny's Child had split. And when Robin Antin wanted to turn the LA burlesque show she'd created into a global brand, she signed with Jimmy Iovine and

Ron Fair at Interscope Records, who made the Pussycat Dolls a household name.

There's nothing inherently disqualifying about a man having a controlling stake in media that promotes ideas about women's sexual empowerment. But when there's a man making money off of nearly every prominent Girl Power message, something's wrong.

It's not just in entertainment that men promote women's sexual freedom only when it's in their own interest. Bill Clinton was a master of this maneuver, promoting sexual freedom only when it wouldn't cost him power. He was the first president to appoint gay men and lesbians to high posts in the federal government, and he expanded the definition of hate crimes to include crimes based on gender or sexual orientation, but he also enacted Don't Ask, Don't Tell after catching heat over his campaign promise to lift the military's gay ban. Later, facing a reelection fight, he signed the Defense of Marriage Act. He made abortions and contraception more accessible, but he refused to stand by his surgeon general, Dr. Joycelyn Elders, when she came under fire for saying that masturbation is a healthy way to practice safe sex. When he caved to pressure and signed a law reallocating direct assistance to poor families into block grants that the states had broad leeway to distribute how they saw fit, he paved the way for a massive new abstinence-only curriculum initiative as well as programs that pressured poor women to get married whether they wanted to or not. And that's to say nothing of the way he treated women in his personal life.

But the turn of the millennium would quickly make us nostalgic for Clinton. Even as Destiny's Child was demanding we say their names, George W. Bush and his pals were making abortions harder to access and pay for, both here and abroad, and pouring millions and millions more dollars into abstinence-only "education." On September 13, 2001, Rev. Jerry Falwell blamed the unimaginable violence of 9/11 on "the pagans, and the abortionists, and the feminists, and the gays and the lesbians who are actively trying to make that an alternative lifestyle" for having "caused God to lift the veil of protection which has allowed no one to attack America on our soil since 1812."[13] Most Americans never went that far, but in the months and years following 9/11, the

THIS IS NOT MY BEAUTIFUL HOUSE

attacks were invoked endlessly as conservatives urged the country to turn away from the queer and feminist attitudes that, they said, had left us vulnerable to Al Qaeda and to return to a world of "manly men" who could protect the nation and the docile, feminine women who love them.[14]

And it was in those years that Ariel Levy, then a contributing editor at *New York Magazine*, strode into the fray. Her 2005 book *Female Chauvinist Pigs* was a blockbuster fingerwag, rocketing up best-seller lists and dressing up the new reactionary zeitgeist in seventies-feminist talking points about women, sex, and power. The book starts from a correct premise, and a crucial one: that women were mistaking access to commercial signifiers of sexuality for actual sexual freedom. It's in the details that Levy veers wildly off the rails. She constantly conflates anecdote with data. She thinks the young women flashing their breasts in *Girls Gone Wild* videos are too dumb to tell the difference between real power and fauxpowerment. Levy never seems to consider that they might recognize the enormous disparities of power between them and the men they're trying to impress, or that maybe they're grasping at one of the only ways they know to feel some kind of sexual power at all. She equates a queer burlesque show with a Maxim Hot 100 party, as if one isn't a direct subversion of the other, as if context doesn't matter and all performances of sexuality are inherently degrading.

It was an argument that went down easy with a lot of people because it made the pearl-clutching cultural mood feel righteously feminist and because judging other women requires us to do no work or introspection of our own. Writing for the *New York Times*, novelist Jennifer Egan called it a "lively polemic" that gave her "an epiphany." But for many younger women, it made them feel more livid than lively. "Intentional or not, Levy contributes to that mean finger, pointed only at girls," charged Jennifer Baumgardner in a review at Alternet, "that says, 'You think you are being sexy, you think you're cool and powerful, but you're not. You're a slut and people are making fun of you.'"[15] Writing for Feministing, Jessica Valenti added, "There's a big difference between a younger feminist who is trying to understand the complexities of sex work and how it informs her politics, and a young woman flashing for *Girls Gone Wild* 'cause boys will like her. And this is not even to say that one pro-raunch action is 'better' than the other—I'm not going to fucking lecture some 19-year-old about who she wants to show her tits to."[16]

It was the old sex wars argument in new clothes: Were women always victimized by the public performance of sexuality, or could sexuality be a path to women's power? But it played out differently this time. Because while the dominant culture was falling in love with burly fire-men and women wearing sweater sets, a new generation of feminists, raised on both Anita Hill and Riot Grrrl (and the more commercial Girl Power efforts), had also become early adopters of the burgeon-ing social Internet. They pioneered the use of each new innovation, first listservs and LiveJournal and then blogs, where, by 2005, a young woman like Valenti, with nothing more than an Internet connection, a women's studies degree, and a lot of opinions, could not only talk back to Levy but also outmatch her audience. (Valenti guesses that Femi-nisting was pulling in "a couple hundred thousand" visitors a month that year, though reliable numbers are hard to find.[17] Still, that's a lot more readers than buy your average nonfiction best seller.) That meant that, although Levy's arguments appealed to many, they couldn't be mistaken for the views of a majority of women, or even a majority of feminists, to anyone who was paying attention.

In its mid- to late-aughts heyday, the feminist blogosphere was a sprawling, messy, multidirectional conversation. Bloggers conversed with, challenged, and amplified each other across platforms, and the commentariat, sometimes hundreds strong on any given post, hashed out the issues in minute detail with the passion of young intellectuals drunk on wine and good debate. Lifelong friendships (and animosities) were formed—I once met a guy in the comments section of a blog I ran and had a two-year love affair with him.

The deeply interlocking nature of these conversations created new channels for people whose voices were often marginalized in main-stream feminist debate—women of color, sex workers, people with dis-abilities, trans people, and others—to insist on being not just heard but also centered. It was on one feminist blog or another (I wish I could remember) that I first encountered the phrase "reproductive justice," though obviously Loretta Ross and her compatriots by then had been developing that framework for a decade. But it was in the early aughts that the idea really took off, and the feminist Internet played a big role.

In 1997, with an eye toward creating a collaboration, a program officer at the Ford Foundation named Rena Marcelo convened a meeting of reproductive rights organizations led by women of color. In fits and starts (and with major backing from Ford for the first three years), that coalition took shape and became SisterSong, the Women of Color Reproductive Justice Collective, with the mission of building capacity in all sixteen member organizations. Unsurprisingly, among those institutions was one Loretta Ross had founded and was running: the National Center for Human Rights Education, which was brought into the fold explicitly to ensure that the other orgs integrated a human rights–based approach into their work so that they could together embody and enact the reproductive justice framework.

After five years of meeting and collaboration, the SisterSong collective decided it was ready for its public debut, a national conference scheduled for 2003. But things had changed at Ford by then, and it was no longer funding SisterSong. So SisterSong turned to the Internet. "I mean, we couldn't even drop a mailing. We had no money to print up anything," remembers Ross. "So we did a call for papers that was distributed over the Internet. We allowed six months for it to get circulated and set, like—first we had a March deadline and then people got back to us and said they couldn't get it back to us in March so we extended the deadline till May, then we extended to June. . . . We were making it up as we go."[18]

It worked beyond the group's wildest imaginings. "We planned for 200, [and] 600 people showed up," Ross told me.

Just as Ross herself was transformed at that first rape crisis center where her experience of sexual violence was named and contextualized, so too was naming reproductive justice transformative for the people who flocked to that conference. "Reproductive justice allows you to talk about the prison-industrial complex, gentrification, sterilization, immigration, all in one conversation. Which you couldn't do under the pro-choice framework. And so . . . people latched onto it like they were in a desert thirsty for water. Reproductive justice is a framework that organizes our existing knowledge into words. . . . Nothing [we were] saying was that new or that original. It doesn't have to be. Because naming itself is a huge power. I mean my favorite quip is that, Newton didn't invent gravity, but, damn, didn't it make a difference when he named it!"[19]

It was also on the feminist Internet—in the comments of the blog Feministe, if I recall correctly—that I first learned the name for a whole different world of things I felt and experienced but couldn't articulate: "enthusiastic consent." It clarified that the "no means no" standard was incomplete and left loopholes in the public imagination that rapists regularly exploited. That it's actually not that hard to make sure you're not hurting someone you're having sex with. That we all have the right to expect partners who will prioritize our pleasure and safety and the responsibility to be that kind of partner as well.

So it's no accident that the blogosphere also enabled me to produce my first book, *Yes Means Yes*, an anthology arguing for a shift to the enthusiastic consent standard and exploring its possibilities. I edited it in collaboration with Valenti, one of the founders of Feministing. We circulated the call for submissions throughout the feminist blogosphere and reached out to some of our favorite bloggers to contribute. It's hard to imagine it finding the widespread audience it did without the trickle-up idea chain that started with coverage in feminist blogs.

Two years later, the feminist Internet struck another blow for sexual freedom. SlutWalk was never intended to be an international movement. It was a local response to a 2011 safety forum at York University in Toronto, where a police officer told those assembled that if women don't want to be raped, they should "avoid dressing like sluts." When Toronto activists Heather Jarvis and Sonya Barnett got wind of the remarks, they decided enough was enough and organized the original SlutWalk, a thousands-strong march to the Toronto Police Headquarters protesting the persistent myth that what women wear has anything to do with whether we're raped. Though organizers encouraged participants to wear ordinary street clothes to underscore the message that rapists choose victims with no regard for what they're wearing, some protesters showed up in sexy outfits to make the point that no matter what we wear, we deserve to be safe from rape.

The idea spread like wildfire through the feminist digital world and quickly crossed over into the mainstream. SlutWalk had a lot of things going for it: a short, confrontational name, a clear message, a certain spirit of playfulness in the opportunity to dress up in any number of ways, media-friendly photos of scantily clad women holding protest signs both cheeky and angry. That first year alone there were over two hundred SlutWalks in forty countries. And though there were outbreaks of handwringing about the protests, overall media coverage was smart and positive, with even the most mainstream of outlets seeming to understand the point of the protests.

In a lacy bra and corset, my hair brushed out wild and enormous, I spoke at the rally following the first Boston SlutWalk, declaiming, "If you use the word *slut* as a weapon against one of us, you're using it against all of us. If you shame one of us, you will receive shame from all of us. If you rape one of us, you will have to answer to all of us." I implored those assembled to claim the word *slut* as an act of solidarity, a kind of slutty I Am Spartacus moment intended to render the word useless and powerless.

But not everyone was inspired. Although plenty of women of color participated in or organized SlutWalks, some women of color criticized the SlutWalk's political use of the word *slut* and association of the word with a mode of dressing, pointing out that Black women, sexualized and sexually abused by white people since the days of slavery, are targeted with words like *slut* no matter what they wear, that because they can't opt out of the idea, they can't opt in to it either. In an open letter to SlutWalk organizers written by the Black Women's Blueprint and endorsed by more than fifty organizations and individuals, they called for SlutWalk organizers to rebrand and deepen their organizing: "As Black women, we do not have the privilege or the space to call ourselves 'slut' without validating the already historically entrenched ideology and recurring messages about what and who the Black woman is."

Because SlutWalk wasn't an organization as much as it was an idea that anyone could use to execute a march, the response to these critiques varied. Some SlutWalks renamed themselves and did the hard work of deepening their racial justice analysis. Some marches remained the same. Some fractured over the issue and fizzled out. Most recently, the format has been reinvigorated by Amber Rose, a multiracial model and actress whose two LA-based SlutWalks have centered on women of color.

Loretta Ross, for one, is a fan. "A lot of people offer critiques of the SlutWalk, [but] I love reclaiming the word *slut*. I love it because that was hurled at me, so many times starting with my own mother. So I have some deep wounds around the word *slut*. When I saw the Slut-Walk and the reclaiming of that, I could not have been more proud. Even though I understand the critiques."[20]

As we head into an era of backlash against women's sexual freedoms, Ross is also here to remind us of how far we've come, even in just her adult lifetime.

> I think the normalization of sexual pleasure for women has really made progress. That a woman who admits to being a sexual being is very important. . . . The first rape crisis center was only founded in 1972. And we haven't stopped violence against women but we damn sure made it not acceptable . . . not only in terms of defining the crime and identifying the perpetrators, but the real impact on changing how women thought about their bodies, their lives, and their autonomy. . . . And it is probably the most successful global human rights movement there is. Because there is not a country in the world where women are not fighting to end violence against women. Much more so than fighting neoliberalism, much more so than fighting underdevelopment, much more than they're fighting for reproductive politics, much more so than they're fighting for anything else. They're fighting to not be violated.[21]

Not that all progress is linear. Reproductive justice, for example, has become a much more popular idea, but not everyone who invokes the phrase understands the framework. "It's a victim of its own success," says Ross. "We've got mainstream organizations trying to co-opt it and de-radicalize it, we have academics claiming to be able to write about it, and they take kind of like the, 'add women of color and stir' approach. But they only want to talk about abortion! And then I'm hearing from so many people who've encountered the framework who don't know about its origin in Black Feminist politics. When people detach it from the human rights framework, they de-radicalize it."

On the other hand, the rise of Trump—or at least the responses his rise has so far inspired—has only energized her. "I'm actually feeling more optimistic than ever," Ross told me when I followed up in early 2017. "The daily acts of resistance, the Women's March, more people being woke. Ain't nothing like a common enemy." Requests for her to speak about reproductive justice have gone through the roof.

Ultimately, the path to women's sexual power in an age of backlash is the same as it would be in an age of Girl Power: not cowering or compromise, but articulating an irresistibly bold vision of pleasure and freedom that's truly for everyone. If we fight only to defend ourselves against losses, every compromise or defeat will take us backward from the starting point of the fauxpowerful status quo we already live in. When we keep dreaming big and working hard toward our real vision, the compromises and defeats are blunted by that forward motion.

We won't all agree on the details—Ross and I disagree, for example, on whether there can ever be real power for women in wearing skimpy clothes and high-heeled shoes. But the basic idea is undeniable. I'll let her tell it. "You can't talk about keeping people safe if you can't talk about sex. . . . If we were defined as the pro-sex movement there wouldn't be anybody left for them to organize except people who are going to be proud of being anti-sex."[22]

## CHAPTER TWO

# WHAT WOMEN WANT

THE TREND LINE should be pointing up.

I'm in a nondescript office in a nondescript university lab three hours east of Toronto, staring at a line describing how much blood was in the tissue of my clitoris over time. Just minutes ago I was reclining alone in another nondescript room across the hall, sensors pressed against my clit and in my vagina, watching porn, getting more and more aroused. But the line depicting the engorgement of my clitoris while I watched people having sex is a downward ski slope. So are the lines of the other women they've tested. And the researchers don't know why. They know the sensor is accurately measuring blood pooling in the bulb of the clitoris. But they have no idea why that tissue is getting less engorged as a woman gets more aroused. They think that maybe blood flows out of the bulb to some other part of the internal clitoral structure as she gets more and more turned on. But that's just a guess. They don't know where the blood might be flowing to, or how to measure it.

I prepared for my day in the lab the way you might for a promising first date. I attended to my personal hygiene with extra care, put on a pair of panties I especially liked (I didn't think the researchers would be seeing them, but you never know), and put on something casual yet charming. I ate a light lunch beforehand: I wanted to be cool, not hangry, but also not bloated.

I don't know what I was expecting, but the door to SageLab—the Sexuality and Gender Laboratory—was just another door in an unremarkable hallway of the Psychology Department of Queen's University. Even inside, there was no sign of anything out of the ordinary—just as I had been warned, the offices were decidedly unsexy, unadorned academic lab spaces. Until I met The Chair.

The Chair is a plush, overstuffed recliner covered in towels and other soft barriers that make it changeable and sanitary. The minute I sit in The Chair I am ready to strip and spread, but unlike at the doctor's office, it takes a while to get going. First, Kelly Suschinsky, a postdoctoral researcher working at the lab, walks me through the details of everything that's about to happen, my rights as a subject, and how to insert and place the probes in their proper places. This takes much longer than you might think, in part because I'm peppering her with questions as we go, but also because of the amount of thought and consideration Sage's staff puts into making sure each subject is fully informed, freely consenting, and maximally comfortable.

The care starts with that chair and those towels. I was expecting a doctor's examination table and a paper gown, not a Barcalounger with soft linens, but the difference is no accident. "We want it to be as comfortable and as natural [as possible]," explains Suschinsky. That thorough thoughtfulness extends to factors you and I might never consider, like the study they conducted to determine how much to pay subjects so they felt adequately compensated for such intimate service, but not coerced into something they're uncomfortable with (by too tempting a sum).

And now they're focusing that formidable care on cracking the mystery of that declining trend line. It's a little exhilarating to stare a genuine medical mystery in the face, like striking off into uncharted territory, vast possibilities in front of you. But the fact that this particular territory is uncharted is also enraging. We're almost two decades into the twenty-first century, and we still don't know the basic mechanics about how the clitoris works. We didn't even know about the existence of the internal clitoral structure until urologist Helen O'Connell studied it with an MRI in the late nineties—more than two decades after men's internal sexual anatomy had been similarly mapped. The clitoris is the only part of the human anatomy whose sole purpose is pleasure. And yet many people still today don't know that the clitoris is much, much more than the little nub we can see and touch on the outside of our bodies. It has curving arm-like structures that extend deep inside the pelvis, two of which wrap around the vaginal canal.

If women are ever going to seize full control of our sexual power, we're going to need total access to everything that's knowable about our sexuality. But our contemporary understanding of women's sexual function is beyond shoddy. Why do some cis[1] women ejaculate, and what are they ejaculating? We don't really know. Why do some women orgasm from penetration, but most don't? We don't really know. Do the hormone regimens given to trans women have long-term side effects? We can't say. Why does hormonal contraception (including emergency contraception) not work as well for fatter women? We don't really know. (And most women don't even know that it doesn't.) Each of those question marks makes women further vulnerable to "experts" hawking their One Answer to the question Freud made famous: "What does a woman want?"

The question persists like antibiotic-resistant bacteria. It drives an entire cottage industry of listicles, like *Men's Health*'s "20 Women Reveal What They Secretly Want in Bed" and YourTango's "These 9 Things Are Exactly What Women Want in Bed." It served as the title of a disposable Mel Gibson nineties comedy about a man who uses newfound mind-reading powers to manipulate women into liking and/or boning him. And it's the organizing principle behind the (surprisingly large) "pick-up artist" community, which has made books like *The Game* best sellers and spends thousands, possibly millions of dollars each year on workshops and programs that promise to teach eager male pupils how to manipulate "women" into sleeping with them. Nameless women, basically interchangeable input/output devices, all of whom are assumed to have the same source code and to be vulnerable to the same hacks.

All that snake oil takes its toll. Many of the young women I meet in my travels are so overwhelmed by so-called experts and personalities telling them "What Women Want" that they're left confused and alienated from the possibility of making their own discoveries about their individual sexual desires and temperaments. When everyone else is telling you what you are, it's hard to hear your own voice above the din.

Any project that has at its heart the question "What do women want?" has already failed. There is no valid answer because it is not a valid question. Sure, we can generalize a few things about women as a category when it comes to sex, though fewer than you might expect. We can safely say that most women fear sexual violence, and that this fear informs our sexual choices and appetites throughout our lives. Cis women as a class are far more likely to orgasm from stimulation of the external clitoris than from a dick (or anything else) sliding in and out of the vagina. We know that women are, statistically speaking, more likely to experience responsive arousal—that is, their desire for sex arises in response to the presence of appealing sexual stimuli and the absence of factors that would make sex unappealing—than spontaneous arousal, the kind where you just feel turned on and then have to go about finding a method of satisfying that craving.

But even these known things are not known for every woman: some women feel spontaneously aroused most of their waking hours. Some women like nothing better in bed than a good, deep pounding. You're going to have to actually communicate with the actual woman you're interested in to find out what she wants (and doesn't) in bed. That requires you to conceive of her as a whole, sovereign human being and not to think of her desire or her body as shameful. If you need help, consider that female genitalia, far from being deformed or disgusting, are actually the norm from which male genitalia deviate. In utero, with no additional hormonal influences, all embryos develop vulva, clitoris, vagina, cervix, uterus, ovaries. It's only when embryos unprotected by the XX gene pair are subject to a hormone wash in the sixth week of gestation that they develop the male analogues of all those organs. Biologically, the clit is the norm. Dicks are the deviants.

Other pieces of "common wisdom" about sex can be debunked by learning our history. Today, the dominant assumption is that men are horndogs, while women mostly just put up with or permit sex. But for most of Western history through the nineteenth century, women were assumed to be the ones with uncontrollable sex drives, and men the poor sods who had to try to keep up despite their less-randy nature. In one story from ancient Greek mythology, Zeus and Hera are having an argument about whether men or women take greater pleasure from sex. They turn for an answer to Tiresias, who lived seven years as a woman thanks to a curse by Hera. His reply? "If sexual pleasure were divided into ten parts, only one part would go to the man, and nine parts to the woman."

Myths about What Women Want hurt everyone. I was once in love with a man who wanted a lot less sex than I did. It didn't start out that way, of course—New Relationship Energy carried us through the first few months—but as that wave of hormones subsided, we settled into a deeply uncomfortable groove. I felt constantly rejected, like I wasn't sexually desirable and like my desire was a problem. Every time I felt sexual want, I felt an immediate internal response: oh, no! Please go away, sex drive. It got pretty fucked up for me, pretty quickly.

My boyfriend wasn't faring any better. He told me he felt constantly pressured, which made him want sex even less. Which I totally understood. When you feel like someone else's desire is more important or more overwhelming than your own, it's not a very sexy feeling, is it?

Needless to say, I felt terrible. Part of that was just the personal agony of the situation, but part of it was that I felt like a freak. What kind of woman wants sex all the time? What kind of woman can't inspire her man to want to bone her? Was my desire grotesque? Was I failing as a woman? That same year, by sheer coincidence, the hot Christmas gift book was called *Porn for Women*. Inside it were carefully lit photos of beefy guys doing nothing more racy than housework, because of course what really turns women on isn't sex at all. Har har.

Google "Porn for Women" today and you'll find listicles on ladysites like Refinery29 and Marie Claire. Follow the links and you'll find a lot more than men vacuuming, but the broad, baseless assumptions remain: women like to look at faces more than genitals. (Actually, men focus on faces more than women do, according to a 2007 study from the Center for Behavioral Neuroscience.[2])[3] Women's erotic response is located in the brain. (Sure, but that's true for everyone, regardless of gender.) We want sensuality, not crass fucking (there's no research on this either way, but plenty of anecdotal evidence to suggest that women aren't uniformly such wilting violets). We want to imagine sex in the context of a loving relationship, not an anonymous hookup (actually, if you control for safety fears and the belief that the outcome will be pleasurable and satisfying, women want casual sex just as much as men do). That old idea about women being turned on by men who pitch in around the house? It was dusted off and reanimated in 2015 by Sheryl Sandberg, who gave it the vomitrocious portmanteau "choreplay." Even purportedly feminist fantasies—like Amy Schumer's romcom smash *Trainwreck*—seem to think that women who sleep around are self-destructive and that we can heal ourselves through heterosexual monogamy.

False assumptions about what women are supposed to be like in bed don't just hurt women in the bedroom. A psychological mechanism called "stereotype threat" actually dooms us to live down to what's expected of us. In one famous experiment, participants were ushered into a fitting room, given either a sweater or a swimsuit to try on, and then asked to take a math test while wearing their assigned garment. The men fared equally well regardless of their outfit, but the women in the sweaters significantly outperformed their sisters in swimwear.[4] In another, mixed-gender groups of eight- to ten-year-olds were shown either sexualized or nonsexualized advertisements, and then asked to take a math test.[5] Once again, boys in both groups performed equally, but the girls exposed to the sexualized ads did worse than the girls who saw neutral ads. In other words: women who are reminded of their expected role as brainless sex objects for men literally can't think straight. What we as a culture believe is true about women and sexuality can genuinely become the truth if it's repeated often enough, locking us into uncomfortable and unsatisfying boxes.

There are surprisingly few scientists trying to unlock those boxes, but Meredith Chivers has made it her life's work. She studies "sexual concordance," a fancy way of saying that she's exploring the extent to which our physical arousal and the arousal we experience subjectively match up. In her most famous study, she showed subjects a wide range of potentially erotic videos, including ones of humans having sex or masturbating as well as ones of bonobo monkeys going at it. Chivers measured both how people's bodies responded to the videos as well as how turned on they reported feeling. The results were fascinating: men were aroused by a more limited selection of the videos, which mapped largely to their stated sexual orientation, and their self-reports largely matched the measurements of their physiological arousal. Women responded physically to almost every video, regardless of their sexual orientation, but those same women self-reported being turned on by a much narrower range of videos than physically aroused their bodies. Since then, she's discovered that the concordance gap is largest in straight women—that while queer-identified women still have a concordance gap wider than an average man's, it's smaller than the average gap experienced by women who identify as heterosexual.

It's no accident that all of Chivers's early mentors were men. In the late nineties, when she was coming up, there was almost no sexuality research of any kind being done by or about women. "I don't think there's been the same kinds of pressures to understand clitoral structure that there have been with making penises hard," observes Chivers, "because for a long time, that was the script: there's going to be heterosexual sex, there had to be a hard penis in order for it to be sex, there had to be penetration for it to be actually sex, it didn't really matter whether the woman is aroused or not. If knowing more about the clitoral structure was going to get more men laid, I'm sure we'd know more about it." Even now, she sometimes resorts to a male-centered Mars-Venus frame when she applies for funding, because a lot of the grant makers are men who believe that knowing What Women Want is most important when it comes to helping men have sex, too.

Chivers told me that she "feel[s] kind of dirty about that," but we should all be grateful she's funding her research however she can. Not only is she among the first to explore the concordance gap, but that device measuring clitoral blood pooling, the one that's producing the mysterious downward line? Chivers is only the second researcher to

ever use it. There's no such brave new world when it comes to measuring sexual response in cis men. "Because so much medical research
has been done to make penises hard again, there's a lot of understanding," she tells me. "You name it, we understand how a penis works."

I met Chivers—tall, self-possessed, and sophisticated—on my first
trip to Kingston, a terrifying visit I made to give a speech on sexual ethics at a time when the campus was roiled in conflict between feminists
and men's rights activists. One female student had been punched by
an unidentified assailant only a week beforehand, and the mood was
so tense that I was assigned a security detail. Chivers was a calming,
can-do presence, quick with a joke but equally understanding of how
stark the stakes were. (She also took me out for some fantastic poutine
the next day.) We've been friends ever since.

Which is perhaps why I was lucky enough to be invited to visit her
lab to learn more about what she and her colleagues do and to experience first-hand what it's like to be a woman whose sexual response is
taken seriously by science.

The study itself works like this: once I'm fully briefed and ready,
Suschinsky leaves the room and I drop trou, but not panties. I take the
probes as instructed—the vaginal sensor looks more or less like a small
travel vibe, and the clitoral one more like a nose made out of some
sort of clear resin—and slip them into place as instructed, pulling my
panties up to hold them there. Then I slide the chair back into a fully
reclining position, reach my right hand toward the keypad I'll use to
communicate subjective data while the test is under way, and tell the
empty room that I'm ready. Suschinsky, listening in on speakerphone
from a room across the hall, starts the test.

Questions flash on the TV screen: How do I feel? Disgusted?
Aroused? Happy? Worried? I rate each emotion on a scale of 1 to 7,
trying to move as little as possible while finding the right keys on the
keypad. (Moving, I'm told, will create a lot of noise in the data.)

Then the questions give way to a video and my heart bangs—am
I really about to watch porn in a lab? Not quite yet. I'm watching a
nature video, all sweeping mountain vistas and bears scrounging for
food. I am confused by this, not sure if it's some kind of a test like the

bonobos were. *Do* I feel aroused at the sight of the lush hillsides and running water? Maybe I do? I'm second-guessing myself, knowing my genitals are telling the researchers their own story, and afraid of contradicting them. I want to have full concordance. I want to overachieve.

Finally, the porn begins, high-quality but banal, a man and a woman enthusiastically pleasing each other in a series of mostly nonridiculous positions. I find myself surprisingly aroused for a woman who can't touch herself while watching porn with sensors on her junk in a lab in the middle of the afternoon, and my finger keeps reaching for the up arrow to indicate my steadily increasing ardor.

Afterward, sensors off and clothes back on, Suschinsky shows me my results on a computer monitor in a cramped room across the hall. It's surprising to me how validating the data are. Seeing a line tracking the measurable rise of my arousal makes it feel real, a thought that immediately embarrasses me. What was it before? All in my head? Who cares? If I experience something as pleasurable, isn't that what matters most? But there they are, the plotted points getting farther apart as my vagina engorges with blood. Even still, the change seems frustratingly small to me. After the first minute, the vaginal plot plateaus, even though I know for sure I felt the action rise and rise in my pussy. And of course, we all know what the clitoral trend line is mysteriously doing. Suschinsky tells me that I'm in normal range, that my data look like the data of the vast majority of women who've run this test. I'm placated, but I had no idea I so longed for scientific validation of my desire.

I'm tempted to explain away this insecurity by telling you about how direct the penis is about its arousal, and how private and inscrutable a pussy can be. It's a satisfying argument because there's some truth to it, but it deflates a bit upon inspection. I've had enough sex with enough partners with different genital configurations to know that penises can be shyer or more mercurial than we give them credit for, even when the penis-haver feels plenty turned on. And vaginas can be quite chatty if you speak the language of scent and color and heat and moisture.

No, I think this surprising craving for scientific validation of my boner has to do with a lifetime of messages about the validity and importance of my desire, or, as a bisexual woman, the erasure and suspicion of it. It has to do with all the people, straight and gay, who've accused me of being a fence-sitter, of lying about my true libidinal loyalties. With watching too much male-centered porn that treats female pleasure as either trophy or afterthought, and fucking too many men who watched that same porn, too. It has to do with Andy, the high school boyfriend who taught me about my clitoris and threatened to rip out my uterus and shove it down my throat if he ever discovered I'd been faking orgasms with him, and with the fact that I had faked every single one, not because I wasn't having a blast with him in our sex life (boy howdy did I love fucking Andy) but because I literally didn't know how to come. That's exactly what it's about: growing up in a world so intent on alienating women from our sexual power that a young woman who loves sex as much as I did could literally not know how to have an orgasm until she's twenty, when a female friend practically shook me by the shoulders and sent me off with very specific instructions. A world in which I never learned about female pleasure in sex ed. It's about how, even as I've developed an identity as a sex revolutionary, I'm still insecure about sex most of the time — should I want it more? Different? Less? Should I be more embarrassed of my rape fantasies and submissive tendencies or the fact that half the time I'm just not as sexed up as I used to be?

I'm not the only person in the lab caught up short by my own responses. Suschinsky remembers a time when, looking for videos of sexual violence and threat for her master's research project, the concordance gap hit too close to home. "I remember watching those kinds of movies and being very aware that my body was responding, but that I was [also] sick to my stomach, and I'd never noticed that before. It was this visceral response where I was nauseous, but my body was responding [sexually]. It was the strangest thing, like, oh my god, this thing is real! Your body can respond and you don't want it."

Still, studying sex has its personal advantages, too. "I think my comfort level with it probably helps in conversations with a partner, or even that comfort with myself," observed Jackie Huberman, another researcher in Chivers's lab. Suschinsky agrees. "There's not a whole lot that can really faze me at this stage. Unless you say that you're really turned on at the thought of killing someone. That might distress me. But other things that might seem taboo to most people, it's not a big thing. And that's not always the anticipated response, so I think that's helpful in a relationship."

That kind of open-mindedness can only help when you're chasing after the mysteries of the human body. Chivers rightly rejects any pat conclusions about what the concordance gap means, especially those that treat the body as truth and women as liars. She has hypotheses about possible factors, but even the questions fly in the face of common assumptions that posit men as healthy and normal when it comes to sex and women as out-of-touch, liars, or frigid. One study found that straight-identified men exhibit a stress response when exposed to gay porn, whereas straight women have no corollary reaction to watching lesbians.[6] Perhaps the concordance gap means that women are actually the more functional gender, and straight men are shutting down any possible physical response to non-het sex because they've been groomed to fear being identified with anything gay. Another study[7] finding that vaginal lubrication can function independently from other signs of physical arousal gives support to what's called the "preparation hypothesis," that cis women's bodies may have evolved to lubricate in response to a wide range of sexual stimuli to reduce our odds of injury if we're raped. Chivers also wonders if the concordance gap is adaptive toward our safety in a broader way, giving women increased flexibility to think clearly even when we're physically aroused. And her recent research suggesting that women with low arousal have a larger concordance gap is coherent with the possibility that women are alienated from experiencing our own sexual desire because women's sexual appetites and autonomy are subject to social punishments.

It's important to remember that these hypotheses are just that— guesses that suggest areas for investigation, not conclusions or facts. If research into the concordance gap is past its infancy, at best it's a toddler. But even as questions, their breadth and creativity illustrate how flatly bankrupt most of our ideas are about women and sex.

That bankruptcy is paid for by women's suffering. Those of us who sleep with men pay every time we encounter a man who treats us like interchangeable vending machines that will dispense to him sexual pleasure if he inserts the secret coin. Because these men think they know What Women Want, they pay little attention to the needs and desires and boundaries of the individual woman in front of them, and women's sex lives suffer for it. And if we have the temerity to refuse to play along with the script in his head, we know we're risking him reacting with violence or abuse.

Some women pay with other kinds of pain. Doctors have worked hard to perfect the "look and feel" of breasts when they're surgically reconstructed postmastectomy so that women's sex partners won't be disappointed, but most of the time they don't even bother to tell their patients that those "perfect"-looking breasts will be completely insensate, leaving them unable to feel for themselves the sensation of a lover's touch or even a child's hug. I have a friend whose otherwise happy marriage almost collapsed under the strain of her undiagnosed vaginismus, a disorder whose sufferers experience involuntary muscle spasms in their vagina whenever anyone tries to penetrate it with anything—finger, tampon, speculum, penis, you name it. There are a lot of hypotheses about what causes vaginismus but precious little actually known. And because most (mostly male) doctors operate under the assumption that (1) women are weak and exaggerate pain and (2) women just don't like sex that much, women who present with symptoms of vaginismus are often written off as frigid or as unknowable mysteries. It took my friend years to find a doctor who would take her seriously and treat her.

Even the very scientific exploration of female sexuality that SageLab undertakes gets erased by the What Women Want framework, as this story of Huberman's illustrates. At a party recently, she told a guy what she was researching, and he took it as an opportunity to ask for the source code to women. "[He] was pretty much asking me, 'How can I pick up women? Tell me. Give me some kind of tip from all of what you do.' I [explained], 'I don't study anything like that.' He's like, 'Well, yeah you do that's what you just said.' So I kept trying to take it back to an explanation of women's responses that we're trying to understand, and what cues are relevant to women. But . . . it didn't matter."

Nothing about women's sexuality mattered except what he could use to satisfy himself.

The mass media, by and large, acts just like that dudebro, translating Chivers's careful work into headlines about how no women are really straight, no matter what they say. "The Lies Women Tell about Sexual Arousal" is the headline *The Daily Beast* went with. Though they changed it (a day later) to the more nuanced "How We Misunderstand Sexual Arousal" after Chivers read them the riot act, the damage was done: the article had been shared and republished across the Internet. "This is why I have pretty much stopped speaking to journalists," Chivers tells me.

The myth that women are lying about sex is a classic. Michael Jackson said Billie Jean was lying about the kid, and uncountable numbers of rape victims are accused every year of lying about how they really wanted it. Men think women are lying about being on birth control (in reality it's men who are much more likely to engage in birth control subterfuge), lying about being lesbians, lying about being virgins. Even when we really are lying, the myths are wrong about why. When I was faking orgasms with Andy, it wasn't some plot to undermine his masculinity. It was because I didn't know how to have an orgasm, and I knew how important it was to him that I did, and I didn't want to make him feel bad. The idea that women's bodies are telling some ultimate truth that we refuse to admit with our mouths is a gendered fantasy, exposed by the fact that men are not treated as lying when they get nonsexual boners. If we believe men when they say, No, I'm not really turned on right now, I just have to pee, why do we treat women whose bodies and experiences aren't aligned like suspect, secret bisexuals? Because it sells papers. And because it makes men feel like women's bodies are "knowable" without them having to treat women like full human beings.

Even the basic language betrays this bias. One of Chivers's pet peeves is when reporters talk about "penises and vaginas" as though they are analogous. In fact, the penis is structurally analogous to the clitoris, and the scrotum to the labia, all of which are contained in the *vulva*, the correct word for the totality of most women's external genitalia. As for the vagina? "Vagina is just a space," says Chivers, sort of blowing my mind in the process. I'd never considered it before, but it's undeniably true that the vagina is essentially an absence. "It's a space surrounded by all of these organs. It's the space where the penis goes, therefore that's how we . . . label women's genitals. You do have vaginal walls, it's true. But . . . it makes way more sense to talk about vulvas."

Part of the problem in translating her work via the media is a problem all scientists face. As the business models supporting journalism have been destabilized by media consolidation and social media, specialized science beat reporters have become an endangered species. The result is that most science is reported on by underpaid writers with not enough time or expertise to properly understand the studies they're summarizing for the public and supervised by editors under pressure to drive as many eyeballs to advertisers as possible.

But even when the rare writer puts in the time, they still seem to get dragged under by the power of our collective mythology about women and sex. Chivers met journalist Daniel Bergner somewhat by accident while he was researching his book *Other Side of Desire*; he had come to interview Chivers's partner (also a scientist) and became curious about her work as well. He spent days at the lab, and Chivers was pleased to have such a smart, thorough journalist interested in her work. "We had great conversations [which inspired] lots of wonderful insights, [and] brought me to all kinds of interesting research ideas." The article he wrote afterward for the *New York Times Magazine* was called—wait for it—"What Do Women Want?" The piece left Chivers "a little cold," though overall she called it "pretty decent." I was surprised to hear her praise it even this faintly, because I had hated its reductive framework enough that I wrote a letter to the editor, which the magazine published. Chivers explained it to me this way: "I [had] to look past the tired trope title [and] the potential gross media misinterpretations. I have to find possibility of good, and the good thing that came out of that article, for me, was that people paid attention, and suddenly were talking about sexuality."

But that article turned into a book deal, and eventually she couldn't look past the final product.

I ended up in his book wearing a low cut top and lace up boots. The sexy scientist. There was no internal consistency in how [my research] was interpreted. The undercurrent was, "we really kind of believe the physical responses because that's . . . the truth of women's desire." And that was very upsetting, especially given how much time I had spent with him, hammering home that that is exactly not the message. He really wanted to paint this picture that women are not necessarily as wedded to monogamy, and he used my data and presented it incorrectly saying that "Oh, women get turned on by sex with strangers so this means that's what they really want."[8]

There's that phrase yet again. By using it to frame his book, Daniel Bergner couldn't help but be sucked in to the black hole of bad assumptions, starting with the idea that there's a grand unified answer to what all women want from sex just waiting to be found.

The good news is that, more and more, younger generations of women are refusing to be lumped together and mythologized about. On Tumblr and Twitter and YouTube, they're educating each other, standing up for each other, and stoking their own unashamed curiosity about their own personal sexuality. Some of them are even turning to new high-tech tools like the Lioness, a new vibrator that teaches a woman about her own sexual response by learning her preferences and tracking her arousal and climax patterns.

Liz Klinger, inventor of the Lioness, got the idea while selling cheap sex toys at Tupperware-style parties to make ends meet after college. As she hustled from event to event, she noticed that many of the women at the parties would pull her aside to ask about their sexual anxieties, questions that boiled down to "Am I normal?" and "How can this be better?" The Lioness serves as a woman's confidante, using sensors inside the vibrator itself to record a range of biometric signals that, when paired with a mobile app, gives the user a map of her arousal and orgasmic patterns.

It's the perfect personal device for exploring the mind-body gap that Chivers's research has unearthed. Like a Fitbit for sexual pleasure, it has the potential to teach women what their unique "normal" is and give them clues to how to make sex better for themselves as well as how to convey that information to a partner.

Klinger explained to me:

> One of the things that we've found through one of our testers, they're a husband and wife where the wife realized as she was using [the Lioness] that she could use it to get some information that she was finding out about herself, like how long she wanted stimulation or foreplay, and bring over the information to talk to her husband about it. They had a pretty good sex life, but there were some things in their relationship that . . . were sometimes hard to convey to him. So she went over to show him this information like, "Hey, remember that we had this conversation about having more foreplay? Well, this is what I mean. This is how much foreplay I want, this is how hard, this is what I need and it's right here." And his response was basically like, "Oh. It's a chart. I get it."[9]

Of course, not all of women's sexual response can be encapsulated in an infographic. Our bodies and desires change over time and fluctuate depending on mood, health, circumstance—all kinds of things. But having data about how your arousal tends to work is clearly a huge boon for women struggling to communicate with a partner. It can also help women understand those very changes for themselves. Klinger related:

> For my mom and for other people who are in her age group, who are going through menopause, there are changes happening to their bodies, and . . . they're trying to figure out, "What's going on? My body seems different than it was before. I want to still have a happy sex life, so how do I make that happen?" There's a huge need in this space for women who are going through menopause to try to understand their own body that's changing, and have a way to be able to understand that without being given just an array of medications and pills and all the other stuff that's being pushed out there.

Beyond the personal power of self-knowledge, the Lioness has the potential to change the field of sex research writ large. Most studies of female sexual response involve a relatively small number of participants for a short amount of time, because inserting things inside the vagina in the name of science is considered pretty invasive by the review boards that regulate experiments on human subjects. By creating a system through which Lioness users could opt in to having their personal data anonymously collected and aggregated, Klinger and her collaborators can provide researchers like Chivers with a far more robust data set than they've ever been able to create or access before.

Chivers is all for it. "I'd love to get my hands on [data like that]," she told me, though she was quick to point out that a set of women all voluntarily using a biometric sex toy and sharing their data with researchers won't ever be a random sample of women, no matter how large it grows. Still, this kind of new approach made her eyes light up. "I don't think the unscrewing of understanding of women's sexuality is going to happen necessarily from the research that comes from scientific laboratories. We're going to do some of that work, but I see so many young women these days who are doing such cool shit around women reclaiming their sexuality and I'm really happy about that. I'm happy to be part of that. And I'm glad that there's lots of opportunities for some people to really engage and have their own voices heard."

## CHAPTER THREE

# FAUXPOWERMENT WILL BE TELEVISED

A S A RULE, Beyoncé doesn't wear pants onstage. And people have opinions. "It's the rejection of norms, an act of self-love," gushed Anne J. Donahue at MTV News.[1] Emma Watson, our erstwhile Hermione Granger and the UN's feminist ambassador to men, disagreed in the wake of Bey's infamous 2014 Video Music Awards appearance, in which she stood, wide-stanced and bare-legged, in front of stories-high letters spelling out FEMINIST. "I felt [Beyoncé's] message felt very conflicted," Watson said, "in the sense that on the one hand she is putting herself in a category of a feminist, you know, this very strong woman and she has that beautiful speech in one of her songs ["Flawless"], but then the camera, it felt very male, such a male voyeuristic experience of her."[2]

There's plenty wrong with a white woman policing the sexual expression and body pride of a powerful Black woman, as numerous Black feminist writers explain at length every time one of these critiques surfaces. There's something itchy, too, about claiming Beyoncé as a feminist superhero, who can usher in a new age of empowerment with a single wardrobe choice. But most of all, it just feels wrong to expect an actual human woman navigating gender and race and power and fame to embody everything that each of us wants to see on our screens. "Are Beyoncé's bare thighs empowering or degrading to women?" is a perpetual think-piece machine because it's an unanswerable question, based on a pair of false premises that infect so many of our conversations about media and women's sexual power: the myth that representation alone can either liberate or oppress us, and the impossible expectation that each individual image we see must satisfy every one of our representation needs.

Representation matters, of course. When *The Hunger Games* and *Brave*—two movies featuring heroic women wielding bows and arrows—did major numbers at the box office in 2012, women's participation in archery spiked over 100 percent in the following two years.[3] But you didn't see handwringing about whether Katniss and Merida were also inspiring girls to go on arrow-shooting sprees in the streets or whether the emphasis on old-school weaponry made them more vulnerable to people who wield guns. Those images were not expected to send every message ever needed about women and weapons. So, yes, Beyoncé has inspired women—most of them other pop stars, as far as I can tell—to go pantsless. But the focus on the meaning of her pantslessness for all of female sexuality is a signal of how hungry we are for images of women standing in their sexual power: if we see one image that doesn't speak to us or doesn't sit right with us, it feels like a crisis, because we don't know when and where we'll find another that does.

That scarcity isn't going to be solved by agonizing over each representation. Representation is just a symptom; it's the tip of the iceberg that we focus on, because it's literally what we see. If we want the kind of wildly diverse representations of women and sex that we deserve—a media ecosystem that doesn't fixate on any one version of women's sexuality but instead collectively represents the infinite ways women experience and express our sexuality—we have to look past representation to authorship. Who is making these images, for whom, and to what end? Who has access to tell their story, and who lacks it? When women, all kinds of women, have as much power as men do to make the media, what we see on our screens will change dramatically.

Put it another way: Beyoncé doesn't exist in a vacuum. As much as it may seem like it, she didn't construct her sexuality out of magic glitter. She grew up a Black woman in a culture that treats Black women's sexuality as cheap, dangerous, and disgusting. She hustled her way to the top of the pop diva game, a game that was already in play, with rules and judges and bosses and other players. Now that she's Beyoncé, we think of her as being able to do whatever she damn well pleases, and maybe that's even true in many ways. But she didn't get there overnight, and she didn't get there without living and breathing the culture around her, whether that's American culture at large or the hothouse culture of the music industry, which has for decades required its female players to use their sexuality as a bargaining chip, to present a fuckable image to imagined straight white men who are, in reality, never the bulk of their fans.[4] It's ridiculous to expect her to invent her own symbology of sexual liberation, free of any influence from the cultures she grew to power in. When we fixate on Beyoncé, we fail to ask a better question about the context in which she's pantless: If female pop stars aren't, for the most part, trying to seduce men into buying their albums, why do they so often perform an idea of naked and gyrating sexuality in ways that their male counterparts rarely seem to?

Like most questions about women, sex, and media, it's complicated. In some ways, it's inevitable. Our cultural imagination about sexuality is deeply bifurcated along gender lines, so when women work out their ideas about sexuality onstage, how could it not look different from when men do it? The most indelible sexual images Beyoncé has produced in the last few years can be read in powerful and subversive ways: yes, I can be sexual and in full possession of my own political power. Yes, my Black marriage is both respectable and freaky. Yes, I have the same vulnerabilities most women do if you betray me, but *Who the fuck do you think I am? You're not married to some average bitch, boy.*

Music can be a place women subvert sexual objectification and use it for their own ends. Just ask Josephine Baker, or Tina Turner, or the Riot Grrrls. But female pop stars from Madonna to Miley Cyrus have often also traded on fauxpowerment, selling the empty idea of "sexual liberation" to their female fans as a way of easy ersatz rebellion. Of course, that path isn't equally open to every pop diva—when Nicki Minaj released the cover art for her derriere-focused single "Anaconda" in 2015, her (Black) ass launched more think pieces than the

61

rise of ISIS, even though *Sports Illustrated* sells (white) female asses just as bare on the cover of its Swimsuit Edition and no one reaches for the smelling salts. And, of course, if fans of any of these women actually dressed and acted like their faves in public, they'd likely be slut-shamed and sexually harassed, possibly be fired from their jobs, and, if they were unlucky enough to be targeted by a rapist, blamed for bringing it on themselves. The idea of "bad girls" may be celebrated in pop culture, but in reality women who break sexual taboos are much more likely to be punished or abused.

Pop divas are also selling themselves as a sexually valued ideal for their female fans to reach for. In a corollary to the way that cars are traditionally advertised to men using "hot" women, when female sexualization is used to sell to women, the idea is that hotness will come along with the product.

But again, let's not get so fixated on the image that we don't ask who shaped it. Not who's in charge of Beyoncé now, but who was in charge of how she got to become Beyoncé. Destiny's Child was famously managed by her father, Matthew Knowles, who also produced her first three solo albums before Beyoncé severed professional and personal ties with him, claiming at various points that he stole money from her and that he refused to treat her like an adult long after she became one. (She has also released a few songs, notably "Ring Off" and "Daddy Lessons," which are widely believed to reference him, but I'll leave the lyrical interpretations to you.) Most of Destiny's Child's music producers were men,[5] as were the bosses who signed them at Columbia. It's a common story across most media: even when women are in the spotlight, men are often in control behind the scenes. The top ten video game companies, according to gaming press leader IGN, share among them not one woman in top leadership.[6] Eighty-three percent of all directors, writers, executive producers, producers, editors, and cinematographers working on the top 250 domestic highest-grossing films of 2015 were men.[7] Even in news media[8] and literary journals,[9] which have seen movement toward parity in recent years, men still dominate.

All of these men think they know what sells. And it conveniently maps to a vision of the world in which women are ornamental. On the big screen, it translates to female characters being twice as likely to wear "sexy" revealing clothes as male ones are and five times as likely to have their appearance remarked upon. Even more disturbing, girl characters as young as thirteen were just as likely to be treated like sex objects as were full-grown women.[10] In video games, female characters are far more likely to be sidekicks than protagonists, and if a female character is playable, she's likely to cost money to play as an add-on option, as opposed to the free-to-play male default.[11] In every medium, women are relentlessly presented as either rewards, ornaments, or obstacles.

And on the rare occasions when our bodies are represented in ways that aren't for sex, the culture hardly knows what to do with us. In 2015, the company that manages ads for the New York City subway system rejected a campaign from the company Thinx (which makes absorptive panties as a reusable alternative to pads and tampons) simply for using the word "period" and cheeky imagery of broken eggs and vulvic grapefruit, even when it happily ran racy ads for breast augmentation and *Fifty Shades of Grey*. It's the same phenomenon that produces a world in which men who happily enjoy misogynist porn in private feel equally free to shame women who dare to breastfeed in public. If "sexy and consumable" is the default for women's bodies, any depictions that don't fit that mold can easily seem wrong.

It's tempting to respond by calling for censorship of the most egregiously objectifying content. But that's rarely a productive response — it reduces the argument to whatever single representation people are freaking out about on this particular day, as though getting rid of that one media product will make us all safe. And it too easily positions those of us fighting for a better media ecosystem as prudish scolds who want to take everyone's fun away. As a solidly pro-fun American, I think of our media ecosystem, instead, like a grocery store. If you went shopping for the week only to find that the only thing available in the grocery store was potato chips and ice cream, you'd be pissed. That doesn't mean that potato chips and ice cream are evil or should be banned from grocery stores. It means that we have the right to demand a full range of media options for our diet, because without them the culture gets sick.

Here are just a few ideas for what that "full range of media options" could look like when it comes to women and sex: women of all shapes, sizes, ages, and races being equally likely to be portrayed as sexually voracious or sexually naive. Women shamelessly pursuing their specific sexual appetites without being punished or mocked. Sexual violence of every kind being treated like a horror, but not used as a lazy plot device to motivate men or make female characters more interesting. Every woman shown being sexual also visibly having a complex, three-dimensional life or, if that's unrealistic, at least parity with men on how many of us are treated as set decoration or plot devices.

It's an inviolable rule that when media representation of women comes up, the bottom line must be invoked. Surely, these high-powered businessmen aren't just doing whatever stiffens their dicks and fluffs their egos. They're just selling what sells. Sex—specifically, a suffocatingly narrow concept of women's sexuality—sells. Women will buy stuff made for men, but men won't buy stuff that's not manly enough. That's supposed to be an immutable fact of life. But it's not. Consider the Bechdel test, which selects for films that feature two named female characters who at some point during the movie talk with each other about something other than a man. (If you're not clear on what a low standard that is, imagine if films in which men talked with each other about something other than women were rare enough we needed to single them out for praise.) In a study of films released between 1990 and 2013, FiveThirtyEight found that films that pass the Bechdel test are a better return on investment domestically for studios than those that fail it, and these films perform equally well internationally.[12]

So why do so many films fail to clear even that basement-level bar? "It's about way more than just box office," says Melissa Silverstein, founder and director of Women and Hollywood. "It's business with gender stereotypes layered on top of it. And it's really hard to break through these stereotypes." Silverstein explains that, because movies have such large budgets and can take so long to develop—a major studio film might take five years or even longer from green light to premiere—executives are reluctant to embrace any information that suggests that their portfolio of films already in the pipeline might not be what audiences really want. Still she remains optimistic. "It takes a long time to turn a ship around, and we've been talking about this for a long time already. There are lots of signals out there from the public that they are really interested in these kinds of movies. Take *Hidden Figures*, for example: it did better box office in 2016 than that year's installments of the *Star Trek*, *X Men*, and *Bourne* franchises. I'm hopeful that Hollywood gets the message."[13]

Of course, not all media is Hollywood, especially these days. If you look hard enough, and you know where to look, you can find a wild smorgasbord of different ideas about women and sex on YouTube channels, in country music, in novels, comic books, indie films, blockbusters, blogs, porn. But most of us don't make a hobby of searching for obscure indie media. Lots of folks just don't have time. They choose from the options they already know about and know how to access. A couple of years ago, when visiting my parents, I noticed a box in the garage from an external speaker they'd recently added to their TV. The box had Netflix, Hulu, and Amazon logos on it, so I asked my folks if they knew that their speaker also could get them streaming television. They had no idea what that even was. When I showed them how to access it and got them logged in, their minds were blown. That's a low-stakes example—my parents' lives haven't been changed materially by binge-watching *House of Cards*. But their attitudes have absolutely been shaped by watching *CNN Headline News* on an endless loop in the morning and a steady stream of crime procedurals at night. They think the world is a more dangerous place than it is and that police are a lot more trustworthy than they are, as a whole.

In a media ecosystem where every option exists, curation is king. Modern media curation has two gates. First, of course, are the traditional curators, the male-dominated power brokers we've been discussing: editors and producers who can greenlight media projects for major outlets with major publicity budgets still have an enormous amount of sway, as do the respected critics and reviewers who decide what is worthy of their attention. Critics are also overwhelmingly male—one survey of film review aggregator site Rotten Tomatoes found only 22 percent of the critics afforded "top critic" status were female.[14] More recently, of course, we have become accustomed to a second set of gatekeepers: our friends and family and even random strangers we've decided to follow on social media, as well as "peer" reviewers on sites like Goodreads and IMDb. But peer review sites are easily skewed by a motivated minority with a mission (see the *Ghostbusters* reboot and the handful of manbabies dedicated to its ruination) or by more stubborn and pervasive implicit biases, which most users aren't even aware they have. (The data crunchers at FiveThirtyEight.com found that male peer reviewers regularly drag down aggregate review scores for TV shows aimed at women, but the reverse isn't true.)[15] As for the social networks we choose? They're usually plagued by homophily, which is a fancy way to say that it's human nature to want to hang out with people who make us feel comfortable, and usually those are people who remind us of us. Without active and careful intervention on our part, we can easily be left with an online life that tells us only things we already agree with and recommends media to us that doesn't challenge our existing worldview.

That brings us back to the traditional media gatekeepers, and we know who most of them are already. They're the members of the Academy that inspired #Oscarssowhite protests. They're the directors who create what I call the Biopic Problem, which is what happens when you complain about the treatment of women in a movie about one or another Important Dude only to be told that it's a true story, that's just how it was. Which ignores the real question: Why are so many biopics made about men who treat women like shit? They're the editors at *Esquire* magazine, who unironically published a list, "The 80 Best Books Every Man Should Read,"[16] which includes seventy-nine books written by men and one by Flannery O'Connor, prompting essayist and national treasure Rebecca Solnit to remark, in her rebuttal at LitHub, "The list made me think there should be another, with some of the same books, called 80 Books No Woman Should Read, though of course I believe everyone should read anything they want. I just think some books are instructions on why women are dirt or hardly exist at all except as accessories or are inherently evil and empty."[17]

When it comes to media depictions of sex, there's also a third type of gatekeeper: self-appointed guardians of "family values," like One Million Moms (with fewer than ninety thousand Facebook followers, it's an organization representing considerably fewer moms than advertised), which regularly pressures sponsors to stop advertising on any show that depicts frank sexuality or even nudity and which famously attempted to boycott JC Penney because it dared to hire Ellen DeGeneres as a spokesperson. The Parents Television Council presents itself as a more respectable option, rightly targeting the rape jokes on *Family Guy* and at least making a passing effort to appear as concerned about on-screen violence as it is about sex. But the PTC shares with One Million Moms the same core belief that any sex on TV is harmful. In an early episode of *Glee*, lead Rachel attends an "abstinence club" meeting and is appalled at the misinformation and religious propaganda she finds there, prompting an exchange that still represents the best sex ed I've ever seen in prime time:

RACHEL: Did you know that most studies have demonstrated that celibacy doesn't work in high schools? Our hormones are driving us too crazy to abstain. The second we start telling ourselves that there's no room for compromise we act out. The only way to deal with teen sexuality is to be prepared. That's what contraception is for.
QUINN: Don't you dare mention the "C" word.
RACHEL: You want to know a dirty little secret that none of them want you to know? Girls want sex just as much as guys do.
MALE STUDENT: Is that accurate?

Instead of applauding, the PTC called it the "Worst TV Show of the Week" and slammed it in the press.[18]

We absolutely should be concerned about what young people are learning from media about sex. But treating all frank depictions of sexuality as dangerous is not the way to express that concern. When you control for other factors (like young people who are already sexually active seeking out media that reflects their lives), there's not much evidence to show that watching sex on TV makes it more likely that young people will have sex.[19] In fact, at a time when most people agree the media is suffused with sexual and sexualized images, when it has never been easier to find media depictions of sex, a 2016 study found that Millennials are having far less sex than the two generations that preceded them.[20]

Of course, having less sex or more sex isn't more or less moral, or more or less emotionally healthy. The questions we should be asking about media and sex aren't "how much sex does this media show?" but "what attitudes toward sex does this media convey?" Are younger adults having less sex because they have other things they'd rather do with their time or because they want to avoid emotional intimacy? Or because they fear they don't measure up to the beauty ideals they think are required to be "sexy"?

It wouldn't be hard to make that leap. Although paternalistic worrywarts like the Parents Television Council have made careers out of wringing their hands anytime youth sex is depicted on-screen, no matter the context, they've been missing the forest for the trees: sexualization. The difference between depictions of sexuality and sexualization is the difference between subject and object. Showing women expressing and directing their sexuality is by and large not dangerous to anyone. Depicting women as props in men's stories about sex is sexualization, and that's exactly what the last several generations have grown up with: media images produced by and for men, featuring sexed-up, fauxpowered women. The American Psychological Association found that sexualization not only leads to negative outcomes like eating disorders and self-esteem issues in women but also gives men unrealistic expectations about what sex with real, human women will be like, which reduces sexual satisfaction for everyone.

There is some hope. Media consumers are growing increasingly savvy at clapping back at offensive representation using social media campaigns. And though the overall number of women in media power positions is changing glacially, a new cadre of powerful women has staked claim both behind and in front of the camera. Names like Ava

DuVernay, Shonda Rhimes, Tina Fey, Samantha Bee, and Jill Soloway have become synonymous with women wielding new power in Hollywood. Animator Rebecca Sugar's unabashedly feminist, queer, and genderqueer kids' show *Steven Universe* has won awards, accolades, and a rabid fanbase and has made her the first woman to independently create a series for Cartoon Network. Beyoncé isn't just a pop superstar—she's producing new artists on her own music label and is a co-owner of Tidal, the streaming service she launched with her husband, Jay-Z. Only time will tell whether these are exceptions that prove the (male) rule or green shoots of real change, but my money's on green shoots.

And you don't even have to be famous to change the media landscape. Just ask Tani Ikeda, an award-winning filmmaker and founder of ImMEDIAte Justice, which teaches teen girls—mostly low-income girls of color—the film skills they need to create their own stories about sexuality, stories they don't find anywhere else, stories that avoid easy, fauxpowerful answers and instead confront the violence and shame they've been made to suffer, and to transform it into something powerful, hopeful, and new. When Ikeda was the same age as the girls she now works with, she had a secret: she had been the victim of a sexual assault. But it didn't stay a secret for long. "I remember going back to school and being completely ostracized," she tells me. "My circle of friends stopped talking to me. I couldn't find myself. I couldn't find passion or anything in all these things that had made me feel alive. I was having these nightmares every night and it was hard to go to sleep."

The one thing Ikeda did still have was art. She had dabbled in spoken word poetry and followed an older cousin to a summer camp for girls interested in filmmaking. So when the dreams started to change ("In one of these nightmares I flew. And after that every night I would go into my dreams and prepare myself like a warrior to fly or to feel secure or to fight"), Ikeda knew what to do with them. First, she wrote them down. And then she started filming. And that singular act of claiming control—of responding to the violent erasure of her agency by literally making her dreams visible—is still changing the path of her life and the lives of countless girls.

That first film of Ikeda's was experimental and appropriately dream-like, featuring shots of her grandmother brushing her long gray hair, of a friend naked in a bathtub, of her own stomach covered in dirt and then in eggshells. "I felt like I was tapping back into my sensuality through the visual image, like it was capturing something very raw inside of me," recalls Ikeda. And because she was a participant in the Reel Girls film camp, her short was submitted to the Sundance Film Festival in a package with a few other films produced by some of the other campers. Even better: when the shorts were accepted, the program flew Ikeda to Park City, Utah, for the festival, and it was there she once again found a place to connect and belong after the painful isolation she had felt at school. Before the festival she was skipping school and blowing off any thoughts of college. Now she was plastering the walls and ceiling of her room with posters of the films she'd seen at Sundance and applying to some of the best film schools in the country. Every single one of them accepted her.

Once she was settled in at USC, once she got her hands on the power and legitimacy to shape the stories that shape our world, she immediately set to plotting what to do with it. "I felt like I was just this one individual coming from my community who has to shoulder the storytelling," she recalls, "and it didn't feel like enough that I'm the only one who gets to tell my story." In search of answers, she joined a circle of queer women of color artists and activists who got together every Friday for a potluck dinner. It was there that she realized her story of violence and isolation was all too common. And it was there that she decided to do something about it.

When Ikeda invited me to spend a day on set with the ImMEDIAte Justice girls, I assured her I'd be a good journalist—seen but not heard, a silent observer in the corner. I don't remember if she laughed when I said it, but it didn't take much time on set to realize what a laughable proposition it was. IMJ is a participatory experience, no exceptions. As the day wore on, I came to understand that expectation of participation as radical and transformative: as girls and women, we've been trained to see ourselves as objects or consumers of media, but not as cinematographers, directors, gaffers, sound engineers. At IMJ, the lines are blurred: everyone is constantly swapping positions in relation to the camera. That fluidity erodes the power dynamics between directors and performers. We are in control of that lens; it doesn't control us.

There are five girls in attendance that Saturday afternoon, a fraction of Ikeda's usual group, but it's spring break and that means scheduling conflicts. Three of them—let's call them Annemarie, Samantha, and Zoe—are high school students, and today they form a giggly claque, scouring the space for the best light for selfies. The other two are young women who attend Claremont McKenna College and are interning with IMJ. While they help Ikeda tape down the cords and unpack the equipment, I steal away with the three high schoolers to a room upstairs where we can talk. (And take selfies for Instagram, natch.)

Once I turn on the recorder, Zoe and Samantha turn awkward and quiet enough that I worry about whether I'll even hear them on playback. I do, but their voices have become indistinguishable in their whispers. The next day, over brunch, I tell Ikeda this story, and she's not surprised. "When they first joined the class, whenever we were in a circle and everybody was sharing, they were so embarrassed and they would just giggle. So I would call them my giggle monsters, and even if they just said one word, that was enough.

"But they kept coming, and then there was this other girl who wasn't a part of ImMEDIAte Justice, and had said something about 'the ImMEDIAte Justice girls.' I don't know what the beef was. And [Samantha] went in. She was like, 'This is our crew, and we film awesome shit.' It was really sweet to see, even though she was just coming and not saying anything, and she was great with composition but other than that didn't really want to contribute, how much that space meant to her in terms of her wanting to defend it."[21]

It's not the only corrective I'll be surprised with that afternoon. Annemarie is working with some other girls on a film about body image, and when I first ask her to talk about it she launches into a monologue about the evils of the new generation of corsets being popularized by the likes of the Kardashians. "You have these waist cinchers and all these crazy things going on," she explains, with the unmistakable energy of a newly converted feminist, "and to fit the beauty standards nowadays you have to be a certain way or maybe a certain height, and you see all these different things that say maybe you're too skinny or too fat, and it's horrible because it's unattainable to get that certain beauty. . . . You want to be like that and you get mad at yourself because you don't look like that and you think it's your fault but it's really not."

I nod eagerly as she says this, my heart glowing with pride and reassurance. Which is why it catches me up short when a few minutes later she praises Kim Kardashian with a similar fervor. "I like how she's kind of coming out clean with a lot of these things that she's doing. It just shows you how unrealistic it is, how she dresses and she shows her cleavage, and it's the kind of dress that you can't wear a bra with and she just duct tapes her boobs." We immediately get distracted by a practical lesson on how one replaces one's bra with duct tape, for the benefit of the intrepid adult reporter in the room, who has never heard of such a thing. But the contradiction stays with me, and I ask Ikeda about it afterward.

"They're all at that age where I see them kind of try to be smaller and take up less space," she tells me. And they are shamed for being perceived as overtly sexual. So Kardashian, in that sense, is a role model, however flawed.

> While there is a lot of critique around the way in which she sexualizes her image, she is oftentimes doing it as a selfie in the bathroom, which is different than in the nineties having a commercial director light your body in a certain way. What's a little bit different in the conversation for me is the interplay between the way people are generating their own brand or their own image. . . . I think the girls are aware of how things are more nuanced, which means a lot of their feelings are very conflicted. It's an interesting time. And it gives us more room to dictate how we express our sexuality.

She also uses some of the IMJ time to help them interrogate their own ideas of aesthetics, pleasure, and sexuality, both in front of and behind the camera.

On a physical level, what do you like, what do you not like? When we're filming something, what colors do you like? What are you drawn to? It starts to build up more of a base of how that looks, how that feels. So if then at that point you can say, "I like taking selfies in this bathroom because it's got really nice natural light," maybe that is an entry point, just feeling like you have more control over the image and how you're projecting yourself. You might take 50 photos and you find the one that you love. That's controlling your image. In the larger conversation are you still subscribing to specific beauty ideals? Probably. But I think it's also a journey and a process. I sometimes feel like in feminist critique there's this ideal that we have to be at some imaginary political, woke feminist selves at all times, and we police each other to be that, and I don't subscribe to that. I was lucky to be socialized as a filmmaker in a very girl environment, where we did want to film our bodies, and there was something so pleasurable about showing our sexuality. That was a part of the desire.

That tension—between the temptation to replicate reductive ideas of women's sexuality and the power of using the camera to capture your desire for yourself—is on full display in the studio that afternoon. The day finds the girls working on two group projects: against a white backdrop, one of the interns is helping Samantha and Zoe create a short video about rejecting beauty standards. The girls take turns on either side of the camera, brainstorming ideas and whispering suggestions, putting on and removing makeup, chucking eyeliner at the lens, dancing charmingly goofy dances of liberation. There's nothing edgier happening here than you'd see in a Dove ad, except for the fact that no one is selling anything. Except for the fact that these girls have total authorship over both their visions and their images.

This is not the big time. The videos produced by IMJ get shared on YouTube or Facebook, and some of them get screened in class by supportive teachers or at special events for families and friends. Their most popular video, a strange and funny one about street harassment called "Catcall for What?" has about 12,500 views as of this writing. But just getting their work seen at all is a big deal for these girls, who

73

all too often feel invisible in their own lives. And whether or not Samantha and Zoe go into film careers, it's clear that this assumption of participation, this opportunity to experiment with their bodies in front of the camera coupled with the chance to develop their vision behind the lens, is permanently relocating them as subjects of media, not simply targets or consumers of it. Becoming intimately familiar with how media constructs ideas better prepares them to resist a lot of the damaging, sexualized ones that they're viewing, because they know that behind every image is an author with an agenda. They know that another idea could just as easily have been constructed. This outsider film school is also an experiential media literacy class.

Just feet from them, Nina, the other intern, has taken off her shirt and is lying on the floor, casually applying electrical tape to her nipples. Annemarie writes on her arm and takes a photo after each letter, slowly creating a stop-motion video that will eventually read, "Every smile, tattoo, bathing suit and crop top is a small revolution. Tell yourself you're beautiful every day, and I promise you will be." It's a quote from body image activist Matt Diaz that one of the girls saw on Instagram. A few of those words will wind up on my own leg before the day is over, but at the time I'm still trying to be a detached observer, and I'm worried about Nina, whether she feels it necessary to get naked and disembodied to make a video people will watch. For an hour and a half, I watch the other girls write on her and photograph her as she holds her body excruciatingly still, and I worry. But then she gets up. She announces that she needs to move, and another of our number assumes the position, and Nina begins to direct, to shoot. And my worry gives way to understanding. This was not a man behind the camera telling her to show him her tits. It's a group of young women of color all collaborating to create authorship, writing their own sexuality and their own rebellion, shifting easily through and around their relationship to the camera. Context matters.

The next day, over brunch, I asked Ikeda whether the girls being so much on camera and not just behind it is an accident of convenience (they're the subjects closest to hand) or something more than that. She tells me about Linda, another of the IMJ girls, who was being inter-viewed by a peer about a mural project they've all been doing lately. "She caught herself by surprise and started crying," Ikeda remem-bers, "and she was like, 'I'm crying because I never thought that I was important enough to have media created about me, and now my face is on a wall, huge. Now [this interview with me will be] screened in an auditorium. I don't see people who look like me celebrated in that way, and it's important.' She was crying and trying to find those words to describe, like, what it meant to her. And so I think it's both. It's visi-bility, but having control over our visibility."

It's hard to overstate the power of that control, and of learning it in community, on developing girls' sense of actual worth. When Ikeda started working with this particular group of girls, she thought she'd start by asking them each to make short films about a personal story. "Everybody was like, 'I have nothing to say, I don't know what we would film about my life, there's no story,'" she tells me with a rueful laugh. So she tried group work instead, developing collective projects to work on together, engaging the girls in technical skills building, get-ting them comfortable in small ways in front of the camera, drawing on exercises from Augusto Boal's classic political theater text, *Theater of the Oppressed*, to help the girls experiment with occupying their own bodies and taking up space in the world.

A year later, she put the same question to them: What do you want to film? What's most important to you? And this time each of the girls had a very clear vision. Ikeda puts it this way: "At the beginning, it's not that these girls didn't have anything to say. It's that they didn't believe that they did."

But if Ikeda is building a bubble around these girls protective enough to midwife their previously suppressed voices into the world, she's also careful to prepare them for life outside of it. Not every IMJ girl goes on to work in the film industry, but some do. Ikeda mentions that one graduate is now working on the set of the Netflix hit *Trans-parent*, another has become part of her crew shooting short films about groundbreaking women for the Hallmark Channel—and most sets are pretty far from feminist nirvana.

"I've had experiences where [cinematographers] treat all the other guys as bros that you go out drinking with, and those are the guys that get hired for the next shoot," recalls Ikeda. "As a woman trying to figure out how to navigate those spaces, you're clearly not one of the guys, so in those ways, sometimes you get cut out of things. In other ways, you're also treated as a set hookup possibility. That's how a lot of women [working on set] are seen. Camera guys are always interested in makeup girls because those are usually the only women on set."

That is one insidious cycle: Hollywood produces stories in which women are props for men's journeys; very often sexualized props. Men who work in the industry see that idea enforced every day in front of the camera, so when they look around on set and see there aren't that many women around, they replicate that same dynamic behind the camera. Which makes it harder for women to rise through the ranks to tell different kinds of stories. Which keeps the cycle in motion.

Even on less-lecherous sets, it can be hard for women to break through. Ikeda tells me that, just like in any other male-dominated field (and, to be fair, just like we've noted most of us do in our own social networks), the men in charge on set tend to favor hires who remind them of themselves. And once a producer develops a crew he likes, he just keeps hiring the same group over and over on every new project he takes on.

So how does Ikeda prepare her girls to get past the gatekeepers of the boys' clubs of filmmaking? She doesn't. Instead, she's prepping them to find the cracks in the gates and wedge them open wider, by finding women of color like Ava DuVernay (and Ikeda herself) to mentor them as they create clubs of their own. "Ideally it's building alternative structures, because things are changing so much in film," she tells me. "It's a lot easier now to make 'niche work' and still have a huge audience for it. On the *Transparent* set crew, they hire more trans folks on all areas of production than anywhere else.

"By having a full saturation of very, very different narratives that exist for a young person at ImMEDIAte Justice growing up, it gives them more choices and more possibilities for who they can become and what's possible. . . . When so much of the rest of the world agrees that you don't matter, it is so hard to stand for yourself. It's so hard to see your worth and to love yourself. So when people say it's revolutionary to love yourself, it is. It's not soft politics. It's huge. It's huge, in a big way."

And that's exactly why we need more than movies and TV and books and music and video games that show women how to love ourselves. We need a media ecosystem that actively loves women at every level, in full possession of our agency and power and complexity. That values a robust and diverse range of women's stories about sexuality (and everything else) and employs a diverse range of women storytellers who wield at least as much power at least as freely as their male colleagues. When we can create that media landscape, we won't have to tell anyone they're worthy or valid anymore, because it will already be reflected at them from a million mirrors.

## CHAPTER FOUR

# MONEY MAKES THE SEX GO ROUND

O UR SEX LIVES are inextricably tangled up with our wallets. Think of that item in your closet that makes you feel like a sex bomb as soon you slip it on, or the song you bought (or stole!) that gets you in the mood every time. Or, not to put too fine a point on it, think about your favorite vibrator. There's nothing wrong with reveling in how things we can buy make us feel. But economic forces influence our sexuality in much more complex ways than that— ways that are often invisible and sometimes quite malignant.

Before age seventeen (the average age of first intercourse, according to the CDC), most young people have been exposed to porn. Some of them have seen quite a lot of it. And because there is otherwise such a taboo against adults talking frankly with young people about sex, what they see when they google "free porn" (or even happen upon it accidentally) is often the sum total of what they know about sex before they have it.

Not all porn is reductive and misogynist. There's fantastic feminist porn, queer porn, and just plain indie porn that isn't racist, that doesn't assume every woman wants cum on her face, that knows that anal sex requires both lots of lube and lots of communication, and that shows sex is about a lot more than just the male orgasm.

But that stuff isn't typically on the free sites, where most young people (and adults!) get their porn. Which is likely why researchers have found that increased exposure to porn among teenagers correlates to a belief that men are inherently sexually dominant and women are subservient, to increased acceptance of sexual violence, as well as to an increased likelihood that male teens will perpetrate sexual harassment. One study found that college men who watch more porn are less likely to enjoy sexually intimate behavior like kissing, cuddling, and caressing. Among teen girls, increased exposure to porn is linked to negative self-esteem and body image issues.[1] And adults are vulnerable to similar effects. The media we consume shapes what we think of as normal as well as what we consider possible.

If we all received comprehensive, shame-free sex ed throughout our childhood and adolescence, and especially if that education included porn literacy, we could blunt the impact that lowest-common-denominator porn has on our personal lives and on our culture. But it's also worth asking why the free stuff any twelve-year-old can find online so often repeats and reinscribes narrow and damaging ideas of what sex is and whom it is for.

In part it's because the independent producers who produce great porn care more about their product. Obviously. That quality costs more to produce, and it inspires loyalty in fans. So when quality porn is stolen and posted to the free sites, fans notice and tell the producers, who are also more motivated to exercise their legal right to have it taken down. The companies that specialize in volume over quality and produce the monolithic porn that's only a "free porn" Google search away? They care a lot less and don't bother with takedowns nearly as much.

There's also just a lot less quality porn out there to find than there is crappy, misogynist porn, and that has to do with economics, too. For one, banks and web hosts often decline to take sex-related businesses as customers, regardless of how legal or responsible a business is. Those financial institutions that do serve "adult" businesses are free, then, to charge extra because their customers don't have the option of shopping around for a better price. And that surcharge — credit card processors that charge porn sites 12–16 percent per transaction instead of a standard 2–4 percent, for example — is a lot more easily absorbed by a megacorporation with multiple revenue streams than by a small indie producer that lives and dies by the margin on each sale.

I'm not correlating size with quality here by accident. Most of the major "tube" sites—the aggregator sites that show up first in almost any porn-related search—are owned by one company: MindGeek. The company formerly known as Manwin (really) has spent the better part of a decade gaining a near-monopolistic control over the porn industry. It started off with a few aggregator sites that allowed users to upload whatever content they wanted, even content from other companies that they didn't have the right to share. Manwin monetized that free content by selling ads alongside its smut. (Because free porn was such a novelty, and therefore a big draw, Manwin pretty early had enough eyeballs to even get the companies whose stolen content was on its sites to pay to advertise.) Of course, the availability of seemingly endless free porn devalued the price of all porn, which devalued the production companies themselves, until Manwin was able to buy up a bunch of them, too. Which brings us more or less to the current day, in which most of the porn from which we construct our sexual worldview is produced and distributed by the minds at one (need I say male-owned) company, whose main motive is to churn out new scenes as quickly and cheaply as possible.

MindGeek's business model isn't just shaping the sexual imaginations of teenagers and adults alike. It also hurts porn performers. The credit card processors that do take on the "risk" of working with porn companies don't just charge more. They require that companies properly document their adherence to basic industry standards that ensure that performers are of legal age, consenting, disease-free, and properly compensated. But because MindGeek doesn't need end-user credit cards, it doesn't have to abide by those regulations, leaving performers more vulnerable to a wide variety of workplace abuses.[2]

There are, of course, other options. TrenchcoatX, a pay-per-scene site that features only ethically produced porn, subverts the tube sites' practice of reductive tagging (think barfy category names like "Ebony," "MILF," and "Shemale" that reduce performers to stereotypes) by instead delivering search results based on users clicking "squicks" (behaviors and themes they don't want appearing in their search results) and "squees" (more of this please!). And Pink Label TV is perhaps the exact photonegative of MindGeek: a site that carefully curates the best of ethically and artfully made queer porn from around the world. Shine Louise Houston, who founded Pink Label, thinks of it as an incubator for the kind of porn she'd like to see more of in the world, and she runs the business accordingly, paying the content creators that make her cut far more than most other video-on-demand sites do. It's an approach that's finding a growing audience, Houston tells me, but very slowly. "Watching porn is now a little more acceptable, so I think people have been demanding different and more quality and I think that's possibly why there's been a flourish of independent artists over the last 10 years. . . . But this movement once again is being drowned out by all the noise from the tube sites. . . . When people are looking for exoplanets, there's a big old sun, and that's the tube site, and the exoplanet is this little tiny thing. It's hard to find us in the glare."

Even when places like Pink Label are visible, the people who find them have to be willing to pay for their pornography. That's a tough sell in a culture that doesn't value women's sexuality in general (if we think sluts are worthless, why should we pay to watch them be slutty?) and that doesn't treat porn like a legitimate cultural product the way it does music and other kinds of movies or even like a legitimate leisure activity to enjoy.

The good news is that this is a trend that's easy to influence. You can decide today that it's worth a little money to ensure the welfare of porn performers and to undermine the monopolistic hold MindGeek has on our cultural sexual imaginations. You can also decide that you're not ashamed of watching porn and treat it like any other media you consume, critiquing the subpar or problematic stuff and recommending the stuff you like to your friends. Stigma is part of what keeps the industry shady and underfunded. But there's nothing inherently wrong with enjoying a video of people having sex. Just because you may have encountered pearl-clutchers who think porn is shameful doesn't mean you have to believe them. Just because neoliberalism treats women's sexual labor as worthless doesn't mean you have to agree.

Neoliberalism is basically the belief that the free market knows best and will give people what they need and deserve. It's a belief in capitalism as a meritocracy in which regulations aren't safeguards against oppression or exploitation but obstacles to the will of the market, which will bring about the Greater Good. It's capitalism as a religion, really, as an article of faith.

What's all this economic talk doing in a sex book? When the economy relied on happy, healthy workers, it invested in a social safety net: Medicaid and Social Security. Infrastructure like public transportation. Strong unions. Widely available sex ed and family planning services, offered free or at low cost. Now that the economy needs fewer workers because jobs can be easily outsourced or eliminated through automation, it cares about people less. And that means we're all on our own, and our problems are treated like individual problems, not structural ones. It's no accident that all of those social safety net programs I just listed have been weakened or eliminated in recent decades. Neoliberalism assumes that the market is essentially infallible, and therefore any suffering must be the fault of the people who suffer. When competition can only produce the correct result, collaboration is suspect. When the market is the source of our happiness, there must always be something we can buy to cure unhappiness.

When we leave our sexual culture up to the "free market," we get all kinds of unintended consequences that extend far beyond pornography. As artificial intelligence increases in popularity, helpmeet apps like Siri are most often default coded female, while Big Thinkers like IBM's Watson are programmed and named to sound like men. The companies producing these devices aren't wrong about what their consumers want: a 2012 study found that people expect robots they perceive as male to have control over their environments, while they expect "female" robots to serve others.[3] What's wrong is that private companies control so much of our sexual discourse, and we barely notice: people feel more comfortable bossing lady voices around, so companies produce lady voices to boss around, so people get ever more used to women's docility. For-profit companies don't seem to care what impact they're having on our ideas about women, sex, and power as long as they're making money.

An old friend of mine, Matie Fricker, moved to New Mexico and opened Self Serve, a feminist sex shop. Self Serve sells only toys it knows are safe to use and ethically made, and it offers classes on everything from healing after sexual trauma to how to give the best blowjob. It's a model business citizen, and it's a force for good in unscrewing the sexual culture in Albuquerque.

Self Serve can't advertise on Facebook, though, because Facebook doesn't allow ads that suggest sex can be pleasurable. "Ads must not promote the sale or use of adult products or services, except for ads for family planning and contraception," reads the Facebook Adult Products and Services ad policy. "Ads for contraceptives must focus on the contraceptive features of the product, and not on sexual pleasure or sexual enhancement, and must be targeted to people 18 years or older."[4] That's right: you can advertise dangerous diet pills on Facebook. If you're savvy, you can even sell a semiautomatic rifle there.[5] But you can't suggest that sex is fun or sell anything explicitly linked to sex except contraception. Theoretically, Self Serve can advertise condoms by saying that condoms help prevent the spread of disease. But it can't say a particular condom feels better than another. That's too close to talking about how nice sex feels. And in reality, it can't even run the disease prevention ad, because it would link to the Self Serve site, which sells prohibited explicit sex things. Won't someone please think of the children?

That is, in fact, Facebook's argument. Because users can be as young as thirteen, it doesn't want to be responsible for those users learning anything about sex. That's a problem in and of itself, because it would be a lot better for those thirteen-year-olds to learn about sex from Self Serve than from any of the porn tube sites. But it's also a bullshit excuse—it would be incredibly easy for Facebook to create an "adult" category for ads and to only show those ads to people older than the age of eighteen, or even twenty-one. Such a category would allow businesses like Self Serve to advertise their wares and do good in the world, spreading the message that safer sex can be fun.

But Facebook doesn't have to be concerned with the greater good, because Facebook is a publicly traded corporation, and any human values its employees may individually have must take a back seat to share prices and quarterly earnings. Because, contrary to what the Supreme Court might think, corporations aren't people. So, that profit motive is what's controlling nearly everything a thirteen-year-old can most easily find on the Internet about sex. Facebook doesn't want to have to answer to angry parents whose adolescents clicked through to Self Serve, and it doesn't seem to want to invest the money it would take to create code that would guarantee sex-related ads are served only to consenting adults. Perhaps it just doesn't think taking money from sex shops is good for its brand image when it also does tons of business in conservative countries. Whatever the reason, Facebook has decided that the most cost-effective policy is simply to ban these kinds of ads. On the flip side, it's hard to imagine that no one has reported MindGeek's tube sites to Google for repeatedly hosting stolen content (a violation of Google's terms of service, which gives Google the right to delist it from search[6]), but Google sure seems to have given Mind-Geek a pass. Both decisions—Facebook's to ban ads for Self Serve, and Google's to allow MindGeek to remain in search results—are well within a company's rights to make.

But what about our rights, as human beings, to the information and products that can make our sex lives healthier, more fun, and more fulfilling? When companies and markets are unchecked, we wind up with sex lives that operate far too much like economics. As it is, the most dominant model of sexuality in the United States treats sex as a commodity exchange in which women "give it up" and men "get some." In this "sexual marketplace," a term used in all sincerity by pick-up "artists" and other assorted assholes, women's sexuality is the commodity, which they must keep safe from theft and only trade for the best possible deal, ideally a man offering marriage. (There are no queer or genderqueer people in the commodity model of sex.) Men are the buyers, trying to get the goods for as little as possible (ideally not even a phone number).

It's not hard to see how damaging this model can be. It's used to erase sexual coercion, because "a deal is a deal," after all. It's used to delegitimize the trauma of rape, equating sexual violence with theft. It's the underpinning of our cultural obsession with women's virginity and purity. If men weren't obsessed with collecting and acquiring a rare gem to display in a collection, virginity wouldn't be seen as an asset in women.

The commodity model encourages us to value women on the basis of their appeal to men. Not just queer people but also older women, women with visible disabilities, any women who lack "marketplace value" to the men who run the market don't exist. Race, age, body shape, and size—they all contribute to a woman's value relative to other women. So too do the choices she makes: if she is enthusiastic about sex or has multiple sex partners, she is, to borrow a phrase from some random Internet troll who once called me this, a "devalued pussy." (I did the only reasonable thing possible when I heard that: I invented an imaginary band by that name, which would only play in cities with dirty-sounding names, like Bangkok, Blue Ball, Atholl. The tour shirts would have been really something.)

Not coincidentally, this model makes most of us feel like utter shit about ourselves when we inevitably fail to be the most valued commodity possible. And that sexual insecurity, the marrow-deep knowing that we're not desirable enough, that there's a formula we could unlock that would make the world value our sexuality more, makes us prime targets for actual commodity markets. From fast-food ads to the Victoria's Secret fashion show, advertisers know just how to push the buttons of our sexual insecurity because, in many cases, they installed them. After all, if we feel sexually powerful and fully actualized without the latest luxury car/kitchen appliance/video game, we're not going to care if marketers tell us that buying that item will make us more appealing.

Sex is such a crutch to capitalism that the market pounces on any sexual trend and finds a way to use it to make us insecure enough to buy the latest quick fix. It does it even if that trend is revolt or revolution, as the Riot Grrrl–Spice Girl–Pussycat Dolls progression demonstrates. But that's only one example among countless others. There's nothing new to what *Bitch* magazine cofounder Andi Zeisler calls "empowertising." It dates back earlier than Virginia Slims selling cigarettes with "You've Come a Long Way, Baby" to the "I Dreamed I Won the Election in My Maidenform Bra" 1952 campaign.[7] It's just as popular today, showing up in spots for everything from Always maxipads to De Beers diamonds.

I once spent a week as the sexpert in residence on a popular message board for moms that I won't mention by name because there are so many boards like it and these same conversations happen everywhere. I was looking forward to days of discussions about the wide range of sexual experiences and challenges that women face. Instead, nearly every woman asked me a version of the same question: Could I recommend a pill that would make her want sex more? I tried to meet these women where they were, tried to ask if there were perhaps conditions in their lives making it harder to access their desire—did they feel ashamed? Did they have a husband (they all had husbands) who was attentive to their needs and desires in bed? Were they overworked and stressed out? Almost to a one, they refused to engage these queries. If they did, they would say something like, yeah, sure, my husband is only focused on his pleasure in bed, and I'm overwhelmed every minute of the day, but can't you just give me a pill so I can just want sex under these circumstances? They had been trained to accept every circumstance of their lives except themselves, to see their sexuality as a commodity owned by their husband, a commodity that was failing to deliver satisfaction. They believed that the only way to fix themselves was to buy something. To purchase a patch. It was a depressing week to be a sex educator.

This was long enough ago that there really was no such pill available. But since then, one has come on the market with great fanfare, only to fail spectacularly. Addyi was supposed to be "the female Viagra," but at its peak it sold only fifteen hundred prescriptions per month compared with the more than half-million Viagra prescriptions written in its first month on the market.[8] There are a lot of factors in its failure, including the exorbitant cost of the pill, the fact that women are forbidden from drinking alcohol while taking it, and the restriction that only premenopausal women can use it. But the number one was that it didn't really work for most women who had libido concerns. For sure, some women have biologically based issues with suppressed libido. They can and do deserve better research into medical solutions. But it's awfully hard to separate them out from the masses of women who don't want sex because they're working second shifts at home after working all day for money or who have learned not to expect that sex will be any fun for them. There is no pill, no market solution for these women. Fauxpowerment is just another empty promise of neoliberalism.

Neoliberal fauxpowerment, what Zeisler refers to as "market feminism" in her excellent book *We Were Feminists Once*, gets in the way of women accessing real sexual power in two parts. First, it distracts us. When we're focused on whether we're buying the most empowering stuff, the pole-dancing classes and Spanx that will make us feel our sexiest, we're distracted from the things that could really make us powerful, like full and equal access to our reproductive rights and a justice system that effectively addresses sexual violence.

I have nothing against women buying things that make them look or feel sexy. I own fancy bra and panty sets and can rarely resist buying a new red lipstick, even though only I can tell the difference between it and the three other red shades I already own. But market feminism convinces us buying these things aren't just fun—they're activism. And except in certain very limited and rare contexts, they're just not. Few things we can purchase make us feel sexually powerful in any sustained way; the effect always wears off, and like any good drug, leaves us craving a stronger hit next time. Empowerment that can be purchased is always an individualistic solution, a day pass out of the fucked-up structures that not everyone can afford. Sexual power is a structural issue.

Which leads us to problem number two: market feminism doesn't just focus on individual feelings at the expense of systemic change. It requires, and therefore cultivates, your sexual insecurity. Companies selling you shit to make you feel powerful always need to find or instill a new insecurity or to reactivate the one they told you the last product would sate. If you feel secure and powerful in your sexual sovereignty, you may still want their lip plumper, but you'll know that you don't need it. It's a recipe for exhaustion and bankruptcy, both the emotional and literal kinds. It's why Dove, having apparently saturated the market for anticellulite cream (yes, that's really what those early Dove Real Women ads were selling), had to recently create a new prerequisite to women's "empowerment," telling us we could really raise our arms in a power pose if only our armpits weren't so disgusting. And it just so happens that they have something to help with that.

To add injury to insult, women are spending our money on all this fauxpowerment from a place of already weakened economic power. In 2015, women earned only 83 cents for every dollar earned by a man. Broken down by race, Asian women made 87 percent what white men made, on average; white women made 82 percent, Black women made 65 percent. Latina women made only 58 cents on the white male dollar. Meanwhile, women who are actually trying to gain power and money through sex are stigmatized as either whores or gold diggers. Meanwhile, rape victims struggle to afford the aftermath of their own assaults, as medical and legal bills and disruptions to work or schooling easily add up to five-figure debt. Meanwhile, poor women are coerced into being sterilized (yes, this still sometimes happens right here in the United States[9]), penalized if they decide to have a baby, and economically bribed into marriages they don't want and that may be unsafe for them. Meanwhile, as of this writing, Congress is attempting to roll back the Affordable Care Act, a move that would strip coverage for contraception and all kinds of reproductive health care from millions of women, even going so far as to enable insurance companies to charge women extra for prenatal coverage, because (cisgender) men don't get pregnant. (The male politicians who advocate this are strangely mum on whether women should have to pay for coverage of Viagra or prostate cancer treatments.)

Even if it survives, the Affordable Care Act's contraception coverage is like Swiss cheese, leaving many poorer women falling through the holes insurers and employers have carved out. Want an abortion? Sure, they're theoretically legal but only really accessible in some states if you can take multiple days off of work, afford transportation, and have adequate private health insurance or enough cash. If you're on Medicaid, you're entirely out of luck: the Hyde Amendment, passed originally in 1976 and renewed by Congress every year since then, says no abortion for poor women. (Technically, it says no federal funding can be used to pay for abortion, but every legislator knows that the practical effect is that Medicaid is barred from paying for abortions, which in turn means poor people are up a creek if they need one.)

Money plays a role privately, too. Every day, money forces women to have sex they otherwise would reject, whether by becoming sex workers or by staying with partners they don't want but can't afford to leave. Far too many men (and women) still think if a man pays for an expensive date, he's entitled to "get" sex from a woman.[10] And the past few years have seen a number of female teachers fired for sexual "transgressions" committed in their off hours, including burlesque dancing and even simply getting pregnant outside of marriage.

Changing the economy and the way money is used to punish and devalue is a long-term project. At best each of us can pick one part of it, and chip away little by little. Support candidates and elected officials who will build a strong social safety net and regulate the markets in ways that blunt the worst impacts. Organize for strong unions and a livable minimum wage. Use our dollars as votes, spending them on what we want to see more of in the world. But there's something else each of us can do in the meantime: resist the narrative of the market. Don't let capitalism decide what you value or who is valuable. If you're having a hard time picturing what that would look like, I'd like to take you somewhere.

On a side street just steps from the chaotic swirl of Harvard Square, there's a nondescript door in the side of a Unitarian church. There, you can ring a bell, head downstairs, and find yourself welcomed into a bright and cozy space about the size of a college dorm's common room. This is Youth on Fire, a drop-in center for homeless and street-involved youth.

It's incredibly common for sexual violence or oppression to have played a role in forcing young people out of their homes. Forty percent of all homeless youth identify as LGBT, and the most common reason they cite for their precarity is that their parents kicked them out for being queer. Around 30 percent of homeless young people have been sexually abused, as compared to 1–3 percent of the general population their age. And once young people become homeless, their sexual vulnerability only increases. Some of them find they have to trade sex for money or a place to sleep. Others wake up to find an uninvited man in their sleeping bag, an experience so common many victims don't even call it rape. If they want to have sex for pleasure, there's nowhere for them to go—you can get kicked out of a shelter for being sexual with another guest, and having sex in public can get you an arrest record and a permanent spot on the sex offenders registry.

The free market is never going to liberate these kids. The free market is what left them to fend for themselves on the street when their homes were no longer safe places to be or ceased to exist. The free market is what marks them now as worthless, as though their financial assets and their human value were one and the same.

This cozy Cambridge basement is a rebuke to that idea. The walls are bold colors; the decor playfully modern. To your left, in the entryway, there are bulletin boards bristling with flyers, where notices for the on-site needle exchange snuggle up against invitations to college fairs. To the right, a list of quick chores, with a dry-erase blank next to each, where members take ownership of their space each day by spending five minutes cleaning the kitchen or sorting laundry. A little further in you'll notice closets full of clothes, couches and chairs, computers awaiting use at cheerful desks, and a wall of brightly colored built-in bunk beds with corresponding storage lockers, for use by the guests of the night shelter that Youth on Fire shares this space with. Across the room from the sleeping quarters, snacks sit out on a counter, beyond which is a capacious kitchen and a pantry full of every kind of food from peanut butter to peaches. In the far corner are offices, a meeting space, and a little medical clinic.

But even more affirming than the friendly space is Youth on Fire's approach to serving the young people it calls members. "Folks can come here, sign in, sign up for that [chore] and sleep all day," says

Mandy Lussier, YOF's program director. "Wake up, grab a pair of socks and grab a bag of ramen and say, 'Hey, thanks, I wiped down the counters and I'm out.' And that is a perfectly successful day. We served that person well that day. That's what they needed. We're not going to tell them what we think they should be doing. We're going to work with them on whatever their goals are."

It's a simple idea, centering the needs and desires of the people the organization serves. But when you're talking about teenagers who've been erased from the culture by their financial circumstances, erased from their families because of who they are and how they want to live in their bodies, that approach is everything.

Lussier gets this first-hand. I've known them (Lussier prefers the pronouns they/them) since 2005, when we both joined the cast of Big Moves, a size-diverse performance troupe in Boston. Back then they had a mohawk in an ever-changing rotation of colors. Today they're much more likely to sport a carefully crafted swoop in the front. But mostly Lussier remains the same: big, easy smile, bright blue eyes, and a perpetual air of both warmth and mischief. If Auntie Mame were a zaftig genderqueer butch dandy, they'd be Lussier.

Back when we met, they were putting themselves through college while slinging coffee at a suburban Starbucks. Looking for something more soul-satisfying than term papers and lattes, they cast around for an internship opportunity and connected through friends to Youth on Fire, where they instantly felt at home.

As a young kid myself I was kicked out of my house around fifteen, just through conflicts with my stepfather mostly. I didn't have a ton of places that I felt like I could go, so I ended up staying with an ex who was really really abusive. But her family was so lovely, and they let me stay there, so I stayed there. It was awful in so, so many ways, but it was what I had. I got into alcohol at fifteen and drank a lot. And so [when] I came here and I was volunteering, it just made sense and clicked. It was working with younger versions of myself. I just felt comfortable here. And the members took to me. Once I did my internship I was like, I'm not leaving this place.

And they haven't. Youth on Fire was so impressed with Lussier that, as their internship was ending, the higher-ups managed to secure some state funding to hire them for a part-time position dedicated to making the space safer and more welcoming for LGBT folks. They've worked their way up from there, first becoming a case manager, then program coordinator, and finally taking the reins as program director in 2015.

But Lussier will always be a case manager at heart. As someone who's had the privilege of having Lussier nurture me through a life crisis, this surprises me not at all. There's nobody better at crawling down into whatever dark hole you find yourself in, making themselves comfortable, and just sitting with you until you're ready to start climbing out—at which point they really swing into action. It's the perfect skill set for their work at Youth on Fire. "I really like meeting [members] on the first day, working with them on whatever they want to work on. For a lot of people that might be finding shelter for the night, or getting a medical appointment." For others it's more the kind of stuff that all teenagers need, including better sex ed than they're likely to find in school.

Though Youth on Fire does run groups and classes, most of the education happens casually, in the context of ongoing conversations and relationships between members and peer counselors or staff. The more members start to feel like Youth on Fire is a place where they're valued, where they can really belong and take up space, the more they become open to the possibilities of their lives and loves. Lussier told me a story about one girl who identified as straight when she arrived at Youth on Fire. Gradually, as she was exposed to the queer-positive space, things started to shift for her. "She started coming to queer coffee hour, which is this group I do with anyone who identifies as something other than heterosexual. We go out to the movies or dinner (I have a little bit of funding to do that). She started coming to that and was like, 'Yo I think I might be gay, I think I like women, what's up with that?' She had so many questions about coming out, about sex, and how to have sex with someone without a penis, and so we had a lot of really real conversations about sex and sexuality."

Those conversations paid off, and not just in helping a young woman find her sexual path. A few years later, after she had stopped coming to Youth on Fire, Lussier's phone rang. It was the same young woman, calling to say thank you and farewell before she killed herself. Because of the trust that had built up between them, Lussier was able to intervene and save her life.

Perhaps this goes without saying, but putting homeless teenagers in charge of their own lives is far from the standard approach of most shelters and drop-in centers. Another (much larger and better funded—there's that market hand again) youth-oriented drop-in in the Boston area takes a very different approach, says Lussier. "You walk in, there's a desk with a schedule, you have to make an appointment, someone has to bring you upstairs to the different floors, and you're going to work one-on-one with a case manager immediately on your concrete goals. And those are the goals you need to work on." Those goals almost always include working toward a GED or getting a job, or both, and if you're not demonstrating that you're working on those goals—if you're not producing—you're not welcome.

You may be made to feel unwelcome even if you are doing as you're told. "They preach that they're LGBT inclusive. And they've got the rainbow triangle at their door. And I've heard some just horrible things that their staff have said directly to members. Staff calling members fags. Making jokes around how people dress and present themselves." And that's not one bad apple; being a woman or a queer person and being in most shelters is a dangerous proposition. Preparing members to navigate the shelter system is a grindingly regular part of Lussier's job. "It's different for different people. So if you're a flamboyantly gay man, and you're going into a shelter, I would tell them, 'Hey, if I were you, I would try to tone that down a little bit.' And to have to tell someone that . . . " Lussier's face cringes with pain. "If you're a trans woman, I'm going to send you to Rosie's Place, because Rosie's Place is a shelter that works with women and they're very trans inclusive. So that's good. But if I have a trans man, I don't know where to send a trans man. So that can be really difficult. I sometimes work with [trans men] who will wear a more androgynous outfit and will go into a women's shelter. Because that's the only place they can go with their current ID."

A new Massachusetts law banning public accommodations from discriminating against trans folks should be helping with this in principle, though of course most of the rest of the country has become much less safe for trans people under the Trump administration. And in practice, the Massachusetts law doesn't protect Lussier's members much. "You send a trans man to Pine Street Inn and try to have them access the male side, if that's the side they feel most comfortable with . . . you have, on a floor, maybe 2 or 3 staff to 50 guys? What if someone calls that person a faggot or a fucking dyke or a number of different things, is that staff person who's completely outnumbered going to step up and say something? No."

I hope Lussier will forgive me for telling you how proud I feel of them as they explain the intricacies and challenges of their work. With a fourteen-year age difference between us, I've often felt a little like a mama bear toward them. When we met over a decade ago, they were still an insecure punk, drinking a lot, not sure of their own purpose or voice. Now they've turned into a proud parental unit themselves. That kind of evolution comes from many places, but there's no doubt in my mind that Youth on Fire can take a big piece of the credit. Growing into yourself in a place that has faith in your leadership, that sees past convention and propriety, that values empathy and human connection, and that wants to help you be your best self and not anybody else? It's hard to imagine a more powerful force.

Youth on Fire does that for every member, not just for tenacious interns with neon mohawks who give great hugs. And it goes far beyond day-to-day interactions. All members are invited to attend a monthly Youth Advisory Board meeting, in which staff listen to members' concerns about the space (recently there's been a little spike in stealing) and ideas about how to make it better. Not every idea makes it through (a recent request to acquire some gym equipment has been tabled for lack of space), but some do, like the new entryway display that features pictures of each staff member along with their name and role to help members get oriented faster. A small cross-section of members is also asked to participate every time there's a new staff member to hire, submitting questions, sitting in on interviews, and holding real veto power over any potential staffer they don't think would make the space what they need it to be.

A few of the members are themselves staffers, employed (and paid) as peer leaders, for up to twenty-eight hours a week. A lot of what they do is informal. They're basically trained as uber-members with expertise in sexual health, harm reduction, substance abuse, you name it, and their job is to be available to other members as a resource as needed. "The peers are able to work with folks in a different capacity than some of the case managers," Lussier tells me, "because they're younger. They've been through this. They're currently going through this. They're just a huge part of the culture here." Some of them also run discussion groups for the members on things like sexual wellness and trans identity, whatever the individual peer leader is passionate and knowledgeable about. All of them get the experience of being paid, being valued in the language of the market, for the very traits the rest of the world uses to justify treating them as though they are worthless.

Youth on Fire also helps members take that leadership and passion out of their cozy center through a speakers bureau. Sometimes members are asked to talk about what their lives are like at local colleges doing homelessness awareness programming or at public health conferences. Last year, the peer leaders educated an adorable audience when a middle school ran a clothing drive for warm winter clothes, and the parents arranged to have the children bring the clothes to the center to meet the people they were giving to, to understand that they're all part of the same community. Whatever the task, Lussier and their staff prepare the members carefully, to great impact.

> These kids who are well dressed, carry themselves well, can stand in front of a room and deliver a really badass speech, [the audience comes to] realize that those are the same people who, after they leave that day, go to their sleeping bag if they're lucky enough to have one. And sleep outside. It doesn't register until you have someone saying,

"I got kicked out of my house and this is how it happened," or "I traveled to Boston for a job opportunity that I thought was going to work out, or a housing opportunity, and it fell apart and I have no safety nets. I have no money to get back."

A few times a year, members of the speakers bureau are even invited to testify at the statehouse or city hall on matters related to homelessness, foster care, or LGBT youth.

The impact goes both ways. It's hard to overstate what it means to a homeless teen to be an invited honored guest at Harvard Law School. "We hear from so many folks that they feel ignored and feel invisible out on the street. That people will pass them by all day; not look them in the eye, or look down on them. So for them to have an opportunity where they can be the educators, they are the experts in the room? It makes them feel important and empowered. A lot of them become more involved in the center and want to do more speaking engagements because it makes them feel good. They feel heard. They feel like they're participating in something bigger than themselves."

I'm no economist, and this book doesn't contain proposals to fix or replace capitalism, or the way it molds and constrains our sexual selves. But Youth on Fire shows us how, in the meantime, we can refuse to be fooled about what is and who are actually valuable. It takes practice to start identifying the myriad ways we're being groped and fondled by the invisible hand of neoliberalism. Once we can see it, however, we can start resisting it, opting instead to value genuine pleasure, consent, health, connection, and sovereignty over commodification, competition, and "sexiness." We may have to pay for our porn, but we don't have to buy into the fauxpowerment marketplace.

## CHAPTER FIVE

# THE SEPARATION OF CHURCH AND SEX

// I HAD A CASE in rural upstate New York in which my client was a Republican police officer," Diana Adams tells me. She's a lawyer who specializes in family law.

It was a child custody case. [My client] was living with his girlfriend before he and his wife had finalized their divorce, which had been waiting for years because neither of them could afford to pay the filing fee. They had been separated for years, but the very first thing that the judge said to me was that sodomy and extramarital sex were crimes in New York State and crimes in the Bible, and I should read the Bible to my client and I might need to read it myself. Immediately I tried to get the case removed from that judge, [but] the only other judge in the county was his brother, and the only court-appointed child attorney, who interviews the child and says what's best for them, was his best friend of 50 years. They had the case dismissed, so I couldn't bring it up on appeal. So basically this dad was losing custody because he was living with his girlfriend before his divorce had come through, and they thought that just wasn't Christian.[1]

Because too many people seem confused on the matter, it pays to say this plainly: We are not supposed to be living in a theocracy. The Constitution is clear on that matter. Only 20 percent of the country goes to church on a regular basis. But you wouldn't know it by looking at the federal government, where 92 percent of US House and Senate members identify as Christian. Our president openly campaigned on giving Christians preferential treatment.[2] Our vice president's entire political career has been bankrolled in part by a family, the Princes, who are openly working toward a Christian Right takeover of the US government.[3] Our secretary of education is literally a member of that family and has said she wants to use public education to "advance God's kingdom."[4] Long before Betsy DeVos's nomination, our nation's public schools have used tax dollars to fund abstinence propaganda developed by explicitly Christian organizations and curricula that teach that girls bear primary responsibility for not "tempting" boys into sex. For a country founded by settlers fleeing religious persecution, our government is strangely tangled up with a particular right-wing strain of the Christian church, and that entanglement is constantly limiting the ways we can be sexual.

Our government wasn't always so subservient to right-wing Christian agendas. For most of the twentieth century, the evangelical church considered politics too earthy and mundane to sully itself with. That was until 1976, when the IRS revoked the tax-exempt status of Bob Jones University, citing the Christian school's policy against interracial dating.

With the backing of evangelical leaders, the school refused to rescind its racist rule and instead filed suit to retain its tax-exempt status. Even before the case reached the Supreme Court (where the school lost), the suit galvanized religious leaders, who saw the IRS ruling, and the Civil Rights Act from which it drew its authority, as "government interference" in their segregated, white fiefdoms. They wanted to put politicians and bureaucrats on notice. But they knew that organizing ordinary rank-and-file evangelicals to explicitly defend racism would be a harder sell. So they cast about for other issues to organize around and decided, for reasons we can only guess at, to go after abortion.

It took a while to take hold. Evangelicals were unaccustomed to thinking of themselves as political actors, and they didn't much care about abortion, either. (That was Catholics. In fact, the Southern Baptist press praised *Roe v. Wade* when the court handed down the decision, saying "Religious liberty, human equality and justice are advanced by the Supreme Court abortion decision.") But the leadership persisted, and as evangelicals began to stir, Republican politicians took notice. A deal was struck: evangelicals would help elect Republicans, and Republicans would become the party that opposed abortion and sexual freedom in general while, of course, defending the church's right to be as racist as it wants to be. The Religious Right was born.

It should be no surprise, then, to find that hypocrisies abound at the intersection of church and state. The year 2016 found the Religious Right throwing its weight behind a twice-divorced, previously pro-choice modelizer who couldn't even name his favorite Bible verse over evangelical poster boy Ted Cruz and, for that matter, lifelong Methodist Hillary Clinton. But Religious Right hypocrisy extends far beyond their choice of candidate. The Republican Party platform, which attracts the overwhelming support of voting evangelicals, advocates for increasing the death penalty, giving tax breaks to the rich, making it harder to qualify for welfare, opposing any minimum wage increase, and doing everything possible to punish, criminalize, and keep out immigrants and refugees. I don't pretend to speak for Jesus, but it's hard to find evidence that he would support a single one of these positions.

Nowhere is the hypocrisy of the Religious Right clearer than in its use of "religious freedom" arguments. The Religious Freedom Restoration Act was a fairly innocuous piece of legislation, passed in 1993 in a bipartisan effort to shore up the "Free Exercise" clause in the First Amendment ("Congress shall make no law respecting an establishment of religion, or *prohibiting the free exercise thereof . . .* "), after a much-criticized Supreme Court ruling allowed a private employer to discriminate against two Native Americans who used peyote as part of their religious ritual. RFRA was drafted as a rebuke to that idea and a return to the constitutionally protected idea of free exercise. Over the years, it's been used appropriately in a few cases, including ones involving Orthodox Jewish prisoners wanting kosher meals and churches that would be otherwise barred by state or local ordinance from feeding the homeless.

Until 2012, RFRA was mostly dormant, a little-used statute that no one much thought about. Enter Hobby Lobby, a chain of craft supply stores owned by an evangelical Christian family who objected to the Affordable Care Act's provision mandating employers include contraception coverage in their health care plans. Hobby Lobby filed suit against the mandate, claiming it violated its religious freedom, as protected by RFRA, to have to pay for contraception that it believed, science be damned, to be a form of abortion.

It's worth diving into the science here briefly. The five forms of birth control Hobby Lobby specifically objected to are three kinds of IUDs (Paragard, Mirena, and Skyla) and two forms of emergency contraception (Plan B and Ella). None of them actually causes abortions. Some of them can prevent a fertilized egg from implanting in the uterus, which prevents a pregnancy from occurring. These are scientific terms, and words have meaning. Also meaningful: until just before it filed suit, Hobby Lobby's health insurance plan covered Plan B and Ella.[5] That's right. The drugs it so morally opposes that it was willing to sue the federal government over being forced to cover? Hobby Lobby was supplying those very drugs to employees for years without even bothering to check. So why the sudden conversion? Given the roots of the Religious Right, could it be that it was less invested in the fate of fertilized eggs and more invested in using women's bodies as pawns in an effort to undermine the authority of the first Black president? I'll let you come to your own conclusions.

Regardless of motive, Hobby Lobby pursued its case all the way to the Supreme Court, where it paved the way for a monumental shift in the use of RFRA. Writing for the conservative majority opinion, Justice Alito claimed that RFRA freed the justices to draw "a complete separation from First Amendment case law" — even though RFRA was explicitly drafted to prevent its being used in this way and the Court has never interpreted it this way in any previous case. What this meant in practice was that the Court has given itself cover to ignore previously settled case law in the interpretation of the "Free Exercise" clause, most specifically a precedent case in which the Court ruled against an Amish employer who refused for religious reasons to pay Social

Security taxes, on the grounds that "granting an exemption from social security taxes to an employer operates to impose the employer's religious faith on the employees."

Far from defending religious "freedom," that religious imposition is exactly what the Supreme Court endorsed in the Hobby Lobby ruling. And a flood of legislation has followed, mostly in the form of state-level RFRA laws designed to permit "Christians" to discriminate against LGBT people in every conceivable way. In 2015, Arkansas made it illegal for cities to pass nondiscrimination ordinances that protect LGBT people on the grounds that requiring people not to act like homophobic bigots infringes on their religious freedom. In Michigan, it's perfectly legal for a private adoption or foster care agency to refuse to place a child in a home that runs afoul of that agency's religious beliefs, whether the agency is against gay marriage, unmarried couples, or single parenthood or whether it simply finds that the wife in a heterosexual couple is insufficiently submissive to her husband. Mississippi's Protecting Freedom of Conscience from Government Discrimination Act is so broad that it protects therapists from having to treat clients who may be too queer or too slutty for their tastes, protects any business that refuses to provide wedding-related services to gay couples getting married, permits state and local employees to refuse to process any paperwork or do anything at all related to gay marriage, permits businesses and schools to institute "sex-specific standards or policies concerning . . . dress or grooming, or concerning access to restrooms, spas, baths, showers, dressing rooms, locker rooms, or other intimate facilities or settings," and much, much more.[6]

And those are just some of the laws that have passed. Despite the fact that most Americans oppose these kinds of laws,[7] in the two years post–Hobby Lobby, state legislatures considered nearly two hundred bills to expand religious "freedom." Most failed, but the ones that have become law are daily making many citizens less free by forcing us to choose between ongoing legal discrimination and adherence to a faith to which we do not subscribe. (If you're still not sure whether RFRA laws are actually "Christian Conservative Freedom" laws, ask yourself this: Would the federal government allow Quaker business owners to refuse to pay taxes on the grounds that their religion prohibits them from supporting war?)

Surprise, surprise: this is all a play straight out of the Religious Right's longstanding racist playbook. Christian "religious liberty" has been invoked since the seventeenth century to defend racial segregation on trains, in housing, and on campuses and to defend bans on interracial marriage. It was the very argument the Christian Right used in defending Bob Jones University against the IRS in 1983.[8] These days, the same folks suing for religious freedom in every court they can are also doing their best to block the construction of mosques across the country and support Trump's ongoing efforts to ban Muslim immigrants and refugees.[9]

More genuinely surprising is the pushback they're getting of late from an unexpected quarter: the Satanic Temple. Despite the name, these are no devil worshippers but a nontheistic organization that takes its inspiration from the idea of Satan as "symbolic of the Eternal Rebel in opposition to arbitrary authority, forever defending personal sovereignty even in the face of insurmountable odds." In practice, much of what the Satanic Temple does is defend actual religious liberty by freaking people out. Sometimes they use performance art to do this: they've performed a "Pink Mass" featuring two men kissing over the grave of the mother of Fred Phelps, founder of the Westboro Baptist Church, claiming the ritual turned her gay in the afterlife (they do not actually believe in an afterlife). They have whipped each other while wearing baby masks and fetish gear in front of antiabortion protesters, to "expose the anti-choice protest as an act of fetal idolatry, highlighting the fetishization and abstraction of the 'baby.'"[10] Sometimes they equip individuals to stage their own protests, like the letter they provide to members (and anyone who downloads it for free from the website) to exempt them from so-called informed consent laws that require people seeking abortions be given state-mandated messages that often contain false or misleading information. The letter claims, "The communication of Political Information to me imposes an unwanted and substantial burden on my religious beliefs." It continues:

As an adherent to the principles of the Satanic Temple, my sincerely held religious beliefs are:

My body is inviolable and subject to my will alone.

I make any decision regarding my health based on the best scientific understanding of the world, even if the science does not comport with the religious or political beliefs of others.

My inviolable body includes any fetal or embryonic tissue I carry so long as that tissue is unable to survive outside my body as an independent human being.

I, and I alone, decide whether my inviolable body remains pregnant and I may, in good conscience, disregard the current or future condition of any fetal or embryonic tissue I carry in making that decision.

Compared with the Religious Right, the Satanic Temple is small, with about twenty chapters (some more active than others) and just over sixty thousand followers on Facebook. But post–Hobby Lobby, it's aiming big league at "religious freedom" laws. Invoking the beliefs in the letter, it's filed a pair of pointed lawsuits, calling into question whether religious freedom laws are really meant to protect everyone, or just right-wing Christians. In 2015, it filed suit on behalf of Missouri resident Mary Doe, who was denied when she brought the letter to the only abortion clinic in the state and demanded she be exempted on grounds of religious liberty from the state-mandated seventy-two-hour waiting period and antiabortion propaganda. A federal judge dismissed the claim a year later, on the fairly ridiculous grounds that Doe was no longer pregnant, but the Temple is appealing. More recently, the Temple filed suit against the 2016 Texas law requiring mothers provide burials for the fetal remains of their abortions. That case is pending as of this writing.

The Satanic Temple's approach may be too idiosyncratic for your tastes, and that's fine. But know that we're going to need to utilize everyone's idiosyncrasies to get out of this mess: the Religious Right's tendrils are so fully entwined in our government that it would take a machete to sever the two. In 2009, Colorado began offering free birth control to anyone who wanted it. Over the following five years, unintended pregnancies in the state dropped by 40 percent, abortions fell by 42 percent, and the state saved millions of dollars in related public health spending from the unintended pregnancies it prevented. You'd think the GOP would be thrilled with the savings and the drop in abortions, but instead a group of Republican state senators, with the support of groups like Colorado Family Action (motto: "Your Christian Voice at the State Capitol"), fought to defund the program, falsely claiming it made girls slutty. (The program just barely survived the attempt.)

Or try to follow the money on this one: In 2016, Utah passed a law declaring pornography a "public health crisis," which enabled the state to spend money from its public health budget on anti-porn campaigns. (You can bet it wasn't differentiating between misogynist tube-site porn and the carefully curated stuff at Pink Label.) The Utah bill was drafted by a nonprofit going by the anodyne name National Center on Sexual Exploitation, which turns out to be just a recent rebrand of Morality in Media, a longstanding anti-porn advocacy group that, until said rebrand, brazenly spouted on its website things like "In His death on the cross, Jesus gave the world the perfect model of what true love is."[11] It is funded in part by—you guessed it—the Religious Right. (Morality in Media also was funded for a few years by the federal Department of Justice, which outsourced all of its investigations of illegal obscenity to the group for two years. Three hundred thousand taxpayer dollars later, it had turned up zero prosecutable cases.) Just after Utah's anti-porn bill passed, Dani Bianculli, the director of the "law center" at the National Center on Sexual Exploitation, told the *Washington Post* that she'd already fielded requests from people in ten other states interested in implementing the same law.[12]

Our government doesn't always bother to hide behind third-party nonprofits when it tries to control our sex lives. Some programs spend federal welfare dollars, funds that are earmarked to help families out of poverty, to promote heterosexual marriage. And it's perfectly legal, thanks to a gap—way too big to be called a loophole—in the way the funding is distributed. It works like this: When welfare was reformed under Bill Clinton, one of the changes implemented was a shift from federal to state control. Previously, if a family fell below a certain income level, it became automatically eligible for cash supplements from the federal government. But since 1996, what we call welfare and what the Clinton law calls TANF, or Temporary Assistance to Needy Families, is distributed via block grants to states—chunks of money the federal government gives to states to distribute as they see fit within a set of guidelines. And those guidelines have a lot more to say about marriage than you would expect.

With some technical exceptions, all states have to spend their TANF grants on programs that support at least one of the following "purposes":

- Provide assistance to needy families so that children can be cared for in their own homes
- Reduce the dependency of needy parents by promoting job preparation, work, and marriage
- Prevent and reduce the incidence of out-of-wedlock pregnancies
- Encourage the formation and maintenance of two-parent families

All of that marriage language is there because of the common fallacy that marriage itself lifts families out of poverty. It doesn't, and decades of marriage promotion efforts have never produced a demonstrable decrease in poverty.

The TANF language leaves states free to take money that used to go to help poor families pay for child care or utilities or food or transportation and instead to spend it on all kinds of vaguely defined "healthy marriage initiatives." Take, for example, Oklahoma's "Forever. For Real." classes, which teach couples, regardless of that couple's wealth or income, how to better understand each other's "love styles" and divvy up the household chores. With essentially zero oversight from the federal government, such programs siphon hundreds of millions of dollars every year from the pockets of the poorest Americans.

Here I would like to say something about how simple the solution to all of this should be: we should be able to just vote out politicians who bring the pulpit to their public service. And we absolutely should refuse to vote for them in the first place, and organize others to do the same. We should be grooming and supporting strong candidates to challenge them, or supporting organizations that do that work. But many, many of us are already doing these things, and it hasn't been enough so far. Not because we're outnumbered. Because conservative Republicans have been systematically disenfranchising dissenters through gerrymandering (deliberately redrawing the geographic boundaries of congressional districts so that they favor Republicans) and other voter suppression tactics.

Their efforts have not gone unchallenged. Earlier this year, a district judge in Texas ordered the state to redraw at least three of its congressional districts. In North Carolina, a federal judge found that districts had been so severely rigged along racial lines—forcing almost all African American and Latino residents into a few tightly packed districts and leaving the rest to be dominated disproportionately by white voters—that the state had to hold special elections in twenty-eight newly drawn districts in 2017. And in late 2016, a federal court found that Wisconsin's 2011 redistricting "was intended to burden the representational rights of Democratic voters" and therefore was unconstitutional. Wisconsin is appealing the ruling to the US Supreme Court, whose decisions will affect not just that state but many of the others where Republicans redrew districts last time they had the chance.

The Supreme Court, though, has been uneven on the issue of voting rights. In recent years, it has rejected attempts by Republican legislators in several states to implement strict voter ID requirements, eliminate or reduce early voting, reduce the number of polling places in left-leaning (and often majority-minority) districts, and use other tactics designed to discourage or bar people of color, who lean heavily Democratic, from voting. But those attempts by right-wing lawmakers would not be so prolific if the Supreme Court hadn't itself overturned key parts of the Voting Rights Act of 1964, which had previously protected against this kind of systematic disenfranchisement.

Whatever the high court decides in the Wisconsin case, one thing is clear: until we find a way to erect strong systemic protections against voter suppression and gerrymandering, we're going have to keep fighting lawmakers backed by the Religious Right on multiple fronts. That certainly seems to be how they like it. In the last decade, their efforts to roll back abortion rights have taken the form of ever-multiplying state-level battles with a growing arsenal of tactics. Some states have attempted to pass TRAP laws, which target abortion providers with stringent medical standards that don't apply to any other fields, with the intent of making it too expensive or just plain impossible for the clinics to comply. Others have pushed personhood amendments, which grant full human rights to a fertilized egg, even before implantation. Still others have passed onerous mandates forcing people seeking abortions to have invasive ultrasounds or wait for days between when they tell a provider they want an abortion and when the provider can perform it, rendering abortion too expensive for people who can't afford to take multiple days off of work for the procedure.

These infringements on our bodily sovereignty are always couched in moral mumbo-jumbo. Don't believe it. In January, the Arkansas legislature passed the most draconian abortion restrictions in the nation, effectively banning abortions after fourteen weeks. The lawmakers who voted for this claim they're just trying to protect children. But the same lawmakers who sponsored the unconstitutional ban also voted to pass legislation that made it legal to carry a concealed weapon on school property and that cut both the weekly amount and number of weeks that struggling families can receive unemployment benefits if a provider is laid off.

Until we can fix our broken democracy, I believe that the single most effective way to beat back the Religious Right's incursions into our bodies and our bedrooms is to expose that hypocrisy. You too have a right to religious freedom in this country, and that means your government shouldn't be in the business of imposing someone else's dubious religious code on you. Don't cede an inch of the moral high ground. The Satanic Temple's confrontational theater and lawsuits are one approach to doing that. But you don't have to be a nonbeliever to fight the Christian Right. In fact, it may help if you yourself are a Christian.

It has certainly been more than helpful to Cherisse Scott, one of a growing group of leaders advocating for reproductive justice from an explicitly faith-based perspective. Her passion for this mission comes from personal experience: years ago, when Scott needed an abortion and didn't know where to get one, she just called the first place she saw in the phone book. It was hours into her appointment there that she realized she wasn't at an abortion clinic at all. She was at a crisis pregnancy center.

Crisis pregnancy centers (CPCs) are businesses that pose as abortion clinics but instead try to shame or scare pregnant women out of their decision to abort. They traffic in misinformation and outright lies and operate from an explicitly right-wing Christian perspective, though they do their best to mask their religious agenda until they have women cornered. And many of them are funded by state and federal dollars. That's right: I'm paying for this abusive charade, and if you're a US taxpayer, you are too.

At least eleven states directly fund CPCs out of state family planning budgets. Another twenty-plus sell "Choose Life" license plates and send the proceeds to CPCs, or require that women seeking abortions get ultrasounds in advance, driving traffic to what's usually the only place that ultrasounds are offered free of charge. South Dakota goes so far as to literally require that anyone seeking an abortion visit a CPC first. States also manage to divert federal funds to CPCs through the very same pesky welfare block grants that fund "marriage promotion."

Despite the fig leaf excuse that CPCs serve state interests by supporting poor expectant mothers, vanishingly few states regulate or monitor whether or how CPCs do that. Some even incentivize the opposite: a *Cosmopolitan* investigation found that the state of Pennsylvania "reimburses a center just $2 each time a woman receives food, clothing, or furniture—a maximum of four times. That's a $24 cap for an individual pregnant woman's material needs." On the other hand, the state pays them upward of $1 per minute for all the ideologically driven "counseling" they can force a woman to endure.[13] Unsurprisingly, CPCs vary widely in terms of how accessible they make diapers, parenting classes, baby clothes, and other things that might actually support good outcomes for new parents and their children. But uniformly, to a center, they manipulate and abuse women seeking abortions, often forcing them to watch terrifying and violent videos and spreading actual lies, like the common false claim that abortion is linked to breast cancer and depression.

When Cherisse Scott unknowingly visited a CPC in search of an abortion, the woman who did her intake asked her multiple questions about whether she was poor or needy (she wasn't), and then tried to talk her into choosing adoption instead of abortion. When that didn't work, Scott was made to watch almost an hour of graphic videos of fetuses' heads appearing to get crushed during abortion procedures and stories about women who regretted their abortions. Finally, she got the CPC staff to admit she wasn't at an abortion clinic at all—but then they convinced her she could get care at a second location across the city. There, a staffer gave her an ultrasound and (wrongly) convinced her that an abortion would sterilize her, leaving her feeling she had no choice but to have the baby.

Of course, once she was a single mother struggling to make ends meet, they were nowhere to be found. But the experience also put her on a path to her life's calling: using her faith to organize for reproductive justice. She began volunteering at Black Women for Reproductive Justice in Chicago, eventually joining the organization's board of directors and becoming a trained health educator on its staff. But when an illness in the family called her back home to Memphis, she discovered a very different landscape than that of the relatively liberal Chicago.

"I was trying to find places to connect," she tells me, in a nonstop patter that reveals most of what you need to know about her internal drive.

> The only place I could find that was close to reproductive justice was working at an abortion clinic here. And that still was not enough, even though I was able to still do education and still talk with women and do a lot of the outreach for them, some of the outreach work that they had, it just was not enough. There was no leadership of women of

color, especially Black women, talking about our own issues from our perspective, from our culture, from our point of economic view, our point of cultural view. So I did a needs assessment for about a year, and I went ahead and incorporated Sister Reach.[14]

Five years later, the organization she founded has come into its own. In 2015 alone, Sister Reach ran a "pro-woman" billboard campaign insisting that Black women know best how to make their own reproductive decisions, hosted a reproductive justice summit, successfully organized to block expansion of some state abortion restrictions, and released a report on research it had conducted, funded by the National Institutes of Health, on the need for comprehensive sex education in Tennessee. (This directly confronted Tennessee's draconian and sadlariously named Gateway Sexual Activity Law, which not only mandates a strict abstinence-only curriculum in public schools but also imposes fines of $500 per child on any teacher who offers students any kind of sexual health information outside of the approved abstinence curriculum.)

Though they do rent a small business space, most days Sister Reach is run out of Scott's home in a modest residential neighborhood of Memphis, which is where I met up with her on a mild January day. Her home office is a cozy, light-filled room, the walls hung with paintings from Black women artists and, in one corner, just above our meeting table, a vision board speaking dreams of funding and expansion.

Cherisse Scott was born to do this job. Raised in a deeply Christian family but exposed to a variety of denominations, she's both profoundly faithful and profoundly ecumenical. And some mysterious engine within her turns even her most painful wounds into testimony for a Christianity that's squarely on the side of women's sovereignty. Throughout her childhood, she suffered sexual molestation at the hands of several adults. Somehow, she found a way to transform that trauma into a commitment to never taking for granted the pleasures of consensual, healthy sexuality. She was forced to rely on food stamps to support herself and her son for years, an experience she draws on for a first-person appreciation of what it means to force a woman who can't feed the child she already has to have an additional child. A boyfriend who sabotaged her contraception taught her more than she wanted to know about what it feels like when a man tries to control a woman's reproduction. And the three abortions she's had? They could have been avoided if she'd belonged to a congregation that encouraged open conversations about sex: she always avoided condoms because they hurt her to use. But she never had anyone to talk with about it. Turns out, she has a latex allergy.

Those common church taboos about abortion and sexuality in general that kept Scott from getting help earlier are simply not grounded in scripture. In fact, the Bible doesn't say a single word about abortion, which I found almost impossible to believe when Scott told me, so constantly have I heard the Bible invoked to oppose it. My surprise creates the perfect opportunity for her to do a little impromptu Bible study with me. "I would say around what does the Lord say about these things, what is in the Bible about these things, is, first of all, love thy neighbor." Her face softens with pleasure as she thinks about the idea.

> That's the very first thing, the most important piece for us. . . . And in that love, there is no Black, there is no white, there is no man, there is no woman, there is no power dynamic, there is no space for domination. . . . One of the things that's really important for us to lift up is there's more than one narrative when it comes to biblical scripture. It behooves us not to kind of fall into this kind of singular way that we want to talk about God or the Lord, and also, behooves us not to try to box individual situations and say "but this type of woman does not deserve to be humanized because she uses drugs," or "this type of person doesn't deserve to be humanized because she was raped and now she needs an abortion" or "she wasn't raped but she still needs an abortion."[15]

Scott was ordained as a nondenominational minister in 1997 but quickly realized that her ministry wasn't the pulpit kind, and so she set about finding her calling. Along the way, she discovered key things about herself, and not just at that CPC. "Once upon a time I was anti–marriage equality, because that's what I was taught." Today she identifies as bisexual, a discovery that caused a bit of a faith crisis for her at first. "[I had] to truly search the scriptures for my own, to see 'Am I going to Hell or am I going to Heaven?' I had to search them for myself in order to find the answer, and [that's] something that is still not encouraged, that is still not done."

That taboo against questioning the conservative Christian party line won't last much longer if Sister Reach has anything to say about it. In early 2017 the group released a reproductive justice and faith toolkit, which contains a wealth of language and tools that people of faith can use to advocate for reproductive justice. And it's developed a cohort of over two hundred members of the clergy, in Tennessee and across the country, who regularly convene in reproductive justice Bible study groups, webinars, and individual coaching sessions. It also provides clergy with liturgy and talking points for sermons that draw on Tupac lyrics to address slut shaming, sex work, and poverty and dive deep into the Gospel of Mark to draw very modern lessons about HIV stigma and domestic violence. No matter the text, the challenge Sister Reach puts to its holy charges is the same: to look past traditional or common interpretations in order to approach the stories with fresh eyes and with the real struggles of their congregants in mind. Scott thinks of it as an "army of clergy that will be able to not just stand against that [Religious Right] foolishness but to stand on the Bible against that foolishness."

It's working, according to John Gilmore, spiritual director of the Open Heart Spiritual Center in Memphis and one of the clergy in Sister Reach's cohort. He tells me that the group's programs offer him both intangibles, like the fellowship of like-minded peers, as well as brass-tacks skills, like the ones he learned from Sister Reach's training on talking with news media about sensitive issues such as condom distribution. He also recently used Sister Reach materials to preach a new kind of sermon about the classic story of King Solomon splitting the baby, in which the hero of the story wasn't the wise king but "the real mother of the baby, [who] believed so strongly in her position and stood in her truth."

In fact, Gilmore's only complaint regarding Sister Reach is that more of his colleagues aren't signing up. "They'll say 'oh yeah that's a great idea, I'm going to come,' but they don't," he tells me.[16] "I think a lot of them have the perception that they would get backlash, that . . . may not be there, or to the level that they think." But he won't stop trying to recruit, because he's seen first-hand the kind of difference Sister Reach has made for his own ministry, and he knows that his colleagues' pews are filled with real people who need the real information and guidance Sister Reach offers. Memphis consistently ranks among the top ten cities with the highest rates of new HIV infections, and the rate of chlamydia is similarly off the charts. The city also regularly occupies the number one or two spot on lists of the poorest cities, and new research suggests a link between poverty and sexual assault.[17] Cherisse Scott teaches clergy to lead by example, being vulnerable about their own lives as a way of inviting others to do the same.

Scott does not mince words when she talks about the Christian Right's obsession with forcing women—especially poor women, especially women of color—to have children, calling out their lack of concern for those children once they come into the world and their racist propaganda that accuses Black women who have abortions of committing "Black genocide." "Okay, so then here's our babies, what can you do? What will you do?" she asks rhetorically, with anger flashing in her eyes. "They've shown what they will do. Which is absolutely nothing. Because our babies been killed in the streets since Trayvon and even before that. . . . We've been seeing death after death after death on Facebook and Twitter. And I've seen no pro-lifers come for our lot. Where are they now? The same pro-lifers just said that every 21 minutes the next . . . leader was aborted. Well, looks like to me that every 21 minutes the next leader is murdered at the hands of police. Where are you?"[18]

But, ultimately, Sister Reach's work isn't about opposing the Religious Right. It isn't oppositional at all. Instead, Scott sees her ministry as one of healing and restoration, working to strengthen oppressed communities and return women and girls to their rightful place as leaders of their own lives. Whether you believe in God is not ultimately her concern; Sister Reach serves people of all faiths and those of no faith at all. But for those who do believe, or want to, for those suffering from what Scott refers to as "church hurt" after having been shamed from the pulpit or the pews for their sex lives, Scott wants Sister Reach to offer a particular kind of healing: "I hope that I am a testimony to folks that first of all you can still love God and God can still love you and you can still have access to God and be gay. Or you can still have access to God and have an abortion. You can have access to God and you know, have a miscarriage. Put your child up for adoption, leave your husband, leave your wife. Whatever. Those things don't separate you from God."

As far as the laws and policies of our government are concerned, it shouldn't matter what the Bible says about sexuality. But until we can get the church disentangled from the state again, it behooves all of us to reject the idea that right-wing radicals have a monopoly on interpreting the Holy Book or, for that matter, on God. That's why it also behooves us to support the work of Sister Reach and other organizations like it, which refuse to cede Christianity to those who wield it as a weapon against the most vulnerable among us. If they can succeed in building an army of clergy and congregants marching in support of sexual and bodily sovereignty, they could help free us all, regardless of what we each believe.

## CHAPTER SIX

# SAVING OURSELVES FROM RESCUE

FELL IN LOVE with my high school boyfriend Andy at a youth group party. He was funny and smart and weird and handsome and he had his own car, a red VW Rabbit. I say all these things as if they're the reason I fell for him, and I suppose they played a part. But the number one reason was this: he liked me. I was chubby and socially awkward, and he wanted to make out with me anyhow. That he was actually a pretty good guy was icing on the cake.

And he was a pretty good guy. It took many years for me to realize how lucky I'd been. If he had been manipulative or abusive, I would have been a great victim. Not just because I was so grateful for his attentions but, ironically, because the very rules and norms that were supposed to keep me safe were actually making me more vulnerable.

So much of the way women's sexuality is policed is done in the name of keeping us out of harm's way. Victim-blamers love telling women to keep our knees closed and our hemlines long if we don't want to be raped. Most national sororities forbid their chapters from hosting parties at which alcohol is served. (This rule has the unintended effect of forcing sisters to socialize only in places where they are someone else's guests, which reduces their control over the tone and direction of the partying.) Abstinence "educators" shame sexual women under the guise of protecting us from getting "used" by men.

It was only marginally more subtle in my house. Boys and sex were essentially forbidden. We were allowed to date only under strict rules, and couldn't go to a party if our parents couldn't call the parents of the kid hosting the party first. As you might imagine, we didn't get invited to many parties.

I have no doubt that my parents had these rules in place for what they thought was our protection. In reality, though, what they were doing was locking me into an isolation chamber. When I started being sexual, there was literally no one I could talk with about any of it. My few friends were the kind of "good girls" my parents approved of—maybe they were doing their own sneaking around as well, but that idea never occurred to me at the time, and it certainly would have been a huge risk to guess whom I could out myself to. There wasn't even an online world to connect with back then. There was no *Rookie*, no Scarleteen.com. There was literally no one but Andy to confide in. If he had meant to harm or control me, I would have been in his thrall.

Today, there are so many more things for worried grownups to "protect" teen girls from when it comes to sex, and just as many ways that "protection" can backfire. We can all agree, for example, that teen sexting has led to some terrible outcomes, up to and including girls literally killing themselves when photos they meant to keep private are made public. But the solution is not to "rescue" teen girls from their perfectly normal impulse to send sexy pictures to their boyfriends, both because there's nothing wrong with teens expressing their sexuality and because it's unlikely to cause harm—one study found that more than three-quarters of eighteen-year-olds who had sent a naked picture to someone said that nothing at all bad had come from it. It was the 12 percent of girls who had been pressured into sexting who had been overwhelmingly likely to suffer for it—and whose photos were much more likely to have been shared against their will.[1] What girls need isn't to stop consensually sexting, it's for boys to stop trading their intimate images like playing cards, and for men to stop coercing girls into sharing images of their bodies they didn't want to share in the first place.

Teen girls also need adults to stop compounding the violations in the name of protection. Nearly twenty states have passed laws that penalize teen sexting, ostensibly to protect teens from being charged under child pornography laws, which would otherwise apply. But, as of this writing, not one of those "new and improved" sexting laws differentiates between consensual sexting and violations of consent. That is, the laws treat two girls who privately and happily exchange nude photos and never show them to another soul as equally culpable as a boyfriend who pressures a girlfriend into taking and sending a private photo she doesn't really want to take, or boys who nonconsensually collect hundreds of naked selfies of girls from their school and post them to Instagram. That's bonkers.

And it leads to situations in which teen girls are grilled about their private pictures by adult men wearing badges and carrying guns, which can and does create trauma where there previously was none. All because lawmakers and law enforcers can't bring themselves to admit that anything about teen girls' sexuality might be healthy. In an interview with Hanna Rosin for her longform story "Why Kids Sext," you could practically feel prosecutor Rusty McGuire stagger for the fainting couch as he declaimed, "What do you do? Turn a blind eye? You're letting teenagers incite the prurient interest of predators around the country . . . [and that interest] can only be met by the actual abuse of real children." But there's no link whatsoever between the rise of sexting and child sexual abuse. In fact, overall rates of child sexual abuse are on the decline in the United States.[2]

It's not just public officials who misplace their interventions. Rosin tells the story of a girl she calls Briana, who was coerced into sending a boy a picture of her breasts on condition that he would immediately delete it. She blew the whistle on some classmates when she found out they'd posted the pic—as well as the private photos of many other of her female classmates—on Instagram. But it was not the boys who were made to pay. Her classmates almost uniformly turned on her as a snitch, even girls whose pictures had also been stolen.

The adults in Briana's life were no better. "During arguments [Briana's mom would] say, 'You have no reason to have an attitude after everything you've done,'" Rosin recounts. "One time, after her younger sister had misbehaved, her mom yelled, 'Don't end up like your sister!'

while Briana stood close by. (Her mother later apologized.) Briana told me she has tried to make amends. She cleans up the kitchen every night after dinner, cleans the bathrooms. . . . Briana used to babysit for one of the teacher's kids, 'but then his wife wouldn't have anything to do with me.'"

Meanwhile, neither school administrators nor police punished the boys who nonconsensually shared girls' photos with anything more serious than a stern talking-to, and they were hailed as heroes by their peers.

Do girls and women need support as we navigate a sexual culture that's stacked against us? Yup. Do some women need urgent aid when other people do us harm? Absolutely. Does that make us damsels who need someone else to decide what's best for us? Not even if we're literally tied to train tracks. Helping women should inherently mean listening to women, trusting us to know what we need. Instead, men pass laws that force us to incubate babies against our will, because they think the alternative—access to abortion—isn't something our lady brains can properly comprehend.

If women constantly need saving from terrible, horrible male sexuality and its side effects, then why are men never held accountable? In the rescue narrative, any bad consequences of the kind of sex women need saving from are almost never men's fault. It's the fault of porn, or other women, or the culture at large. All three of those factors have been invoked in recent years as the furor over the increasing sexualization of girls has taken hold in the popular imagination. On its face, sexualization is a useful concept in a culture that overemphasizes girls' values as ornaments and playthings and underemphasizes our humanity. But in practice, as Danielle Egan illuminates in her book *Becoming Sexual*, the idea of sexualization is increasingly used as a blunt instrument, separating the innocent girls in need of rescue from the culture from the terrifying young women who have succumbed to it and become part of "the problem."

Most sexualization narratives propose innocence as a natural and uncontested state in which girls are without sexual curiosity or desire. But that's a fiction on multiple levels. "Sexual innocence" is inherently classed and raced, so most sexualization narratives concern themselves primarily with white middle-class heterosexual girls. But even those girls aren't without their urges. There is no age at which we don't have sexual experiences or curiosities—they just evolve over time. We can help our children know when and how it's appropriate to explore their sexual desires as they grow, but insisting that they have none doesn't make it true and instead only instills shame and repression.

As Egan writes, it also does girls a profound disservice by splitting them into two warring camps: the good girls versus the sluts. The good girls are conceived of as passive blank slates who neither have nor can acquire the skills to actively consider or critique the sexual messages they encounter, and they certainly have no preexisting sexual interest or agency. They must be protected at all costs from a culture that would brainwash them, lest the media they consume or the "deviants" they meet turn them into the horror of all horrors: the sexualized girl.

The tween who succumbs to "sexualization" is imagined as a terror in a thong. Think of Briana, whose only "crime" was once being pressured to show her breasts to a boy. Once it was revealed that she had done so, she was shunned and shamed not only by her peers but also by her own mother and by other parents who would no longer let her near their child. Like some kind of werewolf, this victim had become a monster capable of infecting "the innocent" if they come too close.

Sexualization, is, of course, a problem. It doesn't take a scientist to conclude that it's not good for girls to grow up surrounded by messages telling them their values lie either in their purity or in their appeal as an ornament or sex toy. But young women and girls aren't just passive receptors for media messages. They are—and we can help them be—active consumers of it, with nuanced thoughts about whether it is harmful or helpful, silly or serious. Some young people for sure feel pressured by the media they consume to be sexual in a narrowly defined heteronormative way. But the age of sexual debut isn't falling; if anything, it's rising.

That's not to say that the opposite swing of the pendulum is good for girls, either. Glossy magazines and sex-positive propagandists alike are constantly pushing everything from G-spot orgasms to polyamory as the sure path to women's liberation. In reality, some women like anal sex, some women find power in learning how to pleasure themselves, and some become fully embodied in pole dancing classes. But other women don't like any of those things, and it's not always because they're hung up or repressed—we're all just different people, and different things appeal to us. What's more, the idea that sexual experiences should always be "empowering" women is an unrealistic amount of pressure. Sometimes sex is just fun, or comforting, or mediocre, or laughably bad. Teaching girls and women that they need to be "rescued" from their repression if they're not leading the most outré sex lives possible only adds another straw to the mountain of expectations placed on women that mortal humans can never live up to.

Still, the more we invest in the protection of women and girls' sexual "innocence," the worse it gets for those who fail that test. Consider just one week in 2016. In Paris on October 3, Kim Kardashian was tied up and held at gunpoint in the course a robbery during which she thought she might die. Internet commenters responded with messages like "Should had killed her We don't need a cheap hoe any more."[3] The New York Daily News crowed, "Kim Kardashian's Paris robbery is too good to be true."[4] Conan O'Brien quipped, "No one was hurt, but in a mansion in Paris, Kim Kardashian was robbed at gunpoint. Kim was bound and gagged, then the robbers broke in." Get it? She was already tied up because she's a slut! Fox News went so far as to speculate that Kardashian had staged the ordeal for attention.[5] One company produced a Halloween costume.[6]

Just days before the assault on Kardashian, Donald Trump took to Twitter to get something off his chest. He had sustained days of criticism about his abusive treatment of a beauty queen led by Hillary Clinton, who invoked Alicia Machado's story in the first general election debate on September 26. It seems Machado, a Miss Universe winner hailing from Venezuela, had gained some weight during her 1996 reign, and Trump, who owned the pageant and therefore was her boss at the time, humiliated her for it, dragging her in front of the press corps for a mandatory workout, and calling her names like Miss

Piggy and Miss Housekeeping in private. Machado subsequently had a relapse of bulimia, which it took her some years to recover from.

Back in 2016, Trump denied none of Clinton's debate-night story about Machado, instead defending himself by insisting that she really had gained weight, and it really was a problem for him. When that argument failed to quell the outcry, he took to Twitter, ranting, "Hillary floated her as an 'angel' without checking her past, which is terrible. . . . Using Alicia M in the debate as a paragon of virtue just shows that Crooked Hillary suffers from BAD JUDGEMENT. . . . Did Crooked Hillary help disgusting (check out sex tape and past) Alicia M become a U.S. citizen so she could use her in the debate?"

Thing is, Clinton never spoke of Machado's virtue or painted her as angelic. She merely said she was a woman in Trump's employ whom Trump abused. It's clear that Trump believes only women who are virtuous and angelic deserve to be heard from and treated with respect. He also evidently thinks a woman who has a sex tape (Machado didn't, but that didn't stop him from claiming it) is "disgusting," and therefore deserving of whatever abuse he felt like heaping on her. Meanwhile, he himself can be seen in a (clothed) cameo in a 2000 Playboy porn video, and he's on record as having watched the infamous Paris Hilton sex tape, a tape that was released against Hilton's will and that depicted her having an encounter she says she did not consent to. "Fun" fact that will make you vomit a little: Trump has known Paris since she was twelve.

Women shouldn't have to earn freedom from sexual humiliation and abuse with our virtue. We deserve it simply because we are human, whatever we choose to do with our bodies. And no: we really don't need to be saved from our sexual decisions any more than men do. The abstinence pushers will tell you that women's hormones are different, that a substance called oxytocin causes us to form strong emotional bonds with our sex partners in ways that men don't, and that overexposure to oxytocin (from slutting around) renders us unable to ever connect with a partner again, like tape that's lost its adhesive. What they don't tell you is that that research was done on prairie voles, not humans, and even then they found an effect only in voles that had too little oxytocin; no negative effect was shown for an overabundance of the hormone. Humans produce oxytocin in a wide range of situations, including when we pet our dogs and when we sing together in groups. If we got less able to pair-bond every time we sang in a choir, I think we would have noticed by now.

When we scratch the surface, we find that propaganda promoting women's sexual vulnerability is almost always being used to control women or other vulnerable groups. In the rare instances where men are blamed for women needing "rescue," the myth of white women's fragile femininity is often used as an excuse for oppressing Black and brown men. That the Trump administration publishes an ongoing list of gender-based violence by "foreign nationals" (a category that makes up a tiny fraction of all the gender-based violence in the United States) while working to defund the Violence Against Women Act speaks volumes about this dynamic. US history is stained with the blood of countless Black men who were lynched as "rapists," when the vast majority of the time the worst "crime" they may have committed was consensually getting it on with a willing partner. Sometimes, as in the case of the 1955 lynching of fourteen-year-old Emmett Till, they had done nothing more than be friendly to a white woman.

Even more often, the rescue narrative pits the "deserving" and at-risk women against some other "terrifying" kind of woman, as when the specter of cisgender women being raped is used to bar transgender women from using women's bathrooms. There's no evidence that predators use the existence of trans women as an alibi to get into women's restrooms. There's already nothing stopping a man intent on finding a rape victim from walking into a women's restroom. There's not usually a guard at the door, after all. Why would he need a disguise? In fact, it's trans women who are most vulnerable to violence: studies repeatedly find that at least half of all trans people have been sexually assaulted.[7] Forcing them into restrooms full of men certainly isn't making them safer. And if you look into the records of the politicians most invested in telling trans people where they can and can't pee, you won't find a history of anti-rape leadership. To the contrary:

conservative lawmakers who are concerned for cis women's safety when it comes to persecuting trans women are often the same ones hand-waving away concerns about rape when they don't suit political purposes. Mike Pence, who sued the federal government to maintain the right of Indiana schools to prohibit trans students from bathrooms, is of course now the second-in-command to a serial sexual predator. Attorney General Jeff Sessions, who supported that same lawsuit, went so far as to question whether grabbing a woman's pussy without her consent (at least as described by his soon-to-be boss Donald Trump) even constitutes sexual assault.

But you don't have to be a misogynist lawmaker to buy in to the idea that women and girls—some or all—have to be rescued from nefarious sexual forces. And whatever your intention, buying in to the rescue narrative always results in women being shoved into ill-fitting good girl/bad girl costumes and pitted against each other. Among sex workers, there's even a neologism for this dynamic: the whorearchy. (Sadly, that's not an amazing new form of government. It refers to a whore hierarchy.)

"The person at the top of the whorearchy—the person who is least likely to be affected by anti–sex work stigma—would be the 'high-class call girl,'" explains Tina Horn, a sex educator and journalist who has worked in the sex industry. "She wears Agent Provocateur lingerie, her clients are high-powered, high-class, wealthy business men, for whom hiring a prostitute is a sign of status. She's always skinny, she's almost always white; if she's not white, then she's maybe Asian, or the color they make Beyoncé look when she's on the cover of a magazine." On the bottom rung, the most stigmatized sex workers are

> the people that we see on *Law and Order*, when they want to show a police precinct and there is always a hooker in there, smoking and handcuffed to a chair. People who are working in exposed and more dangerous zones. Of course those are the people who are more likely to be people of color, trans women, working class, or impoverished people, because they don't have access to fancier clothes [that would give them] access to advertise in a place that screens the girls. Clients

are racist. Clients are classist. A client who is paying $2,000 an hour expects class signifiers that some women might not be able to provide and so they have to work on the street.[8]

Between those two (forgive me) poles, you'll find pro BDSM workers (who rank relatively high because they don't tend to have sex with their clients), porn performers (who have the benefit of their job being legal but who bear the stigma of the permanent public evidence of their job), strippers, cam girls, and more. What you won't find is enough sisterhood. Instead, you often get more of the same pernicious assumptions about women and sex, and the same concomitant pressure for the "good" whores to define themselves in opposition to the "bad" ones, as a way to stave off the greater stigma that comes from ranking lower in the whorearchy. Horn puts it this way, "A lot of times, whorephobia manifests in this savior complex, this concern that a woman is doing something that is going to taint her. That it's going to spoil her precious jewel. When I say to my dad, 'I'm a dominatrix,' I'm able to say 'Oh, I don't take my clothes off, clients are always tied up or groveling on the floor beneath me.' Even though obviously I could be fucking a man for money and feel just as (if not more) powerful as I do when I am whipping them in a full body rubber catsuit."

You may think all of this has little to do with you if you have no connections to the sex industry. But that assumption is itself part of the whorearchy, which extends far beyond those who make money in the trade. Consider the word *whore* used as an insult. Much like *slut*, it has a slippery definition, often meaning simply that the target of the word is being sexual in a way the person hurling it disapproves of. Sometimes it's used as a sexualized bludgeon in situations that have nothing to do with sex, as when Trump supporters at a Cincinnati rally surrounded the Press Corps and chanted the word at them over and over until the police had to escort the journalists from the venue.[9] But it only works if we think poorly of actual whores. It's not enough that you yourself wouldn't want to do sex work. I've never called anyone a filthy doctor, even though I would never, ever want to go to med school. *Whore* only has power when we agree that whores are evil or "fallen," or pathetic, abject victims. If we want to uproot the rescue narrative around women and sex, we have to destigmatize sex work. And that means not just fighting against the whorearchy or the general idea that women can be tainted or devalued by sex. It means we have to talk about the ultimate rescue story: the anti-trafficking narrative.

No one but a monster could oppose anti-trafficking work in principle. After all, trafficking is when people are forced or coerced into engaging in some kind of labor against their will to profit the person or organization controlling them. People are trafficked into domestic and agricultural labor, the garment industry, construction, restaurant work, and more. But when people and organizations decry human trafficking, they're almost always talking about sexual labor, even though the United Nation's International Labor Organization estimates that sex trafficking accounts for only about one-fifth of the total trafficking that happens in the world.

That's in large part because, as feminists have successfully pushed back on the demonization of women for being sexual, it's become more socially tolerable to claim to want to save sex workers than to punish them. In New York, for example, lawmakers have created "human trafficking courts" that have been designed to treat prostitutes as victims instead of as criminals. Trouble is, most of the time sex workers are neither. Most sex workers aren't "trafficked" at all, in that they're not being forced into the industry by someone who is profiting from their labor. And what most of them need more than prison or mandatory therapy is job training, safe and stable housing, and economic opportunity.

"It's easier to say there are bad guys who are forcing women to do this horrible thing," explained Audacia Ray, former executive director of the Red Umbrella Project, an organization she founded for sex worker mutual aid. "That paints a picture that's easier for folks to handle than single moms who are escaping an abuser who are just like, 'Look, this is better than McDonalds.' So there's this overhang of the morality of it that everyone functions within, when most people who are doing sex work, wherever they are on that spectrum of choice/

circumstance/coercion, are doing it to get by. They don't necessarily think of themselves as being victims and are hustling to get what they need for themselves and their family."[10]

Even for sex workers who experience trauma or posttraumatic stress disorder, treating them as helpless victims in need of saving is doing more harm than good. "A really basic tenet of supporting women transitioning out of abusive situations is that they should have choices and options," Ray told me.

> Even if those choices are like, "We have this pile of free clothing. Do you want the blue sweater, or the red sweater?" That's part of how you regain your autonomy, your self-confidence, all of that. And that seems to go out the window when we're talking about trafficking. Judges and social service providers seem to believe that people who are trafficked have lost all ability to make good decisions, and they get pushed into these mandated programs where the program and the social workers know best. That's a really huge problem. Because it's not supporting, respecting, or building up women's autonomy at all. . . . I've heard judges personalize it in ways that they wouldn't about intimate partner violence. Last year I heard a judge ask, "What must go wrong in a woman's life that would make her sell the thing that's most precious to her?"

In a 2014 Truthout investigation of "50 of the most prominent domestic groups founded or organized to limit or eradicate human trafficking, or to assist trafficking victims," writer Anne Elizabeth Moore found that, although anti-trafficking efforts often lack respect for sex workers or even a nuanced approach to their work, they certainly are lucrative. What's a lot less clear is what they're doing with the money. "Given the $686 million anti-trafficking budget shared by 50 of the most prominent organizations (which doesn't count federal costs)," Moore writes, "this breaks down to an average budget of $343,000 per case—certainly enough to secure each victim a safe place to live for at least a year. Yet a 2013 report found only 682 beds available, nationwide, to victims of trafficking." They also play fast and loose with statistics, ginning up numbers to keep the money flowing: "Slightly less than half of the top-earning anti-trafficking organizations in the United States claim to have saved 8,676 total individuals from sex trafficking: in other words, over four times as many victims as there were potential cases of both labor and sex trafficking investigated in the United States, at federal and state levels, in 2013."[11]

And those are the "respectable" efforts. Others don't even try to hide what lies beneath the anti-trafficking "rescue" narrative, like the short-lived A&E show 8 Minutes, which featured cop-turned-pastor Kevin Brown posing as a client, ambushing sex workers with a camera crew, and trying to convince them to "escape" sex work in eight minutes or less. Numerous sex workers "featured" on the program have since come forward to say that they were not given the help with jobs, housing, and other basic needs they were promised in exchange for saying for the cameras that they had been "saved" from prostitution. In part, that's because the show set out looking for trafficking victims but doesn't seem to have found any. The crew did find independent sex workers who were not being forced or coerced and who didn't qualify to be served by some of the anti-trafficking resources the show had identified. But it's also because the show didn't seem to care what happened after the cameras stopped rolling—the point was to show a heroic white man saving pathetic lady victims. I could find no evidence that the show invested any resources whatsoever in increasing the capacity of any of the agencies it referred sex workers to, instead just putting more strain on already overburdened programs.[12] Several of the women featured on the show reported having their lives meaningfully harmed by their appearance—their families ostracized and abandoned them when they learned about the sex work, or the women were targeted by police (who of course also watched the show) and now have a criminal record.[13]

Nonconsensually identifying sex workers as victims is just another form of stigma, and stigma doesn't make anyone safer, whether it's the stigma of having a criminal record or the stigma of sex work itself. Instead of trying to save sex workers, or save "good girls" from "dirty whores," what if we listened to the women who exchange sex for money or other items like shelter or food or drugs when they tell us what they really need?

Cyndee Clay, the executive director of HIPS, a program in Washington, DC, that provides client-directed services to sex workers, puts it this way: "If your motivation is that you don't want anyone to have to exchange sex for money, awesome. Then help them build a life where that's not a thing that has to happen. If you do that in a way that affirms them as an individual and affirms their goals, I don't actually care what your internal motivation is. Set up a program that helps women in sex work learn new skills. Set up a program that helps them address their finances. Set up a program that gives them food. Or helps them figure out child care. Do that."[14]

With its big windows and huge pink lettering, you could mistake the HIPS storefront for a boutique that sells clothing for zaftig women. But open the door and you're sucked into a whirl of energy—dozens of people are here on the Wednesday afternoon I visit, hanging out and talking, watching TV, doing laundry, showering. There are couches and chairs in the vestibule, and just beyond that, separated only by a garage-style door now in the open position, a room with a meeting table and lots of chairs. Off to the right, near a front window, a few computer users are typing away. Just beyond them is a large desk staffed by two or three receptionists who field phone calls, help connect clients with staff support or other resources, and clock newbies like me at record speed, all with a warm smile. Down a short hall and in the back are private rooms to meet with visiting lawyers, social workers, and others; today there's a medical clinic happening.

I've been invited to sit in on a session of "Real Talk." It's a regular group chat hosted by staffer Miss Paula, a tall, Black woman with short blonde and black curls. Miss Paula radiates warmth and competence and gives me a compassionate warning about the kind of language I might hear. When I reassure her I'm not easily scandalized, we head over to the conference table, where a few people have already gathered.

It only takes a few minutes for the room to fill. There are trans women and cis women and gender-nonconforming folks and a few cis men, over a wide range of ages. Almost all of them are brown or Black. The subject today is about health and relationships, which participants take as an invitation to riff on everything from their own physical health to the importance of friendship in their lives. The conversation runs this way and that, with Miss Paula sometimes calling on people who've been quiet and encouraging them to share, but mostly letting the talk evolve how it will. In many ways, the conversation sounds a lot like what my friends and I talk about when we have time and get philosophical—there is genial ribbing and pointed critique across generational lines, and talk of how hard it is to really change habits for the better. Trans women tell funny stories about children identifying them in public, to the horror of their parents. People grapple with their romantic relationships, struggling to sort out when to compromise and when to stand firm. Several women talk about how the men in their lives are so needy and rail against the stereotype that women are the ones ruled by our emotions. One woman speaks eloquently about how she's learned that the most important thing in or out of relationships is to love yourself first.

Of course, this is not a group of my middle-class friends. Most of the participants in this conversation are or have been street-level sex workers, the kind that even other sex workers shit on. They have been or are homeless, or they've struggled with drug addiction, or both. When you ask them about their health, they tell you their HIV status. Many are positive; some have been for decades. One woman shares that she started taking her HIV treatment more seriously when her seven-year-old asked her if she was going to die. Another tells a story about going to prison after stabbing someone during a manic bipolar phase. She says how thankful she is to have been imprisoned, both because it gave her a chance to stabilize her mental health and because it protected her from people seeking to retaliate on behalf of her victim. Several others echo what a positive intervention getting locked up has been for them at a key moment in their life. It's a hard narrative to digest when I have so many critiques of the prison-industrial complex, but then I just think: imagine how chaotic your daily life would have to feel to be thankful to be locked up.

When people in the group talk about sex work, they mostly say they used to do it and are working to stay away from it. When I mention that to Clay afterward, she tells me that's incredibly common, even among people who are still actively working, because even here, at the bottom rung of the whorearchy, people are shaming each other and keeping silent to avoid that shaming. And the isolation that comes with that silence just makes the work more risky. In Boston recently, a group of sex workers attempted to organize a check-in system so they could tell each other where they were going to meet clients and when they expected to be done, and if they didn't check back in by a certain time, someone would know to be concerned and take action to find them. Smart, right? But they quickly discovered that such a safety measure is illegal because it's construed as conspiracy to commit a crime.

Clay is a small, white woman with graying temples that give way to pale blue dreadlocks. Her face is open and you feel at ease with her immediately. She's been with HIPS for twenty-one years, originally enticed into volunteering when a band she liked did a benefit show for the organization. At the time she joined, HIPS operated from an abolitionist framework—the idea that sex work should be entirely eradicated. But as the organization worked with its clients and focused on helping them with what they really needed, it discovered that an eradication mind-set wasn't helping the people it set out to help.

Today the staff of sixteen full-time employees plus fourteen volunteer fellows and peers operates from a harm reduction model that focuses on supporting people in making decisions that are healthier and safer for them. On average, they get twelve hundred visits every month from people who value that approach. And they oppose the ongoing criminalization of sex work because it's just another way of stigmatizing whores.

"I have people working in my drop-in center as volunteers who got fired from food service jobs because they couldn't pass a background check because of a misdemeanor prostitution arrest from fifteen years ago," Clay tells me. "You can't be a licensed massage therapist if you have a solicitation charge on your record. You can't be a real estate agent." And criminalization doesn't just keep sex workers from finding jobs outside of sex work. The fear of arrest and a permanent criminal record keeps sex workers vulnerable to clients who hurt them or refuse to pay them—what sex worker is going to call the police in those circumstances?

The rise of the rescue narrative has encouraged more people to drop a dime on sex workers. Before the anti-trafficking boom, neighbors might complain about not wanting to hear high heels on the street late at night or find condoms in the azalea bushes. But the anti-trafficking narrative gives people moral cover for profiling and criminalizing people who just don't seem to "belong" in their neighborhood. Clay tells me that she hears all the time about cases where someone says to themselves, "'I'm going to call the police because I'm worried about [this person], I wonder if they're being trafficked. But really I just don't want that person walking down my street.' And the trafficking movement has allowed us to clothe all of those racial, class, gender issues into, 'They might be trafficked, we should save them.'"

The rise of anti-trafficking programs has also hurt HIPS directly, by funneling funds it used to receive into projects that seem much more "upstanding" to the average citizen because they sell a black-and-white narrative of helpless victims and permanent rescue. Clay gets a hard glint in her eye when she tells me, "We had a city grant that we were [using to help] probably twelve hundred women a year, on violence issues, and crisis services and counseling services. All of that went to an anti-trafficking organization that helps like twenty." When I ask her what that anti-trafficking organization is doing with the funds, she tells me she doesn't know. But she does know this: "There is a large anti-trafficking organization, which I will not name, and literally their hotline calls us and asks us to take referrals from them." But HIPS doesn't see a dime of that organization's funding.

This isn't just a turf war over money. What's at stake is how sex workers are treated by the culture and by the organizations they turn to when they need support. Make no mistake: many HIPS clients would love not to be doing sex work. As Clay puts it, "I don't see a lot of people leaving hundred-thousand-a-year jobs to go do sex work." It is often an option of last resort. But so too is agricultural work or taking a job at McDonalds. And we don't outlaw those jobs or treat everyone doing that labor as victims. Those of us working to make the world better make sure that people in tough jobs are being paid adequately and that there are humane working conditions and opportunities for workers to move on to work they will find more satisfying. These very labor protections, which are afforded only to professions with legal standing, make it easier to identify and prosecute those who are genuinely enslaving workers.

One of the most common feminist arguments against decriminalizing sex work is that the more sex work is normalized, the more it encourages men to think of women's bodies as a commodity they can buy and sell. That's a real dynamic: most sex buyers are men, and most sex sellers are women. But literally policing what women do with their bodies is not the way to teach men that women are not things. On the contrary, if we decriminalize and destigmatize sex work, women could set better terms for themselves, the way massage therapists and other people who perform intimate physical labor do.

Notice I said both "decriminalize and destigmatize." That's because decriminalization alone isn't going to get us there. "Stripping is a completely legal form of sex work," points out Clay. As is porn. "But can dancers unionize? Not very easily. How many people are totally proud and talk about how their partner or girlfriend or sister is an exotic dancer? [Not many], because there's still all of that shame. And all of that stigma. Legalizing it isn't going to change the way that our community feels about a trans woman walking down the street." That's because we're so busy hunting individual boogeymen that we too often lose sight of the biggest abuser: our oppressive institutions.

Before I leave HIPS for the day, there's one more person I need to speak with. Mz. Bambi White is sporting a pink-brimmed baseball hat with an American flag on it. Her long, brassy blonde hair falls in curtains around her face, which is taut and alert. She's wearing a tight pink shirt and acid-washed skinny jeans. When I introduced myself to the Real Talk group earlier, she fixed me with an intense look from across the table and told me she wanted a "one on one" with me. So when I head to one of the tiny private rooms to meet with her, I do so with some trepidation.

I needn't have worried. White only wants to tell me how great HIPS has been for her and to get us both amped for her future. She wants to be a music producer. "There's a lot I need to know, but I do have a good ear for music," she tells me. "I'm trying to get a job because I need real money to start my record label." But to get a job she needs to have a place to live and the right paperwork. HIPS has already helped her secure the former: after years of homelessness, she finally got a subsidized apartment a few months ago. And now it's helping her get the documents she needs to apply for work. In the meantime, she eats lunch here every day, socializes, gets medical care and emotional support. She tells me that she's learned things about running a business by watching the way the HIPS staff functions together, lessons she'll apply when she's finally the boss. She even found her new boyfriend at HIPS, and they're helping keep each other motivated.

As a Black trans woman who has literally worked the streets, there is no one below Mz. Bambi White in the whorearchy. And no doubt, her life has been hard. Her mother threw her out to make room for a man, and three years ago, her own boyfriend tried to kill her. She's the kind of poor most people can't imagine. But she's no damsel in need of rescue, nor is she any danger to anyone else. She's a human woman who needs to live in a culture that values and honors her humanity, who in the meantime is doing the best she can under excruciating circumstances to build the life she envisions for herself and for her family. "I want better for my family. I know if I'm better, they're better. . . . I'm the oldest on my father's side, there's no one older than me but my father's siblings . . . so I have responsibility to make sure my family is intact. Then when [Grandma's] gone, she can be on her deathbed and [saying], 'Thank you, because I know you're going to take care.'" And she includes HIPS in that family and her future planning. "When I make it big, when I really really make it big, I'm going to donate. I'm going to give HIPS a house."

When we devalue White, when we try to flatten her into two dimensions to fit whatever role makes us most comfortable, whether that's "helpless victim" or "filthy whore," we make life harder for her by making it easier for potential employers to discriminate against her, for men to beat her, for lawmakers to criminalize her life and her body. That should be reason enough to stop doing it.

But if it's not, here's one more: whatever ways we treat Mz. Bambi White, those are the ways we ourselves will eventually be treated. There will always be someone who thinks they're better than us, who wants to tear us down, using sex and gender as weapons. There will always be someone who wants to treat us like a whore or a damsel. It's on us to make those words meaningless.

## CHAPTER SEVEN

# ONLY HUMAN

IMAGINE THIS: DANIELLE, an eleven-year-old white girl from an afflu-
ent suburb of Washington, DC, is raped by a twenty-year-old man in
the neighborhood. Her parents help and support her in reporting the
rape to the police, but the police ignore her medical reports, which
are consistent with sexual assault, and refuse to analyze the DNA evidence. In one internal email, a lieutenant calls her "promiscuous" and
the "sex" consensual, even though she is five years below the legal age
of consent. And then Danielle herself is charged with making a false
report, manipulated into accepting a plea, and taken from her parents
to become a ward of the court, living in and out of detention and secure
treatment centers between episodes of running away.

That's not the plot of a dystopian novel. But it also didn't happen
to a well-off white girl. It happened to Danielle Hicks-Best, an African
American girl being raised by adoptive parents of modest means in
the economically and ethnically diverse DC neighborhood of Columbia Heights, where she was struggling with chronic emotional troubles
stemming from abuse at the hands of her birth mother.[1]

Those distinctions matter because here in the United States, as
throughout much of the Western world, the ideas of "innocence" and
"purity" are not afforded to people of color, especially African Americans and Latinas. The stereotype of African American girls, even very
young girls, as wild, animalistic "creatures" who have to be controlled

137

dates back at least to the enslavement of Africans by white Westerners, who used it as a justification to rape them and generally treat them as subhuman. It's no surprise, then, that when girls of color are sexually abused they themselves wind up in juvenile detention at an alarmingly high rate—a rate much higher than that of their white peers.[2]

We all know in our guts what it feels like to have our humanity recognized, but it's hard to talk about without reverting to tautology. What does it mean to be seen as fully human? Is it, in part, a question of complexity, of whether I am afforded the space to contain multitudes? Can I be emotionally unstable and also be telling the truth when I say I was raped? If not, I'm not being afforded my full humanity. It's also about empathy, whether or not other people consider my feelings, my well-being, and my perspective when they interact with me or take actions that affect me. And it's about singularity, the recognition that I'm a specific person, not a symbol, and that my specific history and opinions and weird sense of humor are a reflection on no one but me.

It's perhaps easiest to understand the experience of being recognized as fully human by considering counterexamples. Most of us know what it feels like to be crammed into an overheated bus or plane that's going nowhere fast, with no personal space, not even enough room for our bodies, really, no control over when we'll start moving again, possibly not enough to eat or drink. That's the entry level of feeling dehumanized—feeling like there is no room for us, we have no autonomy, our basic needs are not only not being met but are invisible to the people who have power over us. But for some of us, dehumanization gets much, much worse than a bad bus ride. For trans women, it means staggeringly high chances of being murdered just for living your life. For Black undergraduate women, it means their white counterparts are likely to abandon them to potential rapists.[3] For men of color, it means being treated by police as inherently suspicious and knowing that every police encounter could quickly turn violent or even deadly. Some studies have shown that the part of the brain that produces empathy, which is the process of imagining another person as equally human and thereby imagining what their mental state might be, was activated less when subjects looked at people they considered far "below" them, like drug addicts or homeless people.[4]

However you define it, the right to be treated as fully human is a tenacious yet constantly shifting cultural fault line. And one of the forces that makes it quake is sex. If strange men have ever yelled sexual come-ons at you as punishment for the crime of walking down the street and existing as a woman, you know what it feels like to have sex used as a tool of dehumanization. If you've received rape threats as a reward for expressing an opinion online while female, ditto. Type the name of any prominent female politician and "porn" into a search engine and you'll see how dehumanizing sexualization can be.

The farther you stray from the white, straight, cisgender male norm, the less leeway you have to navigate a sex life that feels true to you. The dehumanization of women via sexuality is even used to police masculinity itself: think about what it means for a man to be called a "pussy"—he's being reduced not just to a woman, who has less social status than a man, but to a disembodied body part that a "real" man should be treating like a commodity, something to be acquired for as little value as possible.

Sometimes the insults to humanity close in from both sides, like the infamous trash compactor room in *Star Wars*, leaving targets with the distinct impression that they are not intended to exist at all. Black girls like Danielle Hicks-Best, who are criminalized when they speak up about violations of their own sexual humanity, are treated like they're worthy of protection only when they can be used as a bludgeon to shame grown Black women. When Beyoncé released "Partition," an ode to going down on her husband in a limo, Bill O'Reilly tore into her repeatedly on behalf of imaginary Black girls, on separate occasions calling her a "thug,"[5] saying, "Teenage girls look up to Beyoncé, particularly girls of color. . . . Why would she do it when she knows the devastation that unwanted pregnancies . . . fractured families . . . Why would Beyoncé do that?"[6] and further charging, "She knows—this woman knows—that young girls are getting pregnant in the African American community. Now it's about 70 percent out of wedlock. She knows and doesn't seem to care."[7]

Writing about the incident in her book *The Sisters Are All Right: Challenging the Broken Narrative of Black Women in America*, Tamara Winfrey Harris exposes the layers of erasure required to sell this kind of concern narrative:

> Raised middle class in a traditional nuclear family, Beyoncé has been famous and wealthy all her adult life. She may be found on stage slinging vocal runs, but not thuggin' on the corner slinging dope. She has been with the same man since she was eighteen years old, and their child was born after they were married. Beyoncé would seem to fit the mainstream requirements for respectability. But that doesn't matter. Even a married black woman, singing about sex with her husband, is a whore, a bad role model, and possibly a criminal. . . . At the same time, O'Reilly maligned Black girls, intimating that they are particularly promiscuous and fertile.[8]

To the contrary, the pregnancy rate among African American teenage girls declined 56 percent between 1990 and 2010.

And it's not just white conservatives like O'Reilly who insist that Black women subjugate their sexuality in order to be acceptable "symbols" to imaginary Black girls. When Brittney Cooper, a prominent Black feminist theorist and cofounder of the influential blog Crunk Feminist Collective (CFC), explored what it meant to be unmarried, Christian, and a sexual woman at the same time in a 2011 CFC essay called "Single, Saved and Sexin'," she faced such a wave of backlash from her own community that she spent a weekend crying on a friend's couch. CFC commenters and other Black Christian bloggers told her that "young Christians who read this and accept your words as gospel and fall into sin will be on you"[9] and the very Christ-like "someone needs to pimp-slap [your] pastor."[10] Winfrey Harris recounts story after story of Black people taking on the policing of Black women's sexuality, like the female BET executive who banned a "mildly spicy" video from R&B artist Ciara but allowed much more explicit videos by Black male musicians to be aired. After all, learning to play by the rules of the dominant culture is a survival skill for most marginalized communities.

Or, as Winfrey Harris put it, "Knowing that their daughters will be presumed guilty of lasciviousness until proven innocent, black parents can hardly be blamed for teaching girls to keep any appearance of sexual desire, no matter how benign, under wraps, the same way that they teach their sons not to give police officers or wannabe community watchmen reason to kill them."[11]

It's a Russian nesting doll of dehumanization. Lift off the head of the impossible standards for sexual respectability that many Black women have internalized (and taught their daughters), and you'll find white people using the idea of innocent Black girls to shame grown Black women who dare to insist on their right to their own sexuality and humanity. Open that one, and you'll see Black girls like Danielle being treated as criminals because their actual bodies are never afforded the presumption of sexual innocence. Inside that one, discover African women stereotyped by white slavers as sexual "animals" to justify dehumanizing them into bondage (and, not incidentally, raping them while enslaved).

It is the bankrupt fauxpowerment of respectability politics that led Cooper to call for a third way, a place where Black women's humanity has room to unfold. In her 2012 essay "Disrespectability Politics: On Jay-Z's Bitch, Beyoncé's 'Fly' Ass, and Black Girl Blue," she spells it out this way: "We must consider the potential in the space between the diss and the respect—the potential (and the danger) of what it means to dis(card) respectability altogether. This space between the disses we get and the respect we seek is the space in which Black women live our lives. It is the crunk place, the percussive place, the place that makes noise (and music), the place that moves us, the place that offers possibility in the midst of two impossible extremes."[12]

We'd all do well to help her build it. Replacing Black women's rightful sexual sovereignty with cardboard cutouts onto which white people can project stereotypes has impacts far beyond sex. A few years ago, when casting was revealed for the first *Hunger Games* movie, some fans were outraged to discover that Rue was a Black girl, complaining that her pivotal death was less sad because she was Black.

Why, when a twelve-year-old girl is murdered, would her race make her death more or less tragic? In part, it's because when confronted with

actual Black girls, too many of us fail to imagine they could be innocent, and that perceived lack of "purity" is regularly used to deny their
full humanity. Meanwhile, the white supremacist who murdered nine
Black people in a Charleston church in 2015 invoked the specter of
Black men raping "pure" white women as justification for the ultimate
erasure of humanity. The concept of sexual "purity" is itself gendered
and dehumanizing—whatever my desires, whatever I have or haven't
done in bed, has nothing to do with the moral quality of my soul. Both
white and Black women are being reduced to two-dimensional symbols in these contrasting examples. But in both cases, those flat symbols
are being used to justify ending Black lives.

It's not just at the intersection of race and gender where sexuality
and humanity collide. For example, young people with intellectual
disabilities are often excluded from the sex education that their peers
receive in school because the adults in charge erroneously conflate
their intellectual limits with a limit on their ability to experience a
full range of human emotions and desires. That denial of education
not only leaves them extra-vulnerable to sexual abuse, it also hobbles
their ability to form and negotiate healthy sexual relationships.[13] The
ties that bind our sexual freedom to our basic humanity play out in
so many different ways for sex workers, trans and queer women—the
human rights of any one of us are fully entangled with the myriad ways
sexuality is regulated.

Sometimes that entanglement yields surprising results. Heather
Corinna, founder of Scarleteen.com and longtime sex educator, tells
me that the young women she works with in homeless shelters are
some of the most sexually empowered she encounters anywhere. "The
young women at the shelter will talk very candidly—and without
shame—about their bodies, about what they like and don't like when
it comes to sex, about what gets them off. If they have a partner, and
the partner is not interested in their pleasure, or they're just not having
a good time, they're much quicker to pick somebody else" than young
people she works with from middle- or upper-class backgrounds.
That's anecdotal, of course—one symptom of selective dehumanization along class lines is that there's no real clamor to fund studies of

the sexual health of homeless young women—but it makes a certain sense to Corinna, and to me, too. "If you're in foster care or you're homeless, probably your whole life has been super unstable. . . . When so many things are earnestly out of your control, who knows where you're going to be living and with whom from week to week, [then] what your friends think about you, or what your parents think about you, matters a lot less," observes Corinna.[14]

Of course, many young women without permanent homes find themselves in that precarious position precisely because they have already been sexually dehumanized, through sexual abuse and/or because their families rejected them for being LGBT or sexually active. Homelessness or foster care increases their risk of further abuse and decreases their access to quality health care, birth control, safer sex supplies, and sex ed. (If they rely on charities run by the Christian Right, those last things will be in even shorter supply.) The young women Corinna works with may not care much about their sexual propriety, but often, neither do the people in charge of their well-being. Corinna puts it this way: "[As a sex educator,] I can do what I want at the shelter, and one of the reasons I can do what I want is a terrible reason, which is that I'm working with a group of people that people don't give a shit about." But turning that dehumanization on its head is powerful and genuinely empowering. "Even if they're coming to some of this from a place of, this stuff doesn't matter because they're devalued, they're valuing themselves through it. So to say, *I'm not going to be with a boyfriend who just wants me to give him blowjobs all the time, and nothing for me is them valuing themselves.*"

It's too bad that there aren't more resources to study the sexual lives of homeless young women, because it would be instructive to know what gives them the resilience to resist the messages that most of the adults in their lives are trying to send them: that they're disposable and worthless and need to be different before they can be valued. Too often, members of groups that are subject to mass dehumanization resort to respectability politics. Just as fauxpowerment can sometimes make individual women feel more sexually powerful, respectability politics can sometimes (temporarily) work to increase the status and safety of individual practitioners. But they never work to reverse the dehumanization of groups, because by definition, they're about saying, "I'm not like what you've heard about the members of my group. I'm better." It's a lot harder to stand secure in your value in ways that expand the umbrella of humanity to cover more people than it is to kick people out so you don't get wet. I found that out myself on my way out of the closet.

In the spring of my junior year in college, Rachel appeared to me. Not as a vision, but as a fixture in three of my four classes. I had never seen her before, but suddenly she was everywhere, and everywhere she was the smartest person in the room. A short, blue-eyed butch with a penchant for blazers, she wore her blonde hair in a close crop. In statistics class, I sat behind her and became fascinated with the fuzz covering the back of her head; as we became friendlier I started to touch it, to rub it against the grain the way you would a plush carpet, to feel the soft bristle against my fingers. Her gruff voice was tempered by a Southern lilt, and she encouraged my attentions.

I had never had a crush on a woman before, and I didn't know I had one then. But by that fall, we were making out in the office we shared serving as lab assistants for the same professor.

Rachel and I didn't last more than three months; she had some family issues to attend to and couldn't indulge in the endless patiences involved in easing a baby dyke out of the closet. But she changed my life, which has never regained its previous shape since. I remember clearly going to fetch her a Diet Coke late one night in the lab, early in our entanglement, and thinking "I never have to rely on men for anything ever again." It was a profound moment of actual power—and it was bound up in feeling I had new choices.

By the time I graduated, I was on my second girlfriend (Leslie), and I was out and proud on campus. But my family was another story. I wasn't sure how they would react to my interest in women, and I was too scared to tell them until after I graduated, lest I jeopardize their willingness to pay my tuition. So I waited to spill the beans until after the cap and gown were packed away and Leslie and I were settled in our new life in Boston. When I went to visit my parents that summer,

I had my suitcase packed and a local friend on call in case they threw me out. And I had a story concocted that was a lie.

It's a real irony, coming out with a lie. But I was worried that if I told them the truth—that I was attracted to both men and women and was choosing for now to be with women—that they wouldn't accept me. That they would insist I choose men instead, if they knew I was still attracted to them. So instead of telling them how delightful my sexual self-discovery was, how much power it had given me over my life and my future and my personal and political choices, I told them I had discovered that I was a lesbian, with no interest in men. And I told them I was born this way.

I was hardly alone. In a 2013 survey conducted by the Pew Research Center, only 28 percent of bisexuals said most or all of the important people in their lives knew about their sexual orientation, compared to 71 percent of lesbians and 77 percent of gay men.[15]

In practical ways, the Born This Way argument makes sense. The Supreme Court has ruled that "immutable characteristic[s] determined solely by the accident of birth" should receive stricter scrutiny under the equal protection clause of the Fourteenth Amendment. In plain language, that means that it's easier to win legal rights for LGBT folks based on a Born This Way argument than it is if we argue a right to privacy.

But the Born This Way argument is inherently dehumanizing. It says that the law should take pity on us, because we can't help ourselves. By doing so, it tacitly agrees that if we could help ourselves, it would be okay to insist that we do so, and that everything we *can* do to seem more straight, we should do. (Hello, respectability politics.) That leaves bisexuals like me in an incredibly precarious cultural position and has real impact on our lives. The stigmatization and erasure of bisexuals from both straight and gay cultures leads us to disclose our bisexuality to health providers at rates much lower than even gay men or lesbians do. The result? Bisexuals face elevated rates of cancer, depression, and STIs and, among bi men, HIV.[16]

That kind of social pity and silencing is also profoundly dehumanizing for rape victims. I hear from them often at speak-outs and vigils, women who say that they've kept silent for years, that they had convinced themselves they'd just had bad sex or made a set of bad decisions, anything to avoid confronting the depth of the violation they'd experienced or the social stigma that comes with being a rape survivor in America. Of course, that kind of denial doesn't mute the trauma experienced by rape victims, it only prevents them from getting support, healing, and justice. And when the veil of denial is finally lifted, the fact of that denial can be used to further refuse humanity to rape victims.

This dynamic was at play in the trial of popular Canadian radio host Jian Ghomeshi. In the fall of 2014, a few women, under cover of anonymity, reported to his employer, the Canadian Broadcasting Company, that Ghomeshi had been brutally and nonconsensually violent with them in the midst of sexual encounters. Then one woman, actress Lucy DeCoutere, put her name on the allegation and went public with it. With that, the floodgates opened, and eventually twenty-one women came forward describing similar experiences with Ghomeshi.

When three of those women agreed to be witnesses in a criminal case against Ghomeshi, his defense relied on attacking the victims' credibility, in significant part by trotting out emails and letters that showed the women saying affirming things to Ghomeshi after he had hurt them. Even though there's a growing body of social research showing how typical it is for sexual assault victims to try to placate their attackers and convince themselves out of victimhood by pretending nothing happened, the prosecution didn't bother to present any expert testimony to that effect. So it was not much of a surprise when the judge, while claiming he understood that he should "guard against applying false stereotypes concerning the expected conduct of complainants," found Ghomeshi not guilty in part because the victims' behavior after the fact seemed "out of harmony" with the assaultive behavior they had described.[17]

There's an enormous amount of irony in men deciding a woman's account of gendered violence is invalid because she didn't behave the way he thought she should. To many victims, it's a second trauma, so related are the experiences of being dehumanized by a man who overrides your control over your body, and then being dehumanized by a man who tells you that the choices you made after that dehumanization render it moot. And those kinds of decisions have a real impact: Anne Munch, an attorney who assisted the team that prosecuted basketball star Kobe Bryant, once told me that, because of the rape myths perpetuated in the media coverage of that case and two other high-profile rape cases that hit the news in 2003, reports of rape to the campus police at one Colorado university dropped from forty-seven in 2002 to six in 2003. Calls to a Colorado rape crisis center fell off by a third, with callers expressing "a specific hesitancy to report to the police or to victims' assistance due to the fear of their case being made public."[18]

And thus the cycle begins anew. It's not hard to imagine a woman who followed the media coverage of the Ghomeshi trial being discouraged from reporting. If she then comes forward months or years in the future, that reluctance will be held against her in court. Those same myths that kept her from reporting will also make it easier for cops, judges, prosecutors, and jurors not to take her claims seriously. Worst of all: unreported and unpunished rapists are free to rape again. And the findings of researchers David Lisak and Paul Miller suggest they're likely to do just that, each an average of five more times.[19]

The dehumanization of rapists themselves also enables them. When we conceive of rape as a crime that could only be committed by monsters, we miss the real rapists in our midst, who may have many fine qualities and who may seem quite the opposite of monstrous. Ghomeshi was a charming and beloved cultural icon, which is why it took so long for anyone to believe he could also be hurting women.

And if you think our general cultural approaches to female desire and rape are dehumanizing, they're nothing compared to what we put Native women through. Native women suffer the highest rates of rape in the United States. And not just by a little: in a 2010 study, 49 percent of Native women surveyed by the Centers for Disease Control and Prevention reported a history of sexual violence.[20] To make matters worse, rapists who attack Native women are more physically brutal than those who choose white victims, using weapons on and hitting victims in the course of the rape at elevated rates. These trends apply to Native women who live both on and off reservations. No one knows why for sure, but centuries of legal impunity for whites who raped Native women and the ongoing systematic dehumanization of Native Americans by white churches and governments have certainly played a part in giving would-be rapists the (nauseatingly correct) impression that they can do whatever they want to Native women without much fear of consequences.

The story of how Native women became the country's most popular rape targets also reveals a lot about the directional relationship between humanity and sexual sovereignty. Most Native tribes, prior to contact with white folks, had much healthier, more holistic attitudes toward women's sexual sovereignty than we do today.

It's important to note that tribes weren't some kind of feminist utopia—they had rape laws, so, clearly, they had rape. Romanticizing Native people is just a different kind of dehumanization. But things were undeniably better for women and sex before white settlers butted in, which we know because the settlers themselves found Native approaches to female sexuality notable. "As for the young girls," marveled French settler Diron D'Artaguiette in his journal, "they are the mistresses of their own bodies (to use their own expression)."[21]

We also know that Native tribes took rape seriously. When forced by the early American government to write down their laws, Muscogee leaders wrote this astonishing statute regarding rape: "And be it further enacted if any person or persons should undertake to force a woman and did it by force, it shall be left to woman what punishment she should satisfied with to whip or pay what she say it be law."[22]

We of course know now that people of all genders can be raped. And I, for one, wouldn't welcome whipping as an appropriate sanction for rape. But can you imagine a more survivor-centered law? Can you imagine a law that more affirmed and restored a rape victim's sovereignty?

Wave after wave of white settlers certainly could not. They viewed the Native population in general as savages—inherently less than fully human—and as such felt free to rape Native women without consequence. European settlers often made it explicitly legal to enslave Native women for sexual purposes and universally sanctioned sex slavery in practice. The legal rape of Native women by white settlers was so rampant that it was the cause that incited some of the best-known "Indian uprisings."[23] US troops systematically raped Native women during westward expansion and forced migrations, often singling out the most powerful and respected women in a tribe to efficiently devastate the spirit of the entire community.

Dehumanization begets further dehumanization, and so after forced migrations, white men thought nothing of marrying Native women to gain access to friable farmland, oil profits, or other valuable resources. Once her assets were securely transferred to him, these men would often abandon or abuse their wives,[24] who, after all, had only ever been a useful object, not a person. Then, early in the twentieth century, almost an entire generation of young Native children were taken from their tribes and forced into government- and church-run boarding schools, where child sexual abuse was rampant, all in the name of "civilizing" them. In a perverse kind of job training, many Native young women who had been abducted and placed in these schools were also forced to do domestic work for non-Native families for little or no pay. Such work also taught them to internalize Victorian-era social codes about how girls should behave, further training them to be good victims and/ or wives for non-Native men.

White politicians and judges point to these centuries of dehumanization at the hands of white people as an excuse to treat Native people as inept at handling their own affairs. Starting in the nineteenth century and continuing through the 1990s, Congress and the courts have slowly eroded tribes' rights to their own jurisprudence. What that winds up meaning is that non-Native men are free to rape and abuse Native women with impunity on Native lands because, until verrrrry recently, Native tribes could not prosecute them. At all. Even now, shockingly, the most tribes can sentence any criminal to is three years, and that sentencing limitation applies to rapes committed by Native men, too. (In certain cases, the federal government can prosecute a crime committed on Native land, but it has generally proven itself uninterested in doing so.) If you're a man who's inclined to rape or abuse women, the US government has provided you with the perfect place to do that. And so the cycle of dehumanization continues.

But it's not continuing unchallenged anymore. That "until recently" came courtesy of the 2013 update to the Violence Against Women Act, which included a provision to allow tribes to prosecute domestic violence perpetrated on the reservation by nontribe members. (This provision only covers cases in which the victim and the abuser are in an intimate or familial relationship, so cases of rape or child abuse perpetrated by non-Native strangers and acquaintances are still raging unchecked today.) The measure faced steep opposition from (mostly) white men who feared for their ability to get a fair trial in tribal courts. As Senator Chuck Grassley put it, "If you have a jury, the jury is supposed to be a reflection of society. Under the laws of our land, you've got to have a jury that is a reflection of society as a whole, and on an Indian reservation, it's going to be made up of Indians, right? So the non-Indian doesn't get a fair trial."[25] It's a laughable assertion when you consider both tribal sovereignty—you wouldn't expect a jury of Americans if an American commits a crime in Canada—and the fact that people of color face overwhelmingly white juries in the United States on a shockingly regular basis, and we never hear Grassley complaining about their rights to a fair trial.

The fight over the VAWA reauthorization was protracted and bitter, but ultimately successful. And though many, many people helped win that fight, it's hard to imagine them prevailing without Sarah Deer, a citizen of the Muscogee (Creek) Nation of Oklahoma.

With her neatly parted hair, dark frame glasses, and comfortable blazer, Sarah Deer looks like a reasonably serious Midwestern law professor, which is exactly what she is. Her office is bright and friendly, with books with funny titles like *Please Don't Annoy the Indians* face-out, and a print on the wall of Native artist Dana Tiger's painting "Truly Supreme Court," including fantasy Native justices and other justices of color, many of them women. Awards she's won litter the shelves, a dish of chocolates sits out on the work table, and a change of clothes hangs on an unused treadmill. There's not a whiff of pretense in any of it, just the trappings of someone who spends a lot of time at work.

And what work. Deer has spent her career organizing against the systems that have made it so easy to abuse Native women and children. She was the force behind Amnesty International's 2007 report *Maze of Injustice*, which reframed the rape of Native women as an international human rights issue.[26] Her dedication to meticulously documenting the history and present reality of violence against Native women, coupled with a talent for building bridges across factions with disparate backgrounds and sometimes contradictory aims, has resulted in not just the VAWA win but also, before that, the passage of the Tribal Law and Order Act of 2010, which gives tribal courts the ability to hand down slightly longer sentences and increases accountability when federal prosecutors decline to pursue tribal cases that fall under their jurisdiction. It's an impressive enough résumé that she was honored in 2015 with a MacArthur "Genius" Fellowship.

The word fits. But Deer is that rarest of geniuses whose intellect doesn't tower over you as much as it invites you in. In her most recent book *The Beginning and End of Rape*, she proposes her own "indigenous theory of rape," which conceives of rape as an unlawful invasion not just of the body but also of the mind and spirit. She writes, "This theory allows the resulting legal system to address the crime of sexual violence holistically—that is, as a crime against a person in the context of her entire self. . . . In short, rape is conceived of as a violation of a person's humanity."[27]

As a survivor, reading this framework for rape is like realizing you've been holding your breath for god knows how long and can only now finally breathe freely again. Every survivor knows this in our bones—rape is a violation of our humanity at every level—and yet Deer is the first person I've heard articulate it so clearly. To develop her theory, she draws on the best traditions of Native oral history, jurisprudence, and academic rigor. But she also draws her ideas about universal humanity from a source that might surprise you.

"My dad interestingly was, he doesn't like to admit this today, but was a really big part of me becoming a feminist," she recalls, when I ask her where she got her ideas about sexual sovereignty.

And it's a very simple story. *Free to Be You and Me*.[28] We would go to the library almost every weekend, and we checked out the record. I didn't recognize it until later, that not all kids were exposed to this [idea that] girls can do anything boys can do, and boys can cry and all this kind of stuff. [It] was, I thought, very routine, because it's just part of my life, and then when I got older and I realized not everybody shared those beliefs, I was like *Whoa! Didn't everybody listen to this record?*

Deer got turned on to *Free to Be* in Wichita, Kansas, where her mom was a high school biology teacher. Deer was justice-minded from the start, writing letters to her high school paper against the war in Kuwait and rallying for abortion rights. But her turn to anti-rape work was personal. "I had used a rape crisis center, and had a lot of guilt about the kind of burden I put on my volunteer advocates. I was just a mess. A flat-out mess. So when I got my shit together and figured out what I needed to do for myself, I wanted to give back." In law school, a pushy professor helped her connect the dots between her work on sexual violence and her Native identity:

After serving as a rape crisis advocate for several years, [I went to law school] thinking I was going to be a sex crimes prosecutor, thinking "I'm going to put all these bad people in jail," which was a little naive on my part. The Indian Law professor at Kansas (he's since left, but his name was Robert Porter) found out that there was some Indian in Law who was not enrolled in his Indian Law class, and this disturbed him greatly. So he cornered me and got me to go out to a Chinese restaurant, and said, "How come you're not going to take my Indian Law class?" I said, "I'm focusing my career as a prosecutor," and he said, "Listen, it sounds like you're interested in social justice—it sounds like you're interested in making the world a better place. I think if you take my class, I think you'll learn that Indian Law is where it's at." So begrudgingly and because I felt guilty, I took his class, and on the second day I was hooked. It was one of those [moments where] you're just sitting in a room, [and suddenly feel] like oh, this is what I'm doing for the rest of my life.

Being Deer means being patient with white people. The day I catch up with her, she is speaking at an event for the American Association of University Women in Minneapolis/St. Paul, which turns out to be a gathering of mostly white retired professors and professionals who put on a lecture and luncheon series every Monday. To a person, they are courteous and concerned in response to Deer's presentation, but not without constant reminders of otherness. As we leave the theater, one woman accosts her with tearful passion. She takes Deer's hands in hers and does not let them go, all the while asking Deer how she could "save" Native children from their own homes and ignoring Deer's rising discomfort and my attempts to intervene. Nearly every woman we speak with seems compelled to tell Deer about her own remote or rumored Indian heritage, or of a friend of a friend who has some connection to Native lands, whether or not that heritage or those lands have anything to do with Deer's tribe. (If you're not sure why that would be annoying, think of a time you traveled out of state and someone said to you, "Oh, you're from New Jersey? Do you know Bob?" Then add a history of genocide and racism.) These are clearly expressions of a desire to connect across a perceived distance in power and status and humanity. But Deer responds to each of them politely and warmly (if noncommittally), even the woman who had, over lunch, made sure to inform us that those Syrian refugees have a problem with rape, too, you know. *Just awful.* As if rape were a thing that just happens to unfortunate brown people when they are violently displaced. As if there's no rape problem right here in Minneapolis.

When I ask Deer about that moment, all of these moments, later, in her office, at first she says she has no idea what I'm talking about. Pressed, she admits to a certain annoyance at the lack of self-reflection on the part of these women, but ultimately views these interactions in practical terms: "I feel like, here's a group of apparently rich white women, maybe if I give them something to spend money on, they will. I'm willing to put up with some bullshit to educate. Some people go home now and they'll probably email me and want me to speak at their other thing. I'm sure I shook up a few people today, and that's okay. I can put up with some weirdness to do that. And I do like to talk about my work. I like to share what we've done, I think it's amazing."

And it's a good thing she does. To spend any time at all with Deer is also to have one's worldview rearranged. Just reading her book I came across this story that instantly reorganized my ideas of the social location of survivors:

"An Ojibwa tale, published in 1906 by an anthropologist, is an empowering story of the worth and value of women. The story was told by an Ojibwa elder named Mrs. Chatfield in 1894. The main protagonist in the story, an Ojibwa woman, was raped by members of a warring tribe. In the aftermath of the rape, this woman becomes revered among her own people, becoming both a medicine woman and a warrior. She is clearly held up to be a strong and powerful woman."[29]

A little explosion went off in my brain. Having only ever lived in a culture that shamed survivors of sexual violence, having had that shame etched on me even before my own assault, it never occurred to me it could be another way. I thought the best we could ever work toward was elimination of the shaming of rape victims, stigmatization of the stigmatizers instead. But this story goes way beyond neutral. It points the way to a culture that reveres survivors, that recognizes the strength and wisdom it requires to come out the other side of such a profound act of violence. It not only humanizes rape victims; it humanizes all of us.

When I told Deer about my click moment, she told me a story that illustrates the same point from the opposite perspective. She told me about a man she had met, a man who had abused his wife and was in a batterer's recovery program. She tells me that he said, "I looked at my own life, and that I had completely taken on the trappings of this [white] culture. I had become the colonizer in my behavior and I had to relearn what it meant to be a Lakota man." And then another man in the program, a white man, said to him, "I wish we had that. I feel like I don't get the opportunity to say, this was not the way that we did things and we need to go back to that, you know."

"We need to refresh ourselves and figure out what our cultures were doing that made these behaviors so ridiculous." She concludes, "I think Native people are lucky. In a way that we can say, here is the point of origin. We did not treat each other this way."

As optimistic as she remains, it's important to remember that even heroes are human. The work, as you might imagine, backs up on her some of the time, like when she sees progress stall out over the long term. "The first time I started to feel really old," she confesses, "was [when] people started to talk about Roe v. Wade Day, and I'm like, *Do we still need to do that? Oh, fuck yeah, we do. Shit. What? What did I just spend ten years of my life doing?* In the 1990s that's all I [worked on]."

Sometimes it's more grim. A few years back, Deer started trying to document the invisible trend of Native women going missing and turning up mysteriously murdered in the United States:

It started with the story of a Native woman, a prostitute named Casey Pipeston, a member of my tribe. She was found in a creek in rural Oklahoma, and her uncle or her father said something really horrible about her in the news. . . . And I just thought, how many other Casey Pipestons are out there, whose stories are not getting in the newspaper? So I started to really try to find the stories.

I realized quite quickly that I was in way over my head, because I was just doing it as a hobby. I was all by myself with it. I was having nightmares, and I finally said this is not a project I can take on until there's more of a critical mass behind it. . . . I didn't have any money to do it and I didn't have anybody else doing it with me, and I couldn't do it. And I don't know why that's harder than rape. It's just . . . Women in creeks, and I just couldn't.

In some ways it's comforting to know that even someone as inde-fatigable as Deer has her limits. All of us do, especially when it feels like the world devalues us at every turn. The granddaughter of a Jew, Deer's very existence is a story of strength and survival, and she knows it. "Between Hitler and Andrew Jackson," she half-laughs, "I'm not supposed to be here. I mean, both sides, right? I feel very obligated to do work on justice. Because you know, if people hadn't been doing that, I might not be here."

Recently, with some of the MacArthur grant money, she's convened a group of Muscogee academics from a range of disciplines to put together an anthology of their work. It's a contribution toward the positive legacy of the tribe, or, as Deer puts it, a chance to prove that

> we are scholars, we can write, we're not just backwards people who struggle all the time with everything. We actually have an intellectual life. I think I contribute to [the victim narrative] at some level. When I write, I do focus on really shitty things, because they have to be told. You have to tell the truth. But then it sort of gives you the picture that everybody on a reservation is fucked up.
>
> [In my talks,] I make a strong effort to have more positive images, and I talk about the positive actions of Native women, because I don't want to leave my non-Native audiences going, *Wow, reservations suck. What a horrible place to live.* Because, they're not. I mean, Native women have survived and are resilient and are not going away, and they've celebrated their survival, they've celebrated their existence, and if we only portray the negative images and the negative statistics, I think that's as harmful as anything.

This, ultimately, is how we claim our sexual humanity. Not just by playing defense, destigmatizing, rejecting blame and shame and fear and violence—that's crucial work, but it will never be enough by itself. We must also sing the songs of our own powers, of our personal strange beauty, the things we know that no one else does because they're too busy convincing themselves we have nothing to say. We have to sing loudly and long, until we are heard. And we have to listen when others do the same.

It's not enough to reject slut shaming, we must listen to sluts when they tell us that having numerous partners has liberated them from settling for less than they want. It's important to support rape survivors in their healing, but that's not enough until we can also see them as teachers of resilience and tenacity in the face of the unimaginable. It's one thing to "tolerate" gay people, but real change doesn't happen until we celebrate the things bisexuals and gender nonconformists demonstrate about transcending definition. Not because sluts or survivors or queers have the ultimate answers to anything. The choices they make in their lives may not be the ones that work for you. But because being human is like a potluck; it's always a better proposition when everyone is encouraged to bring their special recipe to the party.

## CHAPTER EIGHT

# HOW TO BUILD A BETTER MAN

I SHOULD LOVE *Good Night Stories for Rebel Girls*. A beautifully illustrated children's book, it features gorgeous illustrations of a hundred women who've changed the world, from Ruth Bader Ginsburg to Serena Williams to Frida Kahlo. Each image is accompanied by that woman's story told as a fairy tale. It's basically engineered to appeal specifically to me. Instead, every time I see that cool midnight-blue cover with the bold and funky lettering, my jaw clenches. Because right there the title *Good Night Stories for Rebel Girls* is telling boys to keep out. The creators, Elena Favilli and Francesca Cavallo, double down on that message in the Kickstarter video they made to fund the publication of the book. To close the pitch, they exhort you to "buy it for your daughter, your niece, your friend's daughter. Every girl you know deserves to grow up thinking that she can be anything she wants." It was apparently an effective argument: the pair raised almost $700K before the book was even published, more than ten times their original goal of $40K.

And here I come being a spoilsport. You wouldn't think an inspiring book for girls would be where I'd draw the line. Most of the world is pretty much a boys' club, after all. But why are stories about powerful women just for girls? Why can't we see how important it is for boys to identify with and look up to complex, badass women?

I don't mean to single out Favilli and Cavallo. This dynamic plays out everywhere. When *Star Wars: The Force Awakens* hit theaters in 2015, strangely absent from the toys that hit shelves were representations of the movie's protagonist. Why? Because toymakers assumed that all *Star Wars* fans would want male action figures, but only the girls would want to play as Rey.

Pervasive fauxpowerment narratives teach both boys and girls that sexism is an individual problem for individual girls to overcome by Leaning In and embracing Girl Power, which may be why the Pew Research Center found that 63 percent of men ages eighteen to thirty-five think sexism literally doesn't exist anymore in the United States.[1]

But to actually combat sexism, boys need to believe in Girl Power just as much as girls do. And when we give boys the chance, they love stories about women. My partner and I gave our twin nephews a book called *Rad American Women A–Z* when they were just two years old, and, with the encouragement of their parents, by two and a half they had memorized it and could name women like Dolores Huerta and Kate Bornstein on sight. That's not just a cool party trick: it's going to serve as part of the foundation of their ideas about themselves as men. When boys grow up without identifying with women, when they are allowed to grow into men without understanding that women are complex, three-dimensional people whose stories are just as interesting and valuable as men's stories, boys grow into a masculinity that inherently conceives of men as better—and more human—than women. That happens to be our dominant conception of masculinity in the United States, and it is an unstable one, requiring constant protection from the encroaching possibility that women aren't just disposable sluts or helpless maidens, props in men's plays about their manliness.

You've probably encountered the backlash that howls whenever social constructions of masculinity are criticized in any way. The men who insist that #NotAllMen harass women on the street or treat us like interchangeable objects, and therefore they don't want to hear us complain about it. Men like Dave Hon, who became a viral Internet sensation for a minute when he wrote an accidentally hilarious missive all about how he would never date a feminist.[2] It opens thusly: "If you look for a reason to hate men, chances are you're going to find it."

That feminists hate men is a popular argument among the Dave Hons of the world, men who often identify themselves as "men's rights activists" or "men going their own way" (yes, that's really a thing, though they less "go their own way" and more "yell about women on the Internet"). But these men are confused, and not just because declaring themselves out of reach of feminist affections is like me declaring that I'll never consent to star in *Hamilton*.

Masculinity is the collection of attitudes, behaviors, and roles we tend to associate with men — not anything inherent to men themselves. Masculinity is, in large part, socially constructed and changeable. The open affection and even passion shared between male friends in the nineteenth century would make you blush. (And speaking of blush, little more than a century ago, pink was considered a masculine color, because it was associated with red, which was considered bold and strong.) Think about it: if men were just masculine without having to try, if masculinity were truly inherent to being a man, why would so many men feel so defensive about it? It's precisely because masculinity is an ever-shifting set of cultural standards that so many men feel insecure about whether they're living up to them. They need their tissues to be packaged in a black box labeled "Mansize" before they'll blow snot into them.

As they say: it's funny 'cause it's true. If your gender identity can be undermined by thin sheets of paper, it's fragile indeed.

But underneath the memes and merch is a sort of whistling past the graveyard. Because the fragility of traditional masculinity is also terrifying. Men who feel like they have something to prove about being men are the source of most of the violence in the world. And they're the ones standing in the way of women truly claiming our full sexual power.

That's because traditional masculinity defines itself in opposition to women. Men are strong, women are vulnerable. Men take sex, women surrender it. These are conceived of as zero-sum binaries: if women are strong, that must make men weaker. If women have our own appetites and boundaries, if we refuse to serve as sexual trophies and implements of male gratification, well, that's downright emasculating. That's treating men like "pussies."

The entire world of fragile masculinity is contained in that one epithet. LeBron James had to be restrained from physically assaulting a player who called him a pussy in the middle of a heated game. In the last presidential election cycle, it was going around like the flu: Fox News commentator Lieutenant Colonel Ralph Peters called Obama a pussy, then Donald Trump hurled it at Ted Cruz, then Libertarian candidate Gary Johnson said that, actually, it was Trump who most resembled a woman's vagina. None of these gentlemen was suggesting that their antagonist was warm and strong and flexible and resilient and capable of great pleasure, though all of those things can be said about pussies in real life. What they meant was this: I'm the real man in this situation. My opponent is weak and easily dominated. Like a woman, and her sex organs.

This dominating-women definition of manliness is all too often literal, and we ignore it at our constant peril. Between 2009 and 2015, 57 percent of all mass shootings in the United States were committed by men who were targeting family members or intimate partners, and 64 percent of the victims of those mass shootings were women or children. Even in cases where the killer didn't have such close ties to victims, the attacks are often explicitly fueled by misogyny: think Elliot Rodger, who killed six people in Santa Barbara, California, because he was angry about being rejected by women he considered "high value"; the Orlando shooter Omar Mateen, who may have been animated in part by internalized homophobia and who had abused his ex-wife; and Robert Lewis Dear, who killed three when he attacked a Colorado Planned Parenthood and who had a long history of preying on women. If we stopped treating men's violent domination of women as "natural" or "inevitable," if we started taking women's sovereignty and safety seriously, we could save a lot of lives.

Of course, not many men commit mass shootings. But plenty of them hurt women as a way to shore up their manhood. Even men who think they would never hurt a woman are usually holding onto their masculinity by a thread made of women's souls. Just ask James Knight, an Iowa dentist who fired dental assistant Melissa Nelson because he was too attracted to her; we all know manly men "can't help themselves" around hot women. Or ask any of the million guys I encountered in my online dating days who wouldn't consider dating a woman the same age as they were. A guy who doesn't place himself at the middle of his dating age range is a guy who's telling you he doesn't like women who have as much power and experience as he does. And that, sadly, is most men: in one 2015 study, straight men were asked to consider a hypothetical woman who was smarter than them. These men had no trouble imagining being attracted to her. But when they were told that an actual woman they had met had beat them out in the brains department, most of the men "distanced themselves more from her, tended to rate her as less attractive, and showed less desire to exchange contact information or plan a date with her" than with a woman they were told was their intellectual inferior.[3] In another study, straight men rated "attractive" and "sweet" as some of the most important attributes they look for in a partner, but "independent" and "strong" as their priorities for their daughters, whom they of course will never have to interact with as equals.[4]

Most of these guys are well-meaning humans who've just never been required to do better. On the contrary, many have experienced social shaming and even male-on-male violence when they've dared to be "too" respectful of women. That's the paradox of fragile masculinity: individual men have such a vulnerable sense of gender that it can be undermined simply by buying a box of tampons, yet the rigid culture of masculinity is as deeply rooted as the mightiest of oak trees.

The clearest examples of toxic masculinity replicating itself tend to involve rape and fall into two broad categories: men giving each other a pass for raping, and men pressuring each other into raping. The former includes a litany of judges who've refused to sentence convicted rapists to any jail time whatsoever, mostly because the rapists were "respectable" white men who reminded the judges of themselves. It also includes the cops who systematically disbelieve women when they report rapes, men who don't intervene when they're literally watching a buddy rape someone, sports teams (and fans) who look the other way when the rapist is a beloved athlete or coach, and all the men on the Internet who tell me that Julian Assange couldn't possibly have raped anyone because WikiLeaks. Consider these men the rear guard, ensuring that the barn door stays open once the horse has fled. The van, then, consists of the men who pressure each other to rape: fraternity brothers who compose and circulate guides to "luring your rapebait,"[5] which advise potential pledges, "Here is how to dance: Grab them on the hips with your 2 hands and then let them grind against your dick." Pick-up artists who get rich selling courses and guides that teach men to push past women's "last-minute resistance" to force them to have sex or to get them drunk enough that they're incapable of stopping a man from commandeering their body.

Those examples may be the clearest, but the masculinity police will arrest you for far less. In 2016, Eric Owens posted a series of four photos, each showing his son laying contentedly against him in the crook of his shoulder.[6] In the earliest shot, the son is a baby. In the most recent, he is a young man. The caption read, "18 years later and he still under my arm." The Internet went wild at this show of physical, familial male affection. "This is the weirdest shit ever, girl and her mother is one thing but a man shouldn't be raising his son to lay on him like that," wrote one user. Another put an even finer point on it: "Ain't nothing MAN'ly about that."

In another jaw-dropping example, Aerie, maker of trendy cotton underthings for young women, ran an #AerieMAN campaign, featuring a diverse range of unretouched male bodies in what was purported to be the launch of a new line for men. Except it was all an April Fool's joke, because why would men need something as soft and affirming as body positivity? That's for ladies.

Also for ladies? The responsibility for anything men feel or do. If men harass women on the street, we shouldn't have put on that skirt if we didn't want the attention. Women's dress codes at work and school are often cloaked in rhetoric about not "distracting" men from doing important man stuff. Under toxic masculinity, men evidently have the right to not get turned on at inopportune times, while women don't even have the right not to be raped.

It's enough to make me feel my own kind of oppositional. If men can't get their shit together, if they need us to be subjugated in order to feel right, fuck 'em. Or rather, don't. #BanMen. Fragile masculinity makes me feel like going past *Lysistrata* to full lesbian separatism, leaving men to their own devices at least until they figure out how to exist as men without hurting or degrading us. But the problem with *Lysistrata* (and political lesbianism) is and always has been this: many women like to have sex with men. Refusing to fuck men at all as some kind of punishment of their gender requires most of us to punish ourselves, too. And even if men aren't our lovers, they're our sons and brothers and fathers. They can be real friends and are often our coworkers and bosses and political and cultural and spiritual leaders, too. Disengaging from men sometimes, or from certain men, is a useful survival strategy for many women. Disengaging from men entirely just isn't practical for most of us, and it denies us some of our deepest pleasures.

Besides, when we conflate men with their fragile masculinity, we're falling into the same trap they are. Connecting with men doesn't have to mean playing by those rules if we find men who are struggling to reject them. (Though beware the men who loudly and repeatedly announce how evolved they are. Any man who seeks praise and attention for treating women like human equals is not a man who actually believes that we are.)

However appealing, withdrawing from men also doesn't get us free from toxic masculinity. Like the old Palmolive commercial, women are soaking in it, too, and we take it out on each other all the time. A 2016 study found that fully half of the misogynist bile on Twitter is spewed by other women.[7] Although that study had flaws—it relied on keyword searches, not allowing for the fact that women use words like *bitch* with each other in friendly ways or that sometimes people invoke a word in order to criticize someone else for using it—there's no getting around the fact that lots of women reach for retro manly tropes when they want to exert power over other women. After all, girls are also constantly exposed to men and boys who are disgusted by all things "feminine," and we're just as susceptible to believing it.

Sometimes we aim that toxicity at ourselves, which is why sociologist Lisa Wade, in learning about students' sexual beliefs for her book *American Hookup,* found that her female students were just as likely as her male ones to find the vagina repulsive. Sometimes we enact toxic masculinity in competition with other women, like the Playboy model who secretly photographed a random naked woman at her gym and nonconsensually posted that photo to Instagram with the caption "If I can't unsee this, you can't either."[8] (The most incongruously hilarious example of women wielding toxic masculinity against other women may involve the fifteen-year-old actress who voiced Dora the Explorer, who is alleged to have called a female classmate a "pussy" in an effort to pressure her into vaping.)[9]

So, if opting out of men and building a separatist paradise won't save us, what are we supposed to do about masculinity? Let's start by building a complete narrative about the harms of toxic masculinity, one that includes men among its victims.

I'll confess to having choked on a little bile as I wrote that. The harm done to women in the name of manliness should be more than enough to convince men they need a new way. But it's not. It's just not. And if we can motivate more men by demonstrating how old models of masculinity don't serve their best interests, I'll take it.

A lot of the time when men are injured by fragile masculinity, it's at the hands of other men out to prove their superior manliness. From "hazing" rape rituals on school sports teams to every time a man or boy is called a "faggot" simply for displaying human vulnerability, toxic masculinity requires constant violent dominance. It's also particularly harmful to men of color: Black masculinity is often perceived as threatening and used as license to kill Black men, whereas Asian men are regularly shamed and marginalized for not being "manly" enough.

Even men who dominate are often harmed by toxic masculinity. In a 2016 meta-review of seventy-eight studies on masculinity and mental health that together studied nearly twenty thousand men, researchers found that men who place value on having power over women as well as those who endorse "playboy behavior" are more likely to suffer from depression, body image issues, substance abuse, and other psychological challenges. Perhaps unsurprisingly, they were also less likely than other men to seek professional mental health support for these issues.[10]

If we're willing to move through our anger at being required to help men not be violent assholes, we can help some of them. Karen B. K. Chan, a sex and emotional literacy educator, speaks compellingly of the need to teach boys resiliency in the face of sexual rejection. "How might we empathize with a young guy who is balancing masculinity pressures and the desire to show and receive love?" she encourages us to ask. "How might we normalize and validate feelings of loneliness and insecurity for men who feel isolated or unattractive? What emotional and social tools will a college frat boy need when the girl he just met wants to stop making out and he does not? How can we help him experience bearable rejection instead of unbearable failure? How do we equip him to listen, to continue to humanize her, instead of lashing out in anger or blame?"[11]

For Chan, a big part of the answer rests in humanizing men, even those who might dehumanize women. "Let us offer our audiences the opportunity to be honest about situations that are realistically complex and conflicting. If posing a scenario about a potential sexual partner who is very intoxicated, do not merely push for the 'right' answers according to legal and definitional consent. Move beyond that by discussing how anticipation, excitement, and sexual arousal feel in the face of choosing not to have sex. Empathize with the perceived expectations of friend groups and the pressure to belong. Talk about how disappointment, rejection, and impatience feel."

It's an invitation full of power and potential. If men who are wrapped up in what Chan calls the "Dominance Game" would just relax their bro-borders for a minute, they'd learn that boys really don't have to be "boys." Men can ask for help, and they can change. Even men who've already done terrible things.

I have a friend—let's call him Dave, though that's not his name—who is active in his church, a loving and supportive husband, and a hilarious dinner companion. He's also a former rapist. He confessed this to me in fits and starts, over dinners and phone calls and late-night drinks, after we'd known each other a couple of years. His story matches much of the research my work relies on, but it still forced me to reevaluate some of my core assumptions about rapists and about the role of men in ending rape.

Dave's former MO is familiar to anyone who thinks about sexual violence for a living. He picked victims he knew. He got them alone, encouraged them to have conversations that made them feel vulnerable, and pressed a lot of alcohol on them. And then, when they were too drunk to consent, he "had sex" with them. (That's how he thought about it at the time, though today he will tell you straight up it was rape.)

The research is very clear: most rapists know they don't have consent, and they rape again and again, an average of six times each. Before Dave told me his story, I thought that meant that most rapists were essentially sociopaths. I worried for a long time that Dave, too, must be a sociopath. But I've done a lot of thinking and searching on that idea, and I just don't think he is. I think he's a guy who grew up with some very toxic ideas about what it means to be a man.

Better models of masculinity are everywhere if you know where to look. In October 2016, when Trump claimed his brags about assaulting women were just "locker room talk," a group of male high school athletes in Oregon had their picture taken in their locker room wearing "wild feminist" T-shirts[12] in a rejection of the idea that men's spaces are hostile to women's safety. Thanks in large part to the success of *Magic Mike XXL*, male burlesque is taking off as mainstream entertainment for women,[13] upending assumptions about what makes men hot and whose gaze and pleasure are important. When I polled my friends about where they find examples of the kind of masculinities they want to see more of in the world, the crowdsourced list was dazzling in its diversity and included the following:

- Frank Ocean (for his "openness and vulnerability around sexuality")
- African men dancing together, and skirt-wearing men contra dancing
- Basketball star Steph Curry caring for his daughter at postgame press conferences
- All of Barack Obama's interactions with children
- Queer men of various stripes subverting the very definitions of manhood
- An array of fictional men of film and TV, including Bob from *Bob's Burgers* ("He's so completely unthreatened by other people's sexuality, and clear on what he wants and doesn't. I mean, any dad who would say to his daughter, 'It's your mouth, Tina, you decide who you want to kiss with it and what you want to say with it'—come on, how great is that?"), the men on the show *Brooklyn Nine-Nine* ("respectful and loving dude friendships, totally in touch with their feels and no need to put women down"), a variety of modern superheroes like *The Flash* ("has examples of men bonding and crying and being emotional [and not just over death, which is the only time men are allowed to be emotional and that's usually just rage]"), and *Midnighter* ("gay butch superhero"), and *Steven Universe*.

Every single one of these instances is important—and if recent research out of Kenya is any indication, their presence may well be influencing other men for the better. There, a program called "Your Moment of Truth" managed to reduce the number of rapes the boyfriends and male friends of schoolgirls committed against them by over 20 percent. The program was pretty straightforward, consisting of six 2-hour sessions in which the boys were taught about the impacts and pervasiveness of violence against women, unlearned rape and gender myths, explored the meaning of sexual consent, and learned how and why to safely intervene if they saw someone attacking or abusing a woman.[14] They didn't lock up a single person. They just offered the boys in the program an alternative model of masculinity, one that values women and girls as human beings.

If you curate your life right, you could easily believe that the old ways of being a man are dying, and that we're entering an age of better, more complex, and egalitarian masculinities. But it's much too soon to declare victory. American men may be enjoying more emotional vulnerability in their superhero stories, but they also elected the living embodiment of toxic masculinity as president. Trump has spent his life defining his manliness in opposition to the women he dominates and degrades. He was known to stroll into the changing area of the pageants he owned—even the teen pageants—to ogle the competitors. "It must be a pretty picture, you dropping to your knees" is literally a thing he said to a female contestant on *The Apprentice*, a woman ostensibly in a job interview with him. He has been accused of sexual assault by over a dozen women, including his first wife, Ivana.[15] The men he's installed into power share his attitudes—Chief Strategist Steve Bannon has gotten rich running stories with headlines like "Birth control makes women unattractive and crazy" and "Would you rather your child had feminism or cancer?" at Breitbart.com. When these men talk about making America great again, one of the things they're yearning for is the reestablishment of "traditional" gender values in which men are dominant, women are subservient, and anyone who questions whether that's really the natural order of things is punished.

My friend Dave grew up in a household steeped in those very values. I believe him when he tells me he never thought he was hurting anyone. He didn't think about the experience of those women at all, really, unless it was to evaluate which of their vulnerabilities he could use to manipulate them into bed. He was raised to believe in a masculinity that defines itself not only in opposition to femaleness but also as inherently superior, drawing its strength from dominance over women's "weakness." It was only in learning that there are other, better ways to "be a man" that he became the friend I know him as today.

That's not to say that we should let guys who've already offended off the hook in order to tempt them into the light. If you hurt someone, whether or not you meant to, you should face consequences. In fact, consequences can sometimes help facilitate learning. "I think one of the reasons my behavior went unchecked for so long is that I didn't suffer any consequences," recalls Dave. He mostly picked victims he didn't have a strong relationship or interest in, so if they just faded out of his life afterward, he didn't have to think about why. It wasn't until he lost a friendship he valued that he had to think about his behavior in a new light. "That was the first time I experienced a loss as a result of my actions and I had to take a step back and go, oh, this was bad. It was a wake-up call."

Of course, some men just hit snooze when they get that wake-up call. For decades, conservative kingmaker Roger Ailes used his position of power at Fox News to sexually harass, blackmail, and coerce countless women in his employ. My impulse here is to assure you that Dave is nothing like Ailes, but who knows: it's entirely plausible that Ailes, who similarly grew up in a conservative family, just thought he was being a man, enacting the natural order of things. After all, there seemed to be no shortage of people—men and women—willing to enable and support him. Colleagues say his longtime assistant would scope out new "talent" for him to "develop" and enter fake names in his datebook to cover her boss's tracks. The Fox execs quietly cut checks to silence women who complained and underwrote the construction of a literal wall around Ailes's executive suite to keep anyone from knowing who was coming and going from his center of operations.[16]

That is, of course, until Gretchen Carlson dropped a dime on him. Carlson, a longtime Fox anchor, had been fending off Ailes's advances for years. But when Ailes demoted her for complaining to a supervisor about the condescending tone of her male cohost, she decided she'd had enough and started secretly recording her interactions with him, eventually capturing an entire year of harassment, including the time he told her, "I think you and I should have had a sexual relationship a long time ago, and then you'd be good and better and I'd be good and better. Sometimes problems are easier to solve [that way]." Once she went public with the tapes, more than two dozen women came forward with similar stories of their own. Fifteen days later, Ailes was out at Fox. We've seen the same dynamic in countless rape and harassment cases. When women refuse to uphold it, fragile masculinity can shatter.

Of course, more often, one woman will step up and no one will follow her, allowing her to get crushed by toxic masculinity instead. Even when women do manage to take down abusive men, the victories are partial at best. As of this writing, Fox News is still the most-watched cable news network, and had he not died in May 2017, Ailes would surely still be floating on the $40 million parachute Fox handed him as they shoved him off the plane. I doubt that Ailes or the Fox execs who enabled him for so long had an epiphany anything like Dave's, except inasmuch as they realized they may have to be more circumspect with their misogyny, because perhaps now there are fewer people ready to shore up and cover for abusive masculinity. But that alone is progress.

Not that Dave is any kind of hero, either. Whatever he knows now, he still hurt those women, and if any of them decided to hold him accountable for that, I'd support them. (So would Dave, for that matter, however much it would cost him.) And he has hardly become a full-time feminist crusader. But he does small things that make a big difference. He refuses to laugh at rape jokes or slut shaming or anything that reduces women to commodities for men to judge or consume, and he goes out of his way to explain to other men why these things aren't funny. He doesn't vote for candidates who want to control women's access to abortion or birth control. He's raising his daughter to know that her body is her own, to do with as she pleases as long as she's not hurting anyone, and that no one has the right to control it but her.

These are, of course, small victories, less "revolution" and more "baby steps toward basic human decency." As important as it is to know that these incremental gains are possible, relying on them alone to remake masculinity will take too long and places too much of the burden on the women who are most harmed by it to stick their neck out. For every Gretchen Carlson, there are dozens of women whose names we'll never hear, who object to sexual harassment at work, get fired for their trouble, and can't afford a lawyer or access any real means of fighting back. Dave may have turned inward when someone he valued challenged him to, but how many women did he have to hurt first? And how many "Daves" are there who would have just called that woman a bitter bitch and gone on with their day?

What's more, there's evidence that not all interventions, however well meaning, are created equal. Our brains find it a lot easier to reject information that flies in the face of our existing beliefs than to admit we may have been wrong about something. And the more important that existing belief is—say, the belief that we're a good person who would never hurt anyone—the harder it is for anyone to change it. In fact, sometimes when people with deep-rooted beliefs are confronted with contradictory facts, they can experience what's called a "backfire": not only are they not convinced by the new facts but also they become even more confident in and tenacious about their original beliefs.

Perhaps that's why, when researchers Dianne Berg, Kimberly Lonsway, and Louise Fitzgerald exposed men to either a male or female rape victim telling their story, they found that the men in their study failed to develop more empathy toward rape victims of any gender. And when the participants filled out a questionnaire two weeks after listening to the victim testimony, the men who had heard from the female victim reported being more likely to engage in what the researchers identified as "rape-supportive behaviors" (like using coercion or alcohol to overcome a woman's objections) than were the men who heard from the male victim and those in a control group who merely heard a presentation of facts about rape.

That's worth repeating, not just because it is so counterintuitive but because current approaches to "teaching men not to rape" are so wildly varied and unregulated. So here it is again: a program designed to induce men to have empathy for rape victims actually appears to have made them more inclined to rape.

And the difficulties in divorcing masculinity from misogyny aren't confined to the tricky business of rape prevention. Hostile sexism— the kind that involves calling women degrading names, rape and rape threats, "make me a sandwich" memes, and generally being an asshole to women—is the kind that's most often linked to toxic masculinity. But it's not the only kind of masculinity that relies on the dehumanization of women. After all, if men were just hostile to women all of the time, why would any of us enter into relationships with them? Instead, hostile sexism plays Mr. Hyde to benevolent sexism's Dr. Jekyll, the two of them teaming up to keep women subservient to men's needs.

Benevolent sexism is what happens every time a man invokes his wife and daughters as the reason he's condemning violence against women. It's when Michael Moore floats the patently false claim that women are better suited to public office because "no women ever invented an atomic bomb, built a smoke stack, initiated a Holocaust, melted the polar ice caps or organized a school shooting." Or when Paul Ryan rebuked Trump's "grab 'em by the pussy" hostile sexism by saying, "Women are to be championed and revered, not objectified." Benevolent sexism says that real men protect "good women," who are morally superior angels living on uncomfortably narrow pedestals. It's a kinder, gentler way to force three-dimensional women into two-dimensional boxes and strip us of our humanity. Of course, the moment we fall off those pedestals, it gives benevolent sexism a perfect excuse to turn into hostile sexism and attack. If that sounds like the rescue dynamic all over again, it's no coincidence: the twin engines of hostile and benevolent sexism are always driving that train.

The tricky thing is that it's a lot harder to challenge benevolent sexism, because a lot of women like it, too. It's seductive to feel like, if we perform our womanhood the right ways, we'll be deserving of safety and that all the women we see being harmed and targeted by men have only themselves to blame. That's not to say we should throw up our hands and not try, but to say that we have to get a lot more deliberate if we want to transform masculinity into a healthy identity that doesn't rely on the subjugation of women. Much, much more serious research is needed into what's effective when it comes to making a masculine ideal that's better for all of us.

Also clear? It would be a whole lot easier if we started at the beginning, teaching boys that being strong includes being able to embrace their own vulnerable emotions and that girls aren't teacups or trophies or aliens from Venus but fellow human beings who are pretty dang interesting. I think often of the two men who intervened when they came upon Brock Turner raping an unconscious woman at Stanford—they knew instantly that something was wrong, because she was clearly not moving or participating. Contrast that with Evan Westlake, who in high school witnessed his two friends raping a semiconscious girl at a party in Steubenville, Ohio. When asked why he didn't intervene to stop the assault, he told the court, "Well, it wasn't violent. I didn't know exactly what rape was. I always pictured it as forcing yourself on someone." I'm sure there are many differences between Westlake and the two men in the Brock Turner case, but the one that stands out to me is that Westlake was raised here in the United States. The two men on bicycles in Palo Alto were Swedes, raised in a country that teaches healthy attitudes toward sexuality and gender in school, starting in kindergarten. They knew that a woman who is lying still and not participating in sex is a woman who isn't consenting. And it upset them enough to take action.

There are a lot of obstacles to instituting the Swedish model of sex education here in the United States. But there's no reason that the transformation of masculinity has to wait for our public education system to catch up. Across the country, dozens of programs work with high school and college-age boys to help them rethink what it means to be a man. These programs just need to start younger. We need to shift from an intervention mind-set—trying to shift young men's conceptions of masculinity after they've already been formed—to a prevention mind-set in which we help boys develop healthier ideas about gender to start with.

Because we start conveying our ideas about gender to our kids basically at birth,[17] that's a tough challenge. Not every toddler boy has an aunt and uncle who'll give him feminist board books, and some parents wouldn't let their "little men" near such a gift anyhow. But just because it's hard to design culture-wide gender interventions for those family-only early years doesn't mean we can't do better than we're doing now. In fact, research suggests middle school could be an ideal time to inoculate boys against toxic masculinity. Middle school boys' ability to resist traditional masculine norms is relatively strong but weakens when they get to high school.[18] And other kinds of social and emotional development programs have proven quite effective in middle school.[19]

That's part of why Maine Boys to Men, a program that has long worked with high school boys, is in the second year of developing a curriculum for middle school boys that teaches them to see and side-step the rigid gender roles they're already growing into. And that's only part of their shift from being strictly a training program for high school students to a multifaceted program working to transform masculinity at the community level.

In some ways, this shift is the result of Executive Director Matthew Theodores's very productive midlife crisis. When I meet him, he looks every inch a white guy CEO on a casual Friday, his neatly trimmed salt-and-pepper hair setting off a crisp pastel button-down. I didn't make a note of what kind of pants he was wearing, but in my mind they're khakis. None of this is a coincidence. Until 2012, he was general manager for marketing and strategy at a division of Microsoft, a position he'd climbed to over thirty years in tech sales and marketing. Unfulfilled, he started looking for nonprofits to connect with and stumbled into a board position at Boys to Men. With three boys of his own, then ages six, eight, and eleven, it's no surprise the work quickly got under his skin, or that he saw the potential impact of working with younger boys.

MBTM adapted its high school curriculum for a middle school audience and tested the short, hour-long pilot with a group of boys. From there, it developed a three-hour curriculum that it delivered to ten schools during the 2015–2016 academic year, reaching just over five hundred boys in southern Maine and getting a feel for what worked, what didn't, what had evolved over the year. It tuned it up accordingly, adding more periods of physical activity for the boys and centering emotional literacy as the heart of the program, and wound up with a four-hour curriculum. The program is usually delivered one hour at a time over the course of four weeks and it reaches every boy in the seventh or eighth grade at participating schools (unless parents opt their child out of the program, a vanishingly rare occurrence). The idea is to reset the norms of masculinity for the entire class at once, to build community resilience as they grow up together. MBTM expects to reach a thousand boys in 2016–2017 alone.

The course begins with the "gender box" exercise that's a hallmark of all Maine Boys to Men programs. The idea is simple: the group leader draws a big box on the chalkboard, and the boys brainstorm stereotypes of masculinity. All of those go inside the box. Then they discuss what happens if a guy tries to behave in a way that's not described in the box. Those punishments and threats hover around the outside of the box. The completed visual serves as a jumping off point to discuss how confining traditional masculinity can be and how harmful to both boys and girls, both men and women.

Once primed to move beyond the gender box, the course gets the boys up and moving and interacting with each other through a series of exercises in which they have to decide what they think about topics related to sexism and violence and debate their opinions with peers who both agree and disagree. This gives the boys practice respectfully standing up to each other around issues that matter and also debunks their instinct to assume all of their peers think the same way. They place relationship dynamics on a spectrum from green (healthy) to red (abusive), moving from the abstract—relationships they see in pop culture—to real relationships much closer to home.

Sam Eley, one of the Boys to Men facilitators, tells me that conversation can lead to some pretty powerful revelations.

They talk about cyber relationships and how people don't necessarily respect each other online or via texting. A lot about how kids just switch between girlfriends and boyfriends really fast, so there's not a lot of open communication or respect or time put into those relationships. Because all of the kids, when we actually talk about it, they really value trust and they really value communication and they really value having meaningful time spent together, those are the three things that really come up a lot, and that's not present when kids are just bopping around in a relationship with somebody for a week and moving on to somebody else. So they find that they're valuing that and not seeing it among their friends.

To the uninitiated it may seem to require some kind of dark magic to get middle school boys to be that emotionally vulnerable in front of each other, but Eley assures me that the spell is much simpler: modeling. From the moment they draw a box on the board, he and his co-facilitator (the group is always led by a pair) lead by example, reflecting back on what it was like for them in middle school and telling stories of their own struggles being hemmed in by traditional masculinities. Their emphasis on building emotional literacy comes to a head in the final exercises, which focus on empathy as the glue that holds together all of the other ideas in the course.

The task is fairly straightforward, Eley tells me. "They have a list of experiences on a piece of paper, and we ask them to go around the room and talk to the other guys. . . . So, it says, 'Have you ever lost a pet, or gotten a bad grade, or got an award?' A whole list of things that kids might've experienced." The students simply interview each other and record what they say about their experiences and the feelings that came along with them.

For some, it's a profound experience. "We always ask them, 'What was that experience like? What was it like to talk with your friends about it?'" Eley tells me. "Sometimes they say it was awkward, sometimes they say it was weird. . . . But often multiple kids will say it felt really good and cool or felt comfortable to be able to realize that your friends (or peers that you didn't even know) had some similar feelings to you about those shared experiences. They also will say that it felt good to get to know the kids in the room a little bit better, [that] being able to see how they felt or hear how they felt in the situation allowed them to get to know them better."

You may have noticed that I'm describing all of this second-hand. As an adult woman, my presence would have inhibited those boys as they worked through their feelings about what kind of men they want to grow into. But Maine Boys to Men was kind enough to let me check out one of the programs it runs with high school students. I arrived first thing on day two of a two-day training to find the walls covered with the previous day's ideas, a brainstormed list of traits of healthy masculinity ("Showing emotion," "Healthy male-male connection," "Nurturing,"

"Confidence," "Perseverance," "Bravery," etc.), the Boys to Men mission statement, and, of course, the man and lady gender boxes they generated together.

And then the students flowed in. MBTM's high school programs differ from their middle school work in more than age grouping—the group is mixed gender, a hand-selected bunch of students the school has identified as being leaders or showing leadership potential across a range of social circles, teams, and interests. The idea is to use these teens as a schoolwide vaccine, each inoculating those in their particular spheres of influence. The selected students get two days out of class and off campus to do this deep dive into sex, gender, relationships, and violence prevention. As they file into the plush lounge set aside for us on the campus of Bowdoin College, the mood feels like a field trip.

A lot of the day proceeded as you think it might. Eley was facilitating, joined by a woman named Devon, the two of them young and casual and warm and attractively outdoorsy, as though they had been sent from J Crew central casting. Together they got the group reoriented and walked them through some exercises about the different kinds of relationship abuse.

Things kicked into high gear when the workshop moved from theory to practice. The students were asked to stand and respond physically to a series of hypotheticals, walking toward one side of the room or the other, using their body to indicate where on the spectrum of "healthy" to "abusive" the relationship being described sounded to them. I'm not overselling when I tell you that they were electrified, arguing with each other about red flags, coercion, and consent, making impassioned speeches, and negotiating heatedly with each other in side conversations. One boy developed his own affirmative consent catchphrase, which I'm tempted to adopt: "No 'no' doesn't mean yes!"

The most contentious scenario involved a girl, Lindsay, who gets asked to prom via a very public and elaborate promposal by Ben, who has long harbored a crush on her. She likes him only as a friend. As Devon doles out bits of the story—Lindsay feels pressured to say yes, lest she be branded a bitch; they go to prom and have a nice time; he then invites her to an afterparty with his friends, but not hers—the students shift around the room and make their case to each other: she's leading him on and shouldn't have said yes. She's having a nice time and it seems like she wants to be there. Nothing wrong with an afterparty, but the power dynamic has shifted, so watch out. Just when you think you've seen one too many after-school specials and this story will actually turn out fine (some of the scenarios actually do describe healthy relationships, they're not all morality plays), things start to get dodgy. He plies her with drinks while staying sober himself. (Maybe he's just abstaining so he can drive her home?) She starts to feel woozy and asks if they can go. On the way home, without saying anything to her, he turns off onto a strange side street and stops the car. She pretends to sleep. He kisses her neck, gropes her breast. She pushes his hand away, he gropes her some more.

Stunningly, the three students who take a stand in Ben's defense are all girls. "She kind of led him on," they argue. "She didn't say no." "It all turns out all right." All their fellow students cajole and reason. One boy, textbook perfect, literally says, "It's not on her to say something. She has indicated that she does not want this to continue by pushing the shirt down and she's intoxicated, which minimizes her ability to give consent." Another, referring to the goodnight kiss the pair eventually shares, puts it more frankly: "Putting frosting on a shit cake doesn't make it better." The group, minus the three holdouts, cheers. This goes on for ten minutes, maybe twenty. You can feel how high the stakes are for all of them, that they don't need to be told that this situation is far from hypothetical. I start to wonder about the girls, what makes them so determined to excuse the abuse, even in the face of a wall of critical peers. Is one of them, the clear leader among the three, just a contrarian personality? Do any of them have personal reasons for not wanting to see Lindsay as a victim? Does identifying with male power make them feel stronger, or cooler?

Eventually, Devon ends the stalemate, announcing that what Ben did is sexual assault, in no uncertain terms. The girls remain unconvinced, but the group moves on to the next scenario. It's a stark reminder that toxic masculinities don't just live on in men; men aren't the only ones perpetuating them.

As the day winds down, I get another, much lovelier reminder of how little toxic masculinity is inherently part of manhood. As a closing exercise, Devon and Eley ask the teens to write down what qualities they would now, post-workshop, most prize in a romantic partner and which they want to avoid. Then the students anonymously swap papers and read each other's aloud. "I want someone who has a large personality like myself," "Likes sports, funny, good looking, not controlling," "Someone who communicates well, someone who will trust me, and is trustworthy." With only a couple of exceptions, it's impossible to guess the gender of each author.

After they leave this gilded, wood-paneled room, the students will be assigned an adviser and encouraged to keep working together at school to help their fellow students step out of their gender boxes. That work takes different shape depending on the group of students. At one school, they have chosen to work with every athletic team; at others, they lead age-appropriate exercises at the middle or elementary schools in their districts. Some take it upon themselves to intervene when they see damaging dynamics emerging in their social groups.

It's all part of a focus on making a community project of shifting gender norms that everyone can take part in. To that end, MBTM is also expanding its adult offerings, including a boot camp for new dads that offers both practical parenting prep along with some exercises to help the dads think about how they want gender to play out in their relationship with their co-parent, their parenting style, and the values they pass on to their kids. It's also piloting a new community workshop for adults following on the voracious response to its series of screenings of *The Mask You Live In*, a documentary about boys and men struggling with the strictures of traditional masculinity.

Though the high school program has proven effective through years of evaluation, it's too soon to say what impact the new offerings will have. But the signs are encouraging. Katherine Doughty, who runs MBTM's adult programming, tells me that after the film screenings, "A lot of men stand up and talk, more than anything else we've ever done. . . . There was one young man who was going to have a baby and after the film he came up to me and was like, 'This completely changed my life. My father's an alcoholic and abusive, and I don't want to be like him.'"

That's almost exactly what the middle school boys are saying, too. Feedback from the boys is almost universally positive, with most of them saying they're going to change the way they talk to people or adjust their judgments about how others do gender. "Kids have come up after we're done," Eley tells me, "and said, 'Man, I'm really not going to try and be in a box!'" One told him, "My father is just like that, and I don't want to be that. He is in the box. He sits on the couch and watches TV, drinks a lot. And I don't want to be that."

It won't be just boys learning lessons as the middle school project progresses. The staff at MBTM hopes that it will transform the kind of measurement they can do on the effectiveness of their interventions, by following the students as they grow into high schoolers and beyond. That kind of longitudinal data on transforming masculinities is nearly nonexistent and could light a way forward for many other programs to follow.

And not a moment too soon, because the boys are already being influenced by our Fragile Masculinist in Chief.

"To have such a prominent example of how guys can get away with this and how they're given a pass on terrible behaviors," frets Theodores. "We worry a lot about the leadership example that that sets for young boys. It's an opportunity for parents to have those discussions, for teachers to have it, but without the counterbalance to that it's very scary. All we can do really is more of what we're already doing." And for the rest of us, all we can do is make sure the same kind of conversations Maine Boys to Men is facilitating are happening wherever we are.

## CHAPTER NINE

# STUDENTS OF DESIRE

T HE FIRE DRILL is astonishing in its efficiency. I'm at Thunder Mountain High School in Juneau, Alaska, settling in to watch as two members of the local Teen Council—a group of peer sex educators supported and trained by Planned Parenthood—talk with a class of freshmen about consent. But just after the bell rings to start the period, another sound goes off, and the room springs into motion. The students file out of the room before I can even grab my bag, following one of their own who has materialized from seemingly nowhere with a sign bearing the name of a teacher. We spill out into the hallway and then into the chilly blue day, merging with other classes full of other students following other signs. There's a relaxed excitement to the proceedings, everyone chatting and joking and walking with purpose. They all know where they're going, arranging themselves on the athletic yard in back of the school in some pattern I can't discern. A few minutes later, another bell rings and we file back inside. The whole drill has taken eight minutes.

In any given year, around 3 percent of US nursery, elementary, middle, junior, or high schools will have a fire of some kind. The odds of a student being injured in one of those fires is so small as to be functionally zero.[1] And yet these eight minutes were carved out of the only lesson about sexual consent those students will formally receive during their precollege schooling. Eight minutes lost out of only seventy-five minutes allotted, even though girls aged sixteen to nineteen are four times more likely than the general population to be victims of rape, attempted rape, or sexual assault.[2] (Reliable statistics are harder to come by for male-identified victims of sexual violence.)

I have nothing against fire drills. The one at Thunder Mountain was particularly impressive, and I'm glad those kids know what to do if there's a fire emergency. It's likely that the fire risk to American students is so low in part because we prepare them so well to stay safe. We teach them fire safety in age-appropriate ways every year starting in kindergarten and build on that knowledge with regular drills, until responding to the threat of fire becomes second nature. When I asked the boy who had held the fire drill sign for his class whether that was his designated role, he told me it wasn't—he just knew someone needed to grab it, so he stepped up. Imagine if we prepared students that well to be responsible sexual citizens and to keep each other safe from rape.

By eighth grade, the only information I had been given about my body and sexuality by my public school was at an all-girl assembly vaguely explaining my period to me. (Privately, I knew what I had gleaned from a friend's well-worn copy of Judy Blume's *Are You There God? It's Me, Margaret*, and the more specific instruction my mom had provided on how to wear a menstrual pad. It was the eighties, so these were approximately the thickness of a baguette. She had also issued a blanket order not to use tampons, with the unspoken understanding that tampons were for slutty girls and would take your virginity.)

In eighth-grade health class, however, our teacher had set up a box for anonymous questions. One day, she pulled a question from the box and read it to the class. "What is 69?" it read. Everyone dissolved into nervous giggles. I had a vague sense the question was dirty, but I had never heard the term before. And then calmly, without a hint of embarrassment, anger, or judgment, our teacher drew a 6 and a 9 rotated 90 degrees to the left, so the one was lying on top of the other, and explained the term.

In high school, freshman or sophomore year, I had a biology teacher who every Friday assigned us to read the Science section of the *New*

*York Times* and report to the class about an article we had read. That's how I learned about HIV, then a new and developing news story.

And that's it. Those are the only lessons I remember getting about sex and sexuality in any kind of classroom setting until I got to college. I learned plenty about sexuality at school, though. I learned that I was too fat and Jewish to be considered desirable. I learned that boys could snap my bra whenever they wanted and that seemed okay with everybody. I learned that being one of the first girls to develop breasts and get my period made me even more of a weirdo freak loser than I already was. I learned about the bases, about what made kissing French. I had my first kiss in a classroom — my first boyfriend and I would help out one of the kindergarten teachers during our lunch hour, and it afforded us the only privacy we ever really had. He put his lips all around the outside of mine, like a plunger. I didn't know how to feel about it, but I was glad to have done it. Later he put his hand down my shirt and palmed my breast a little. I sat stock still, stomach in knots, knowing this was a big deal, dying of curiosity, but also slightly detached, like I was watching myself cross this milestone, trying to figure out how it felt. How I felt. It wasn't unpleasant, but it certainly wasn't pleasurable, either.

I didn't know that pleasure was something I was supposed to feel. We didn't talk about pleasure on the rare occasions when we talked about sex, and we didn't talk about consent, either. The clitoris wasn't on our anatomy diagrams. Even that health teacher, though she didn't convey shame, made 69 seem more like an athletic accomplishment than a good time.

What I've learned since then is that I was relatively lucky. Sex ed in US public schools isn't regulated by the federal government, and the resulting patchwork of curricula is such a destandardized mess that describing it winds up sounding like a GRE logic puzzle. Only twenty-four states and DC mandate that schools teach any kind of sex ed at all. No states have an outright ban on teaching sex ed, so that means that the twenty-six remaining states leave it up to the individual school districts to decide, and most of those states don't keep track of district-level decisions, so they literally have no idea what's being taught by whom. Thirteen states mandate that if sex ed is taught in schools that it be medically accurate, but four of those states—Colorado, Illinois, Michigan, and Washington—don't mandate that sex ed be taught at all. (Let that sink in a minute—that means that only nine of the twenty-four states that mandate sex ed also require that it be based in fact.) Nine states mandate that sex ed, if taught, must discuss sexual orientation in an inclusive way, and four require that sexual orientation be discussed, but that only negative things should be said about non-hetero people. (Alabama's statute reads: "Classes must emphasize, in a factual manner and from a public health perspective, that homosexuality is not a lifestyle acceptable to the general public and that homosexual conduct is a criminal offense under the laws of the state.") Nineteen states require sex educators to teach that sex should only happen in the context of marriage. Only twenty-one states require that sex education, when taught, include information on making healthy decisions around sexuality.[3]

There's not a lot of positive change on the horizon, either. In "liberal" Massachusetts, it took until 2015 for the state senate to pass a bill that mandates that when sex education is taught in public schools it "must be medically accurate and age-appropriate. It must teach about both abstinence and contraception, about ways to discuss safe sexual activity, and about the skills needed to form relationships free of violence or coercion. . . . [The bill also] requires teaching about signs of child exploitation and sexual abuse and about the consequences of becoming a parent." Just to be clear, this bill doesn't force a single school to teach sex education if it doesn't want to and gives all parents an opt-out option. All it proposes is a requirement that if schools do teach sex ed, it's fact-based and relatively comprehensive. And even this mild attempt is still in limbo in the House as of this writing.[4]

In Alaska, land of the efficient fire drills, things are worse. In 2016, a conservative senator named Mike Dunleavy introduced a bill that would have required parents to opt their children in to school-based sex education, instead of just letting them opt out. Worse, it specifically banned Planned Parenthood—the largest nongovernmental provider of sexual health education in the state—from teaching in public schools at all. The bill passed in the Senate but then hit an unexpected wall of public opposition, organized in part by that same Teen Council whose lesson was interrupted by a fire drill. They organized dozens of their friends, trained them on how to testify before Congress, and showed up en masse to tell their legislators their lives and health depended on getting accurate, nonjudgmental sex education. The House responded by watering down the Senate bill significantly.

Still, that bill—now law—makes sex ed the most rigorously regulated subject in the state, requiring school boards to review and approve or veto every individual guest speaker a teacher might want to invite to address sex ed in the classroom and every slide, outline, handout, and exercise intended for teaching the subject.

For Alaskan schools with existing sex education programs and supportive communities, the new law mostly makes extra work for teachers, outside educators, and the school board. By the time I visited Juneau, less than four months after the law was signed, the school board had already approved the instructors and curriculum that had been submitted, and they expected no interruption in their ability to teach sexuality in the schools. But the law offers school boards no guidance on what standards they should use when approving or denying educators or curriculum components. That latitude has left the door open for straight-up censorship in districts where sex ed is contentious, as in Fairbanks, where the school board has taken the opportunity to ban health teachers from using anything on the Planned Parenthood website as well as on the sites LoveIsRespect.org and Tolerance.org without first seeking school board approval on each individual web page they want to use.[5] Even worse: a 2014 CDC survey found that only 32 percent of Alaska high schools taught comprehensive sex ed.[6] This in a state with some of the highest rates of sexual abuse and assault (and chlamydia) in the nation. Now the new law makes it much harder for schools with inadequate sex ed curricula to take steps forward.

Even in Juneau, the most progressive school district in the state, the students are learning far less about sex than you might think. I spoke to two school board members, a parent, and a state representative while I was there, and each of them told me how great and comprehensive the sex education was in Juneau schools. But when I asked members of the Teen Council what they had learned about sex in school, they had less than stellar reviews. One remembered that she had a brief sex ed module, but couldn't remember a single detail from it. Another was shown an abstinence-promotion film in which girls who have sex with multiple partners are compared to used-up pieces of tape. Another said, "The only thing that I really remember from the small unit that we had in my health class on sex ed was reading a six-page paper on premature ejaculation . . . and having a slideshow [showing] worst-case scenario STIs." All of them agreed that the sum total of their K–12 sex ed curriculum amounted to one or two weeks in their freshman year of high school.

None of the teens I talked with remembered learning anything about consent, or the clitoris. I always ask young people I meet if the clitoris was included in their anatomy diagrams, because it's a quick test of whether sexual pleasure—especially female sexual pleasure—is part of the sex ed conversation. It almost never is. The idea that sex can be fun and fulfilling is a near-total taboo in high school sex curricula because of the pervasive (but totally false) twin myths that (1) saying anything positive about sex will encourage teens to get busy, and (2) teens having sex—especially girls having sex—is pretty much a catastrophe.

Don't believe it. In the Netherlands, they take sex education as seriously as we take fire safety. They teach age-appropriate lessons in every year of school starting with kindergarten. They don't lie. They don't withhold information. And they don't treat sex like a dirty, hidden thing like too many schools do here in the United States. The result? Teenagers have their first sexual encounters at pretty much the same age, on average, as US teens. But most Dutch young people say they had "wanted and fun" first sexual experiences, and Dutch teens overwhelmingly use contraceptives for their first sexual encounter. That leads to low rates of STIs and one of the lowest rates of teen pregnancy in the entire world.

Our public schools' silence about sexual pleasure is dangerous, especially for girls and queer students of all genders, who are regularly shamed for their sexual wants. In a world that treats straight male desire as the driver of some terrible sexual marketplace in which men "get" sex and women "give it up," those of us who are objectified or erased by that system rarely, if ever, get the message that sex can be a positive experience for us. When schools refuse to acknowledge pleasure, they reinforce the idea that sex isn't really for or about us. Then, when we have painful or abusive sexual relationships, we don't know we deserve to expect better. When we refuse to talk frankly about the good as well as the bad of sex, when we fail to equip girls with the information and skills they need to pursue their own sexual health and set their own sexual boundaries, we aren't protecting them. When all we tell girls is that sex is scary and bad, they expect it to feel that way. We're teaching them to expect abuse.

And all too often, abuse is exactly what teen girls experience. "They grab you, touch your butt, and try to, like, touch you in the front, and run away, but it's okay, I mean . . . I never think it's a big thing because they do it to everyone." That's a thirteen-year-old girl describing how she feels about peer sexual harassment at school in an interview that informed a study by Heather Hlavka at Marquette University. Hlavka studied videotapes of a hundred forensic interviews conducted by a Midwestern nonprofit with young people ages three to seventeen who had experienced some kind of sexual abuse. The study is a jaw-dropping read, revealing how girls and young women in the United States simply expect boys and men to abuse them. Most of the abuse is never reported because girls think it's normal. They think men aren't in control of their own sexual desires. They don't think anything "counts" besides a penis being forced into their vagina. They assume that if they speak up, the people in charge will think they did something bad to bring the abuse on themselves, and that their peers will, too.[7]

They're not wrong to fear that backlash. In 2015, at Spring Creek Community School, a public middle school in Brooklyn, an eighth-grade boy filmed himself orally and anally raping a female classmate and shared the video all over school. Instead of punishing the boy in any way, the school expelled the victim.[8] The same year, a fourteen-year-old girl was sexually assaulted in a stairwell of her high school in Lansing, Michigan. She didn't report the incident because she was afraid she would get in trouble. But when the story came out anyway, she was suspended for "lewd and lascivious behavior." Even though security camera footage confirmed that she hadn't consented, the school decided she hadn't fought back hard enough to not be held responsible.[9]

Hlavka's study demonstrates that, even in schools that teach no formal sex ed lessons, students learn from the administrators and teachers about sex every day. They learn in these most dramatic incidents, but they also learn from how the adults in charge respond (or don't) to the daily drumbeat of "low-level" sexual abuse—hallway gropings, homophobic bullying, "secret" message boards in which boys rate the hotness of every girl in school. And they learn a whole lot from dress codes, in the name of which girls get sent home for a glimpse of shoulder or knee, while boys can go through an entire school day wearing a T-shirt emblazoned with a near-naked woman and a misogynist slogan and not face any punishment.[10]

Run an image search on "sent home from school for wearing" and you'll see a gallery of girls in almost universally nonscandalous dress. Some are wearing leggings with baggy shirts over them. One is in a loose cotton tank top and jeans ripped at the knee. Another, wearing a cardigan and tank top, was sent home for exposing her collarbone. You will not see any boys. That's because, in practice, school dress codes often have many more picayune regulations specifically targeting girls' clothing than boys', dictating minimum skirt length and banning clavicles and cleavage, spaghetti straps and strapless dresses, as though no boy could be expected to control himself at the sight of a naked female shoulder. The codes are framed as devices to reduce "distractions" so that students can focus on their studies. But in practice they distract from girls' studies quite a lot because girls are the ones routinely dragged from class for the smallest infractions, made to miss school sometimes for hours while waiting for the principal, or even all day if they're sent home. Others are forced to wear "shaming" outfits provided by the school. Students of all genders learn the same message: girls' bodies are shameful. If you find them sexy, that's on them. We expect nothing from boys. Boys are ruled by animal impulses and can't be expected to control themselves.

Among girls, dress codes discriminate, too. If necklines are meant to obscure any hint of cleavage, that makes life a lot harder for larger girls with bigger breasts (who are disproportionately Latina and Black girls) than it does for lithe blonde girls with AAs. Every spring, stories run rampant of larger girls being humiliated and kicked out of their own proms for wearing dresses no more revealing than those of their more slender classmates.

Girls of color and queer students are especially targeted by dress codes in ways that go beyond body type. Because enforcement is subjective, administrators and teachers who have an implicit (or, sometimes, explicit) bias toward seeing Black and brown girls as hypersexual will of course be more likely to cite those girls as wearing clothes that are too provocative, even while giving a pass to similar outfits on white girls. Stories also abound about students being found in violation for wearing clothes that don't conform to expectations for their legally assigned gender, no matter how little skin is showing. In some cases, Black girls have been sent home from school just for wearing their hair in braids or in its natural state. And punishments tend to be more severe for girls of color who are found in violation of school codes. According to the Department of Education, Black girls are 5.5 times more likely to be suspended from school as are white girls, and Latina and Native American girls also have elevated suspension rates when compared to that of white girls.[11]

It is schools' responsibility to ensure that every student has equal access to education regardless of gender.[12] By refusing to teach healthy sexuality while simultaneously allowing sexualization, sexual harassment, and even rape to flourish, schools are full-on failing. Remember how stereotype threat works: every time girls are cued to think of themselves as sex objects, it literally makes it harder for them to perform science and math tasks. In the typical American school, girls are getting those cues multiple times a day, from teachers, staff, and students alike. So not only are schools fostering a culture of sexual dysfunction and abuse but also they're giving girls a head start on a lifetime of being intellectually undermined.

And then we give them a diploma and send them off, assuming that, even though we've spent twelve years of education trying to keep them from even wanting to have sex, a switch will flip and those former innocents will suddenly be fully formed and well-functioning sexual adults.

Shockingly enough, it doesn't work out that way. Teens who sign virginity pledges tend to marry earlier (it's not hard to guess why), and people who marry early are at increased odds for both divorce and poverty. And students who head off to college run smack dab into the hookup culture, yet another damaging artifact of our elementary and secondary schools' refusal to prepare young people to be healthy sexual adults.

The idea of hookup culture is a weird collective myth, smoke and mirrors stoked by moral panic and peer pressure. In fact, there's no evidence that the current generation of young adults are having more sex than their parents' generation. But they don't know it. If you ask college students to estimate how much sex their peers are having, they'll paint you a picture of a rolling, four-year bacchanal. But if you ask those same students how much sex they themselves are having, most of them will tell you they're really not having much at all.[13]

The mass fever dream of a hookup culture where college students are having drunken, nihilistic sexual encounters with strangers every weekend (and sometimes on weeknights) is driven, in part, by the very same type of adults who terrorize students about sex while they're still in high school, spinning out nightmare scenarios about what must be happening the minute those young people are out of their reach. I feel for those grownups a little. It's an awkward time. Slut shaming and victim blaming were long perceived as the checks and balances on male sexual aggression, the only strategy that was keeping the "good girls" safe from harm. (They didn't keep any girls safe, of course. But it felt to many like they did.) Those strategies are being rejected by a new generation, but we haven't yet figured out how to actually address male sexual aggression. Sexual encounters aren't any more dangerous than they were back in whatever day you may be nostalgic for—we're just talking about the dangers more.

But we're still talking in powerfully gendered ways that reinscribe the idea that girls need protection and rescue from their own curiosity and appetites. I was once called on by CNN to defend the lyrics of Ke$ha's pop anthem "Tik Tok," which celebrates confident women drinking and dancing until the wee hours and includes lyrics like: "Boys tried to touch my junk, junk / Gonna smack him if he getting too drunk, drunk." To me it sounds like the song of a woman actually in possession of her own sexual power. Yet the CNN host was convinced Ke$ha was a danger to girls for encouraging them to take part in the "hookup culture."

But the fact that the hookup culture is based on a mass delusion doesn't mean that delusion isn't harmful, as sociologist Lisa Wade revealed in her brilliant book *American Hookup.* As part of her research, Wade asked students at a range of schools to keep journals for her about their sex lives in their first year on campus. She found that when students actually get to college and can't find the 24/7 orgy they've been led to expect by handwringing adults, many of them feel like they're doing something wrong and feel pressure to create what they were told was the essential college experience: constant sex without attachment. And though they don't seem very successful at the "constant" part, it's the "without attachment" bit that really stresses them out. Paradoxically, student efforts to conform to the mythology of hookup culture makes some parts of it come true: most of the students Wade studied agreed that, when they do manage to have sex, they face enormous pressure to not "catch feelings" for their sex partners or even show them (or expect in return) basic human decency.[14]

Of course, sex without feelings is impossible. As Wade puts it: "Saying we can have sex without emotions is like saying we can have sex without bodies. There simply is no such emotion-free human state." But students have been told by panicking adults that their peers are all having robot sex, so they make themselves miserable trying to join in, even though most of them would secretly rather it be otherwise, with strong majorities of both genders telling the Online College Social

Life Survey that they "wished they had more opportunities to find a long-term partner."

The good news is that Wade's students of all genders had the basic sense that sex should be fun for them. But for the female students especially (though not exclusively), it often isn't, or their definition of "fun" doesn't include their own physical pleasure. "I want to kind of blow him out of the water," writes Celeste, one of Wade's students. "If they attempt to do the same for me, that's great, though most of the time that does not happen." Another, Izzy, tells a story about a guy she went down on who reciprocated by licking her clitoris one time. One lick. It's a hilarious anecdote about sexual double standards, but also telling is what's missing from the story: it doesn't seem to occur to Izzy that she could ask him to lick some more.

The fact that some sexual taboos have softened doesn't mean that the basic power dynamics of heterosexual sex have changed. Wade's male students still largely viewed sex as an accomplishment or acquisition meant to shore up their social status among other guys. And women are still suffering for it. In casual college heterosexual hookups, men are three times more likely to have an orgasm than their female partners.[15] There's nothing inevitable or biologically determined about this gap: men and women are equally likely to orgasm when masturbating and take pretty much the same amount of time to do the deed. The gap even closes somewhat for heterosexual sex when it happens in the context of a committed relationship. It seems that heterosexual hookups are the worst of all worlds when it comes to women's pleasure, and is it any wonder?

In middle and high school, we consistently fail to even teach students that women are supposed to like sex, let alone equip them to communicate with sex partners to ensure mutual satisfaction and safety. Layer that on top of a college sexual culture where being kind or considerate toward your sex partner is actively discouraged, and you get what we've got: fellatio is expected, but neither gender expects cunnilingus, and when guys do go down on female partners, it's as a play for permission to penetrate, not as an attempt to give her pleasure. One bisexual man Wade heard from laid this dynamic bare, "sheepishly" confessing "that he prioritized his partner's orgasm when he hooked up with men and his own when he hooked up with women."[16]

The hookup culture especially hurts students who are already culturally marginalized. Because it's not cool to involve your feelings in your sex life, students are pressured to pick out their sexual partners almost entirely based on traditional criteria of physical attractiveness. That means we go back to the vile "sexual marketplace" in which women of color, fat women, and women with visible disabilities are all treated as worthless currency. And the party scene is of course overwhelmingly heterosexual, leaving queer students the choice to either opt out entirely or, in the case of queer women, attend but be treated as exotic entertainment for straight men.

The news isn't all bad. Many of Wade's students found that experimenting with casual sex had some positive benefits, including some who didn't have particularly positive hookup experiences. "Hookups made them smarter about sex, helped them to develop more sophisticated sexual philosophies, and left them more prepared to handle whatever came their way," she writes. And the hookup model straight-up works for some students of all genders. Of course it does—human sexual desire is an infinitely varied thing, so inevitably some subsection of college students will enjoy having largely no-strings sexual encounters, for any number of reasons. What's missing is social embrace of a range of equally valid ways of pursuing a sex life, from serial monogamy to abstinence-until-marriage to ethical polyamory to asexuality. The problem with hookup culture is that it's a monoculture, and everyone for whom it's a poor fit suffers.

It also both hides and encourages rape. The expectation that sex is no big deal, something that no one should have any feelings about, combined with a belief in male entitlement to women's bodies and homosocial pressure to score to impress other guys creates a toxic stew that encourages men to give in to their worst impulses. As one of Wade's students so succinctly put it, "A man who hesitates, masturbates." And for genuine sexual predators—the tiny percentage of men for whom lack of consent is a feature, not a bug, who rape an average of six women before they graduate from college—hookup culture is an

ideal smokescreen, one in which everyone from administrators to students seems to blame "the party culture" and victims' "poor decisions"
before they look to the person who actually decided to be violent.
Stanford administrators responded to the Brock Turner rape scandal
by banning hard liquor at undergraduate parties. As if the problem
was access to alcohol and not that a lifetime of schooling still hadn't
managed to teach Turner not to put his fingers inside of a person who
was too drunk to know what was happening. As if the alcohol raped that
woman, not the man.

For those who need it spelled out: absolutely, schools have issues
with out-of-control drinking. But blaming drinking for rape is ridiculous. The vast majority of us have never raped someone while drunk.
Alcohol is not an excuse for rape. If Brock Turner had decided to drive
while drunk and hit another student, no one would let him off the
hook because he'd been drinking. And if the student he hit was also
drunk, that wouldn't make the crime any less heinous.

Just having to explain that makes me feel like a failure. I've been
trying to get schools to take sexual violence on their campuses seriously
since I was assaulted myself as an undergraduate more than two decades
ago. My story isn't remarkable in any way. I was attacked by a student I
knew. Yes, we had both been drinking. When I reported it, the school
proved more interested in silencing me than in making sure the guy
who hurt me couldn't hurt anyone else in the community. The only
thing worth noting about my experience is that it happened in 1992,
and the same patterns are still playing out on every US campus today. A
2010 study by the Center for Public Integrity found most schools were
still fudging their reporting numbers, presiding over byzantine and
biased systems of accountability, issuing lenient sentences for rapists
when they were held responsible at all, and letting victims fall behind
in their studies—or drop out altogether—at alarming rates.[17]

That's not to say that nothing has changed. Today, thanks to the
indefatigable work of a new generation of anti-rape activists who
are leveraging social media to organize across campuses, if victims
choose to speak out about the ways campuses are enabling rapists,
they're a lot more likely to be heard than I was.

It's hard to overstate the impact of student activists now being able to compare notes and form alliances across school lines. When I was at Wesleyan, I thought the problem was with how Wesleyan handled sexual assault, and it was up to me and my fellow Wes undergraduates to figure out how to force our particular school to do better. It never occurred to me that the same exact dynamics were playing out on other campuses, or that I could reach out to students at other schools to share ideas about tactics and compound our power and leverage.

What a difference the Internet makes. In the past decade, thanks in large part to student-led activism, campus rape has become a national conversation, covered by every respectable news outlet and even a few feature films. The number of rape victims filing federal complaints against their schools has skyrocketed, increasing 1,000 percent between 2009 and 2014 alone.[18] And the Obama administration took notice. In 2014, it issued a directive to campus administrators outlining in unprecedented detail what they were expected to do in the realms of transparency, accountability, and prevention if they wanted to stay on the right side of the law, and following up that directive with an ongoing "It's On Us" campaign to encourage bystander intervention and community action.

Meanwhile "Yes Means Yes" laws have passed in California and New York and are working their way through the legislatures of several other states. These laws specifically mandate that colleges adjudicate sexual assault cases using an affirmative consent standard that assumes that consent is not present unless both parties have actively expressed it. (Or, as John Oliver put it, "Sex is like boxing: if both people didn't fully agree to participate, one of them is committing a crime.") These laws could translate into a better sexual culture for everyone on campus because they will almost inevitably result in campuses where the idea of "yes means yes" is more widely understood, and with it the assumption that sex should be a fun, collaborative experience for everyone involved. Even women.

There are signs that it's starting to work. Under the hilarious headline "More Men Are Asking Consent for Sex—and It's Awkward," the *New York Post*, of all places, featured lighthearted stories of young couples' adventures in learning to negotiate consent. The takeaway can be summed up by one young woman featured in the story: "It was so sweet. It made me want him more." If a tabloid like the *Post* gets affirmative consent, the concept is definitely on its way into the mainstream.

But, of course, social norms change slowly, in fits and starts. I constantly hear adults complain that students are confused about affirmative consent and how it works, as though that means the standard is unworkable. Of course people are confused. When you're raised one way and then suddenly you're told to think another, it's destabilizing. Students need help managing that confusion. Problem is, a lot of the adults in charge are feeling destabilized by all this upheaval, too.

Some of them react by rejecting change altogether, claiming that affirmative consent criminalizes "healthy" sexual behavior (as if there's anything healthy about a lack of interest in whether or not the person you're having sex with is a willing participant), and by doubling down on strategies that prioritize covering their asses over student safety. Some school administrators responded to increased scrutiny from the Obama administration by making every student who receives work-study jobs tied to their financial aid a "mandated reporter," meaning that they're obligated to tell the school every detail if a friend tells them, even in strict confidence, that they've been a victim of sexual assault. These policies—directly discouraged by the Obama White House— keep victims from getting the help they need by making it impossible for them to trust even their closest friends. They also suppress the number of rapes reported on that campus, making the school look good even while it's doing bad.

Even more campuses are spending tens or even hundreds of thousands of dollars on the services of "risk management consultants" like Brett Sokolow—over three thousand campuses since 2000, by his estimation. Sokolow seems to specialize not so much in teaching schools how to better prevent sexual assault and support survivors but rather in strategies to cover their asses under federal regulations. And when schools are investigated by the Office of Civil Rights (even in some instances presumably after following Sokolow's advice), schools pay him more money to combat the charges. (He's also been accused of unethical dealings with rape victims who've filed cases against schools, including trying to do end runs around victims' lawyers and telling them he was a neutral arbiter even when he was representing a school's legal interests.)[19]

Perhaps all that money going to keeping administrations safe from lawsuits leaves nothing left for updating student safety strategies? A 2015 survey of "rape prevention tips" found on the websites of forty colleges shows just how far we haven't come: most of the tips—like "Be careful when inviting someone to your residence or accepting an invitation to theirs," "Don't let strangers use your phone," and, literally, "Avoid being alone"—still put the burden of preventing rape on women and do nothing more than attempt to limit women's lives through fear. The four main messages are these: "there are no safe places for women, women can't trust anyone, women should never be alone, and women are vulnerable."[20]

That's not to say that no progress has been made. Last year, Harvard made the shocking decision to sanction members of its Greek organizations and elite final clubs. It announced that any members of those traditionally exclusive and gender-segregated bastions of campus power will be precluded from acting as athletic captains for the school or qualifying to be nominated for Rhodes, Marshall, and Fulbright Scholarships—unless the club agrees to become gender blind. This after the school found that female students who either attend male final club events or who are affiliated with an all-female final club are 50 percent more likely than the average Harvard woman to be sexually assaulted while on campus.[21]

(Of course, fragile masculinity must insert itself in the way of any progress. In response to this new initiative, Charles M. Storey, the fifty-something-year-old president of the Porcellian Club, the oldest and most elite final club, issued what—one hopes unintentionally— amounts to a threat: "Forcing single gender organizations to accept members of the opposite sex could potentially increase, not decrease the potential for sexual misconduct," he told The Harvard Crimson.[22])

There's also not a lot of agreement about what progress looks like. Schools like Harvard, that point to scientific evidence to back up their policy changes, are the exception. More often schools hire outside sex educators of varying quality or pay for online or live prepackaged curricula that promise all kinds of things but offer no data to back up those claims.

But even when schools hire the best sex educators out there, they often use us to check a box. Consent education and rape prevention? Done. And, sure, having me or any other talented and qualified sex educator come to your campus to give a one-time talk or workshop is better than nothing. But just as teaching sex education for a week or two in all of K–12 schooling can't be expected to prepare students for college and beyond, one 2-hour talk-plus-Q&A (or whatever the format) at orientation isn't going to undo the lifetime of bad messages college students have received about sex, gender, compassion, and care. Outside sex educators can play an important role in changing hearts and minds, but to really promote sexual health, schools have to become more concerned with outcomes than with just looking like they're trying.

The good news is that we are starting to learn more about approaches to preventing sexual assault that actually work. The bad news is that almost none of what's being done in US schools qualifies. Out of 140 currently implemented sexual assault prevention programs evaluated by the CDC, only three have proved effective.[23] One, RealConsent, is a six-session interactive online curriculum designed for college-age men. The other two are designed for middle schoolers. In a separate 2017 study by the University of Kentucky, another program—the Green Dot bystander intervention curriculum—was found to lower rates of sexual violence in high schools that implemented it.[24] Which brings us back to the start: college is too late to start giving kids real, healthy, supportive education about sex.

Fortunately, someone's doing something about it: the students themselves. The activist wave that's pushed the issue of campus rape into the headlines is surging into high schools and even junior highs, a kind of reverse pipeline pushing back against the consequences of sex ed malpractice, which amplify with each passing grade. Middle and high school girls are clapping back at sexist dress codes using hashtags like #Imnotadistraction.

And, of course, there's the Juneau Teen Council, one of thirty-five teen councils run by Planned Parenthood affiliates in fourteen states, from Hawaii to Massachusetts. Facilitated by Cori Stennett, with a cheerful, warm energy (sample Stennett quote: "I don't want to call anyone who has not spoken out by name, and put anyone on the spot, but I definitely want to say if you, if you are feeling like you want to share something, now is a good time"), Juneau Teen Council members educate their peers about sexual health and advocate for legislative change while themselves learning skills like community organizing and public speaking. It's equal parts leadership boot camp and youth group, and 100 percent chosen family, as is clear on the night I visit. The room is packed as alumni of the Teen Council join current members in person and by phone to talk out their feelings and fears for the future. One member is fearful for a friend who is undocumented. Another quietly asks what will happen to Teen Council if Planned Parenthood loses its federal funding. It's a good question, because 40 percent of the funding for the regional affiliate that includes Alaska comes from federal grants, and if those funds disappear under the Trump administration, something's going to have to give.

But there's only so much time for worry. After an hour of processing, the alumni take their leave and the current members get down to business, breaking into small groups to plan for upcoming appearances—one group prepping to present a program called "Sexuality and Reproductive Anatomy and Physiology" at a statewide conference for youth leaders that weekend, another rehearsing the consent workshop I'll sit in on the next day. It will be the first time in front of a class for each of the pair leading the next day's session—Sarah, tall and lanky and funny, with an easy charm, and Erin, a quiet girl with warm brown eyes whose face exudes empathy. Stennett rehearses with them, running through all the possibilities of what's likely to come up, how to handle difficult questions, what to do if they feel stuck. She reassures them that she'll be right there to step in at a moment's notice.

That preparation pays off at Thunder Mountain High School, post–fire drill. Erin and Sarah start off shaky with nerves but launch nevertheless into the warmup exercises, and by the time they've moved into the meat of the workshop, the entire class is with them. The main exercise involves groups of four or five students reviewing a handful of cards describing cues they might encounter in a sexual situation and sorting them into one of three categories: "consent," "no consent," or "unsure." After each team posts their answers in the corresponding columns on the board in the front of the class, the class at large discusses. I'm taken aback by how sincere and engaged they are, this mixed-gender room full of fourteen-year-olds talking about sexual ethics in front of each other. They come to agree that nothing anyone wears can constitute consent and that consent given under the influence or threat of violence is no consent at all. Someone saying "that feels nice" is probably consent, but flirting could go either way. At one point, a student raises his hand to object to "Can I kiss you?" being placed in the "unsure" category. It's possible, he argues, that someone would ask that as a way to pivot away from another sexual activity that's being pressed upon them, in which case, it would belong under "no consent." Another boy adds that if someone says yes to kissing, that doesn't count as consent for anything else. I just barely will the happy tears back into my eyes.

But though these kids get the idea of consent, they don't entirely understand what to do about it. When Erin asks the class what they would do if someone wasn't respecting their no, a few girls raise their hands to offer "call 911" or "run away." None of them seem to understand that the people most likely to steamroll over their boundaries will be their peers, someone they like and trust and know. But the bell rings. There's no time to talk about that now. And there won't be again. Although it's wonderful that these students are getting this education, it doesn't change the fact that this is the only time in their entire school career they'll be educated about consent. And they lost eight minutes of that conversation to a fire drill.

Consent, too, is far from the only crucial subject they're still wondering about. The night before, at the Teen Council meeting, I spent some time sitting with a few members who didn't have an upcoming presentation to rehearse. Instead, they practiced taking student questions by reading from those submitted anonymously in previous Teen Council workshops. So many of the questions reveal a profound insecurity, a baseline fear that thrives in our culture of silence about sex. "Is masturbation okay?" "Is it wrong if I like to get attention from boys?" "What do I do if I want to come out but I don't think my parents will like it?" Some of them are funny, like my favorite: "Does an IUD really vibrate the uterus? If not, how does it work?" But even those break my heart a little. These are easy questions to answer. If we were really preparing young people to be healthy sexual citizens, they would know these things before high school.

If anyone's going to make that happen, I believe it could be the young people I met in Juneau. They are so determined to fight, to build a better sexual world for each other and the generations coming up behind them. In the summer of 2016, at the national Planned Parenthood summit for teen council members, the Juneau and Anchorage council members who fought against the anti–sex ed legislation taught their peers from around the country how to effectively lobby legislators. "They didn't reach out to me," recalls Alyson Currey, regional field organizer and legislative liaison for Planned Parenthood of Alaska, with no small amount of awe. "They made their own handouts and it was all from information that they had learned, and it was professional." Already this school year, two members of the Juneau Teen Council have taken the lead in lobbying the local school board to add protections for LGBT youth into the district's nondiscrimination policy.[25]

But at the same time as their leadership and determination make me buoyant with hope, it also makes me cringe a little in shame. It feels profoundly unfair that we've left so much to them, that so much of the future is resting on their still-growing shoulders. Perhaps that's how it has to be. Carole Miller, chief learning officer for Planned Parenthood of the Great Northwest and Hawaiian Islands and creator of Planned Parenthood's teen council programs, tells me that the influence of the Teen Council doesn't just trickle down; it trickles up. "I can't tell you how many families have come back and said I learn so much from my teen, it changed how I vote, it changed how I think about the world. I can stand on a street corner in Olympia, Washington [where the oldest and longest-running Teen Council is located] and interview people and at least one in five would know about the teen council. It's part of the fabric of the culture."[26]

The work also changes the teens themselves. In an essay for MTV .com,[27] Juneau Teen Council member Tasha Elizarde recalls how little she knew about her body growing up, and how gratifying it is now to serve as a sexual health resource to her friends and family. She's also found her voice through Teen Council. She writes:

> I had always been the shy kid who sat as close to the classroom door as possible, afraid to do so much as raise my hand for fear of judgement from my peers. . . . Now, after my first year in Teen Council, little things like this don't bother me anymore. . . . Every time I chose to do something new, I have been supported by the Teen Council community and by my new friends. When I testified for the first time against a legislative attack on sex education, the rest of my Teen Council cheered me on from their seats. When I crafted my first op-ed about access to sex education, my Planned Parenthood Regional Field Organizer reviewed and critiqued my writing. Every time I've taught a sex education lesson in my community, as Teen Council has trained me to do, my facilitator has been there, poised and ready to jump in if I ever found myself at a loss for words.

What Elizarde has found at the Juneau Teen Council is what we owe every young person in America: easily accessible sexual health information, presented without shame or judgment. A community of peers who share her curiosity and determination to make the sexual culture better. Supportive adults who help her grow in age-appropriate ways without treating her like an innocent to be shielded from the subject of sex. A program that persists and grows with her as she comes into her own. She deserves to be at least as prepared for her sex life as she is for a fire.

## CHAPTER TEN

# THE PROFESSIONALS

I HATED GOING TO the doctor when I was in a relationship with a trans man. Not because I had any particular medical concerns, but because I knew they would ask me if I was sexually active, and when I said yes, they would ask me The Question: "Are you having sex with men, women, or both?"

It's meant to be an inclusive question, replacing the old, heteronormative ones that would jump from "Are you sexually active?" to "Are you using birth control?" But it still didn't include me. If I answered that my partner was a man, which was true, it would give the doctor the wrong information about the sexual risks I was being exposed to. But I couldn't bring myself to call my partner a "woman," when he was fighting constantly to get the world to recognize him for the man he is.

It was a small moment, and surmountable—I could and did stammer out some basic information about my partner's gender. But it started off every medical interaction in a way that made me feel small and unwelcome. It told me that my life was illegible to my doctor, which is an uneasy feeling to have about someone you are entrusting with your health. It certainly made me a lot less likely to bring up sex- or gender-related concerns with her and encouraged me to fundamentally mistrust any advice she offered.

When we think about sexual professionals, mostly we think about sex workers—dancers, escorts, porn performers, and the like. Maybe some of us think about researchers or professional sex educators, whether the condom-on-a-banana kind or the kind who terrorize kids into avoiding condoms altogether. But just like my well-meaning doctor, or the gym teacher pressed into teaching high school health classes, there are a surprising number of other sorts of professionals who influence the way we experience sex. Embarrassingly few of these fields require practitioners to have any knowledge of or training in human sexuality.

Most people recognize the need for training in their given profession. Would-be police officers know they need training in firearm safety. Journalists wouldn't dream of covering, say, economic policy without a basis in economic theory. But somehow—whether because most adults have first-hand experience with sex or because we see and hear messages about sex every day through our media consumption—we all think we know what we need to know about sex.

If only that were true. The people in all of these jobs are just people, after all, and most of them grew up in the same half-baked sexual culture that got us into this mess in the first place. And we all carry around moral judgments and implicit biases about sexuality that color our world. (*Implicit bias* is just a fancy name for the ways we may unconsciously be biased against a group or a type of behavior, without even knowing it.)

Police in some cities, for example, routinely arrest women of color—often trans women—on suspicion of prostitution on the basis of nothing more than what they're wearing, whether they're chatting with men, and/or what neighborhood they're in. The same clothes and accessories that will make a cop think a trans woman of color is a sex worker are often considered chic status symbols when sported by white women in the same neighborhood. According to depositions of NYPD officers obtained by the *Village Voice* in an investigation into the abuse of "loitering" laws (which give the cops cover to make these arrests), some of the outfits that have led to arrest include "tight black leggings," a "pink + blue sweater hoodie," a "mini dress, bra strap showing," and "tight jeans and tight tank showing cleavage [*sic*]."[1] I've personally chatted up men in NYC while wearing at least two of those outfits.

Those women swept up by police biased about who gets to act and dress which ways in public will then, of course, face prosecutors and judges with their own miseducation and bias, likely relying on lawyers who are similarly unprepared to defend them.

Lacking training, most professionals fall back on what they think they "know" about sexuality to fill in the blanks, and often that knowledge has been shaped by their lifelong media consumption. All manner of media makers work on sex-related content, from journalists to video game producers to ad execs to filmmakers to novelists, and it would be obviously unworkable, not to mention a violation of the First Amendment, to require storytellers to get qualified in the field of human sexuality before writing a sex scene on television.

But journalists are another matter. Barbara Friedman (no relation), now a professor of journalism herself, tells me that right after earning her undergraduate degree in journalism, her very first assignment as a reporter was to cover a rape. "I had no idea what I was doing, got no direction from my editor, and still cringe when I think about how I conducted myself." When reporters cover sexual assault and don't have adequate grounding in the subject, they can easily wind up retraumatizing the victims they interview. They also are more likely to write headlines like "Bill Cosby Claims Blindness Hinders Defense of Sex Charges" and "Fremont Teacher Arrested for Having Sex with Student," which conflate violence with consensual sex, minimizing the harm done and making it harder for victims to seek justice and for perpetrators to be held accountable.[2]

On the flip side, journalists with barely hidden agendas have made sex "scandals" out of things that are none of our business, like when Gawker outed an executive at Condé Nast for no reason except clicks. Even journalists who mean well can do real damage if they don't know what they're doing. *Rolling Stone* reporter Sabrina Erdely so passionately wanted to expose the rape-enabling culture at University of Virginia that she failed to fact-check her own story, and in so doing not only gave fresh ammo to those who want to claim all victims are lying but also exposed the young woman at the center of her story—who may well have been raped, even if the specific details she shared can't be verified—to international public humiliation and abuse.

There's no excuse for any of this. Recent years have seen the proliferation of media toolkits for reporting on sexual violence, like the one produced by the Chicago Taskforce on Violence Against Girls and Young Women. All of these pitfalls are covered by the guide, and it's readily available to anyone who cares to google for a resource. But newsrooms and J-schools alike still rarely bother to train reporters who cover sexual issues, which is why we see reporters make the same damaging mistakes over and over. Elana Newman, research director for the Dart Center for Journalism and Trauma, advocates ongoing partnerships between journalists and mental health professionals to make reporting on rape more trauma-informed. At an appearance at the 2015 BinderCon conference in Los Angeles, she put it this way, "In Australia, where there had been problems, firefighters have not wanted journalists around, because they were going to make the bushfires worse. So they gave them training—now everyone has to get fire training. I have a vision like that for sexual assault." She points to the success of efforts such as the Center for Public Integrity's 2009 exposé of rape on campus and the *Boston Globe*'s groundbreaking reporting on child sexual abuse in the Catholic Church as proof of concept—both relied heavily on advice from mental health professionals.

Of course, not every mental health professional is going to be equally helpful. Many schools of social work and clinical psychology don't even offer courses on human sexuality, and those that do, offer it as an elective. Nor are professionals required to be certified as counselors or therapists unless they're specializing in marriage and family counseling.

But even if we can agree (please, can we all agree?) that all of these folks should be getting more thorough professionally focused sex ed before they're considered qualified to do their jobs, a lot of questions remain. Who would decide what the standards should be? Who would defray the additional costs of training? What should "qualified" even mean when it comes to sex-related professionals?

It's a question that not even professional sex educators agree on for our own field. It's a question I grapple with myself. I have an undergraduate degree in psychology, a graduate degree in writing, and an enormous amount of independent research and life experience under my belt. Is that enough to prepare me to do what I do?

It hasn't always been. When I first started talking to college students about consent and healthy sexuality, I went out of my way to emphasize how casual sex was great and fine if that's what you want, even if you're a girl. That women shouldn't be stigmatized for being as sexual as they want to be. I was a one-woman anti-slut-shaming brigade. I still am, of course. But in trying to compensate for that injustice, I was also accidentally committing another. Quietly, in notes and private questions whispered in the book signing line, I started hearing that I had made a whole other set of students feel like there was something wrong with them. I was leaving out the kids who weren't that into sex and those who maybe wanted to be but hadn't found the right opportunities yet. The virgins and the monogamists felt shamed by my message of empowerment. At first I was confused, maybe a little defensive: I wasn't saying they were shameful! I hadn't said anything about them at all. And then I heard myself. I hadn't said anything about them at all. They felt silenced, marginalized, erased.

Would I have made the same mistakes if I'd been formally trained as a sex educator? Maybe. Even the most educated people mess up sometimes. But maybe I'd have been given the chance to find my blind spots in a low-stakes setting, where no one would have been hurt by my learning.

It's perfectly possible to get certified as a sex educator. The American Association of Sexuality Educators, Counselors and Therapists (AASECT) provides a rigorous path to certification, involving over a thousand hours of coursework and practical experience. But perhaps because the cost—in time as well as money—to complete the requirements is so high, and because even certified sex educators are still competing in a field that's less than lucrative, many sex educators just go without, and those who hire sex educators rarely require certification. (I've never been asked for a certification in my entire career.)

Instead, sex educators compete for gigs based on word of mouth, creative marketing, and price. That leads to some very uneven results.

Most sex educators are passionate advocates for pleasure as a human right, devoted to ensuring that everyone has the information they deserve to live safe, healthy, happy sexual lives. But we all have our flaws, and any industry based on hustle is bound to reward some charismatic charlatans. So it's also possible to find sex educators who rely on damaging gender and racial stereotypes, who spread actual misinformation, who cheerlead about liberatory blow jobs but have no grounding in sexual trauma, and worse.

In theory, the Sexual Attitude Reassessment (SAR)—one of the core components of AASECT certification—is exactly the kind of tool designed to guard against those biases and blind spots. It's a group process lasting at least ten hours that is designed to make participants aware of their own beliefs and biases related to sexuality to help them correct for them in their professional work.

But the quality of the SAR itself is a bit of a crapshoot. The topics it covers are mandated by AASECT. Every SAR must address "sexuality across the life span," for example, and masturbation, and sexual identity, and eight other general subjects. But how the topic is covered is left up to the SAR leader. That kind of structurelessness can make space for creativity and responsiveness to the needs of a particular group of participants. But it can and does also lead to experiences like the one LatiNegra sexologist, educator, and activist Bianca Laureano had when she participated in a 2010 SAR. "Not only was the data and information introduced and provided to us over two decades old . . . it was also extremely isolating and othering," she wrote in an essay on the experience published at *Rewire*. "The images that were presented were primarily of racially White able-bodied heterosexual people. Only when sexual orientation, gender identity, and disability were presented did we see different representations."[3] When it came to discussing diverse sexual cultures, all of the "differing" cultures presented were from outside the United States, as though the United States is all one culture when it comes to sexual values and experiences.

Aida Manduley, a sex educator and social worker who runs SARs for the Center for Sexual Pleasure and Health in Rhode Island, says that to change SARs, you'd first have to transform AASECT itself, a change-averse, white male–dominated institution. Even if you succeed, there's still the challenge that, because of the intersection of economic inequality with other oppressions, the people often shut out by high certification standards are the women, people of color, and trans and genderqueer people whose perspectives are most needed in sex education.

Manduley points out that the modern quandary around standardization of sex educators has echoes in the past. "If you look at the history of medicine in the United States, who was doing medical care, especially for pregnancy? You had midwives . . . and as doctoring became more professionalized and became more heavy with standards, who could become a doctor, what the role of midwives was, all of that changed. Who was seen as more of an authority changed. Back then they didn't let women into medical schools, period."[4]

Which brings us back to medical professionals. When I asked my friends to tell me stories about encounters with professionals that had affected their sexuality, nearly every story was about seeking health care. One friend, a cis queer woman, wrote, "I have had a hysterectomy and have not had potentially procreative sex in two decades. If I had a dime for every time since the surgery a healthcare provider has asked me multiple times if I was TOTALLY SURE I couldn't be pregnant, I would take us both out to dinner somewhere REALLY REALLY nice." Another told me he "had a therapist I met with three times, each of which contained a portion of me educating her that BDSM is not abuse." A third told me a truly heartbreaking story about being outed to the entire school as a lesbian by the high school nurse.

It should come as no surprise, then, to learn that medical professionals are rarely required to be trained in how to support their patients' sexual health. Bianca Palmisano, owner of Intimate Health Consulting, tells me that even when the biology of sex is taught, medical professionals are still never prepared to deal with their patients as sexual people. "I was looking over the reproductive and sexual health course for a physician assistant's program [at George Washington University]," she tells me. "They know how to diagnose amenorrhea and talk about vaginosis infections. They'll be able to map the entire reproductive system and know the basic progression of obstetric care. But when somebody comes in and they're having sex . . . and it's not going well, there was nothing in there about it." Nor is there any training in undoing biases, whether implicit or explicit, that doctors may have. Pediatricians get no instruction on how to talk to their young patients about consent. If it's not diagrammable or viewable through a microscope, medical providers are on their own.

That's where Palmisano comes in. Intimate Health Consulting trains health care providers to more fully and competently support the sexual health of their patients. Over homemade turkey soup in her cozy home office, Palmisano told me that she started out her professional career as an employment counselor for people who were homeless or at risk of losing their housing. Even then she had an interest in sex ed, interning at an organization called The Garden, which provided pop-up adult sex ed classes around the DC area. The daughter of a nurse midwife and a pharmacist, she swore growing up that she would have nothing to do with medicine when she made her own way in the world. But her experiences working with the sex educators at The Garden drew her in. "Not everybody can shell out $20 to go to a workshop on a Tuesday night at a sex shop in the middle of the city. . . . I said, 'What can be done on a systemic level to improve the way that we are addressing sexual health?' And because I had grown up around medicine, and because I really loved education and I feel like naturally I'm a teacher, this was a very logical place for my efforts to go."[5]

But Palmisano underestimated the fundamental level of services she'd need to provide. Even before she gets to ensuring that medical providers have all the correct factual information to give to their patients, she has to help them become willing to initiate conversations about sex. Providers think that if their patients have sex-related concerns, they'll bring them up, and patients think they're not important unless the provider asks about them. It's a vicious cycle based in fear and taboo.

"Nobody likes to hear this but I say it over and over: talking about sex with your patients, sometimes, is going to feel like giving life advice to a teenager. They're going to be kind of grumpy and awkward about the fact that they have to listen to it, but they're going to take that information back and it's going to be useful two months from now. You have to get comfortable with the idea that there is going to be some discomfort."

That's not to say that providers don't also need Palmisano to educate them on the facts. Even if her contact for an institution tells her that the staff she's being hired to educate are fairly competent already, she often finds that they lack even the most basic understanding. "They don't know what gender-neutral pronouns are. They think that bisexual people [are bi because they] were abused. It's pretty bad."

Combine that lack of education with that unwillingness to even talk about sex and you don't just get awkwardness or offense. You get untreated misery. For example, it takes, on average, more than a year between when a patient first experiences symptoms of vulvodynia, a disorder that can cause excruciating burning, stinging, itching, and other pain in the vagina, and when a doctor finally provides a correct diagnosis so that treatment can begin. In the meantime, those suffering from the disorder often can't tolerate intercourse at all and sometimes have pain when doing things as anodyne as sitting or walking. There is a third factor at play as well. Patients who experience vulvodynia wait so long for diagnosis in part because they often have to see multiple providers until they find one who will take their pain seriously, who won't just pat them on the head and recommend using more lube. That tracks with research showing that women's pain is generally taken less seriously by doctors and other providers, likely because of stereotypes about how emotional and fragile women are.[6] One expert says that period pain can sometimes be almost as excruciating as a literal heart attack,[7] but still period pain management has been little studied, because that's lady stuff.

And even that unconscious bias pales in comparison with the overt misogyny and harassment some women face when trying to practice medicine. In an essay for the *Washington Post*, Dr. Allyson Herbst described some of what she and her female colleagues face on the job every day, including a resident who was supervising her telling her "You're not wearing make-up today. Maybe you should rethink that choice," and a surgeon who, midoperation, locked eyes with her and told his assisting resident surgeon to "Splay [the patient] open like a Russian whore!"[8] It's hard to imagine that this kind of open misogyny doesn't act as a screen to keep sexual minorities out of the field of medicine.

Ironically, Palmisano is self-taught, relying on conferences, workshops, and lots of reading to keep herself and her clients up to date. She certainly seems to know her stuff, but in a second irony, medical institutions penalize her for the certifications she doesn't have even as they fail to provide the content on their own. Though she can sometimes reach the unconverted if they work for an institution where an administrator invites her to educate the entire staff, her lack of accreditation means she can't offer continuing education credits as an enticement to potential attendees, which leaves her with no carrot to offer the most reluctant doctors, who are of course the ones who need her the most.

At the moment, Palmisano mostly advertises via targeted ads on social media, email blasts to places like the American Medical Student Association and the National Coalition of Sexual Health, and word of mouth. Those eclectic efforts are reflected in the audience of the webinar I sat in on, where attendees are MDs, nursing and medical students, and sexual health educators and counselors who want a better grounding for their own work in counseling or behavioral health institutes.

Palmisano has benefited from an incentive built into the Affordable Care Act. If you'll forgive the metaphor, the ACA has provided a ready back door through which Palmisano can slip. Provisions in the law incentivize providers to show that they're having a measurable impact on a population that usually suffers from health disparities, and many are choosing to focus on LGBT patients, "because it's so easy to get data on LGBT people and if you can provide a base level of care, it's not that hard to get LGBT people to be healthier," explains Palmisano.

It's unclear, as of this writing, whether the ACA will survive a Trump administration. "I'm so pissed about that," Palmisano tells me. But there is one silver lining. "The field is notoriously slow to change, and while I'm worried about things like funding for comprehensive sex education and access to LARCs [long-acting reversible contraception], over-the-counter birth control, and Plan B, I'm less concerned that the field of medicine will just throw up its hands and say, 'well I guess queer people and sexual health don't matter anymore!'" It's probably the only good thing about the field's glacial movement—it's so slow that it's almost immune to presidential administrations.

That's good news for patients of all orientations, because much of the information providers need to know and policies they need to enact to make practices more inclusive of sexual minorities and trans people are the same as they need to make their practices more sexually competent in general. Palmisano explains it like this:

> The main thing that makes LGB people different, in a medical context, is who they're sleeping with. . . . So we're already talking about sex, and the reality is this conversation is very broadly applicable. So we can say we want to make a sexual risk assessment that's inclusive of LGBT people, but that means talking about the skills about how to do a sexual risk assessment [with all patients]. It opens up the door to say, "Actually, you have a lot of assumptions about the ways that people have sex, and that's not just about queer people, that's about all people."
>
> I always tell people, never in my life have I had a rectal swab for an STI even though I've reported to my doctors numerous times that I have anal sex. But they see me as a queer woman as someone who is very low risk for that. And so [they think] it does not make sense to do a rectal swab.

Palmisano teaches providers to look past generalizations and engage with the specific patient in front of them. "We don't start with assumptions based on gender, based on sexuality, based on anything. I'm giving a framework for them to be able to ask questions modularly. What kind of sex are you having? And what body parts are you using for it? So if a client says I have 'regular sex,' [the provider should ask] 'What does that mean for you?'"

That conversation is at the heart of the evening's webinar. Palmisano pulls no punches, talking about how to support patients who enjoy fisting, breath play, and BDSM just as matter-of-factly as she talks about strategies for encouraging condom use. But her message comes down to this: it's on you, as the medical professional, to ask your patients about sex. And if you do it openly and without judgment, you will help them be healthier and happier at the same time.

She offers providers two basic questions to ask every patient. "If you're having sex currently, is it pleasurable for you?" and "Do you have any questions or concerns about your sex life?"

I want you to imagine now how radically different our national discourse around sexuality would be if, starting around puberty, you were asked those questions every time you did an intake with a medical professional. For most of us, most of the time, the answers would probably be "yes" and "no," respectively, but that's not the point. Hearing those questions at least annually from someone we consider an authority on our health would teach us to value those questions ourselves. Teaching doctors and nurses to ask about pleasure could have a profound effect on how we think about our sex lives and how we think about our sexual selves.

Even better: focusing on patient pleasure creates better health outcomes. In a 2006 meta-analysis, researchers found that selling safer sex as a boon to pleasure increased people's knowledge and retention of HIV prevention strategies, increased their condom use and their ability to communicate about sex with their partners, and decreased their overall behavioral risk from sex. What's more, they found that emphasizing pleasure when educating about safer sex does not "impact the frequency of sex occasions," in either direction.[9] Translation: using pleasure as an incentive to encourage safer sex practices makes patients safer than using fear, and it doesn't make anyone sluttier than they already are.

Palmisano doesn't have the resources yet to study the effectiveness of her own trainings, but the feedback is encouraging. She hears often from doctors and nurses that they've started having the conversation as a regular part of their practice, and that it's opened up whole new dimensions in their ability to care for their patients. And that physician assistant program at George Washington University, the one that taught only the biology of reproduction, but nothing about sexuality? The school hired Palmisano to add two lectures of her own to it: one on how to take a sexual history, and one on how to help patients with sexual pain and libido issues.

Of course, Palmisano can only reach a tiny fraction of the country's medical schools and providers, and programs like hers are few and far between. But there is a glimmer of hope for the progress of the profession as a whole. In 2014, the American Association of Medical Colleges released a report outlining the competencies all doctors must obtain to properly care for LGBT patients, with videos demonstrating what each of those competencies looks like in practice. The University of Louisville School of Medicine is now developing and testing a pilot curriculum based on that report, with the hope of developing coursework that will be integrated into all medical schools in the future.

The news is patchier in other fields. Despite multiple attempts, I was unable to get any information about any curricula addressing sexuality or sexual violence being taught at a police academy. At professional schools for therapists and social workers, sexuality still hasn't made much of a dent in the core curriculum, but new elective offerings are cropping up at some schools, often thanks to the effort of former students who wish they had been better prepared by their coursework.

Diana Adams, a lawyer whose practice defends the rights of lesbian/ gay/bisexual/trans and other sexual minority clients to form and build families, told me that finding a class on sexuality and the law or LGBTQ family law at any given law school is a crapshoot, depending entirely on the interests of the administration and faculty at each school. That means it's hard to find lawyers who are competent in these areas, and even harder if you can't afford private representation, because you have little choice in who represents you when you must rely on a public defender's office. Because judges almost universally start out as lawyers, it also means that most of the country's judges are unqualified to hear cases involving sexuality.

Adams tells me that when colleagues ask for advice about a case involving a client with a "nontraditional" sexuality, she always asks one question first.

> "Where does this person live?" Because the same fact pattern will be handled differently in different courts in this country. And that's really a challenge, because the standard right now for much of child custody is the best interest of the child, but that's incredibly subjective. I work throughout New York State for example, and I can give you my prognosis based on longitude and latitude. I win below Westchester. North of Albany I have a really hard time.
>
> I've had cases in which a parent didn't do well because they were living with somebody and they weren't married, and that was not Christian. And I've had other cases where my clients in NYC lived in a lesbian collective and threw BDSM parties on the weekend, and there was questioning of why we were even talking about that, why that was even relevant to the parenting at all. It's very dependent on the judges.[10]

The field of journalism remains equally deregulated. One current journalism student at Emerson College told me that sexual assault is covered in their ethics of journalism course, which is mandatory for all journalism students. The only problem is that "most sections are taught by men, who do not have proper training on how to discuss the topic. In my opinion, the discussion about this in class served to place doubt on victims. It harped a lot on the *Rolling Stone* example." But Barbara Friedman, the journalist who botched the rape case she was assigned to cover when she was fresh out of school, is now herself a professor at the J-school at University of North Carolina, and she's making sure to teach the things she wished she had learned. "I make a point of teaching my news writing students how to cover sexual assault (how to read reports, how to generate original data, how to interview survivors, etc.)," she tells me. "As far as I know I am the only faculty member doing this (although I know folks in other units who address this issue in their teaching). We have multiple sections of the news writing class and use a common syllabus—I'm straying from that with my associate dean's blessing, but I wish I could persuade all my colleagues to cover this important topic."

For now, it looks like that kind of slow persuasion is the best tool we have to change the way professionals are prepared to deal with issues of sexuality. So next time you encounter someone "just doing their job" who seems to hold some warped ideas about sex, remember that being an authority in one thing doesn't make them an authority on what you can and can't do with your body. And ask them: Where did you learn that?

## CHAPTER ELEVEN

# OUR INTERNET, OURSELVES

Y OU MAY HAVE heard that the Internet is the best thing that ever happened for women's sexual liberation. You may also have heard that it's a terrifying nightmare for women, a playground for rapists, stalkers, and other violent misogynists. The truth is, the Internet isn't a moral entity. It's just an ever-changing set of tools. At most, it's an accelerant like gasoline: a superfuel for every facet of human nature. For every survivor it enables to speak out against sexual violence, another woman is victimized when a bitter boyfriend leaks private photos or a rapist shares a video of her violation, multiplying her trauma as the scene is consumed as entertainment. For every tween boy who finds misogynist porn when he turns to the Web to satisfy his sexual curiosity, there's a tween boy who finds Scarleteen or any one of the great sex educators using YouTube to bring desperately needed real talk to young people who aren't getting it in school or at home. The Juneau Teen Council used digital connectivity to organize against anti–sex ed legislation in Alaska. Bianca Palmisano wouldn't have nearly the reach she does without webinar technology. The short films produced by the girls of ImMEDIAte Justice would never be shared beyond the smallest circle of friends without the help of You-Tube. But also: digital connectivity enables anonymous hordes to drive women into hiding with coordinated avalanches of rape threats.

I've certainly lived through my share of Internet-assisted human nature. I would never have met either of my most recent boyfriends without it—my current beau and I met the "old-fashioned" way, via OK Cupid, and the guy before him I met because he was a commenter on a blog post I wrote. In between the two, the Internet facilitated many a life-affirming sexual adventure for me (and a few cringe-worthy mistakes as well), starting with the one I'm most famous for, a whim of a hookup via Craigslist's casual encounters. That adventure alone turned into a now-legendary essay called "My Sluthood, Myself," in which I made the case that "Sluthood isn't just a choice we should let women make because women should be free to make even 'bad' choices. It's a choice we should all have access to because it has the potential to be liberating." (Unbelievably, it also turned into a real friendship that has endured for many years longer than our affair did.)

I'm not the only woman who's found online dating empowering. "Dick is abundant and low value" is the new mantra of many a lady dater, meaning that the explosion in dating technology has made it obvious just how many choices women have when we're looking for some fun. We're free to demand that the men who want to be our sex partners treat us more like human people and less like wrapped treats in a sex vending machine. "The truth is," writes Alana Massey in her brilliant *Matter* essay "The Dickonomics of Tinder," "sluts like me are everywhere on Tinder but we aren't impressed by men who are positively beleaguered by the prospect of having to put effort into getting laid, nor do we like it when they mock the boundaries of our girlfriends who want to use Tinder only for traditional dating."

Nearly every woman I've asked has a story about how the Internet has improved her relationship with her sexual self. Some found private postpartum or postmiscarriage communities that helped them heal and reclaim their bodies. Some have physical disabilities that affect their sex lives and use the Web to develop far-flung friendships with others facing similar challenges, helping each other to share not just solidarity but also practical tips and the latest research. One friend spoke for the many LGBTQ people I heard from when she recounted, "I was an introvert debate team captain in the rural South, so I basically learned how to be gay (and later, queer) through Internet research and online interactions. Everything from consent to 'what lesbians do in bed' (pretty sure I actually searched for that) to how to write a Planetout profile that would find me the bookish and brash girl of my dreams." Others spoke of the way web access enabled them to hear from people whose sexual experiences were far different from theirs, expanding both their empathy and their worldview. The sex workers at HIPS have benefited because the Internet has made it possible for them to find clients without having to submit to the control of a pimp.

And it's not just sex—sometimes the Internet gives us space to reject the idea that we need to be sexy all the time. Writer and activist Soraya Chemaly told me this: "What I see mainly in Snapchat that I know confounds a lot of people, especially parents, is ugly girls. Girls who are making their faces not attractive [on purpose]. And I think that's just fantastic. I mean, 20 years ago you just didn't have a way of seeing girls be funny or girls be goofy or girls being sloppy or messy or anything that we all are. And the boys are seeing it too. It's such a refutation of the ideals that are put on them."[1]

That web-enabled rebellion also extends to clapping back against anti-woman violence. The anti–street harassment nonprofit Holla-back! even has an app for it. It's called Heartmob, and it enables web users to have each other's backs when one person is targeted for online misogyny or other kinds of harassment and abuse. But an app isn't even always necessary: Twitter hashtags have become powerful activist tools, as when video surfaced of a passed-out sixteen-year-old being sexually assaulted at a party, and the girl in question took to social media and refused to be shamed, using the hashtag #IamJada. Inspired by her courage, thousands of Internet denizens, including celebrities, posted messages of solidarity and support.

And it's hard to overstate the impact digital connectivity has had on the campaign to end sexual violence on college campuses. "For survivors of sexual violence, the Internet and social media specially, have given us a network of solidarity, but also the validation that our experiences merit not just anger and support but also societal change," reflects Andrea Pino, cofounder of End Rape on Campus and co-editor of the book *We Believe You: Survivors of Campus Sexual Assault Speak Out*. "It allows us a platform to write our stories as we love them; track every day white supremacy, sexism, homophobia and transphobia, even when the media have kept their prevalence well concealed. Access to the internet is a privilege that allows us to seek mentorship, love, and a community that can fight alongside us when our hurdles seem insurmountable."[2]

Of course, tech isn't magic, especially when up against the tenacity of a culture that thinks of women as playthings for men. Just ask any of the rape victims who've discovered, to their horror, that video of their violation is being used to shame and humiliate them rather than bring their perpetrator to justice.

And sex suffers from some of the same tech dynamics that play out in other areas. You can't make an app for everything, but people keep trying. My most fervent pet peeve is the "consent apps" that seem to spring up every six months, each a different iteration on the idea that you can record sexual consent with a partner before you get down with them. These apps not only fundamentally misunderstand how consent works (you can't just say yes once in the beginning to "sex" and have that cover whatever happens next) but also provide no protection against victims being forced into recording their "consent." Even apps whose ideas are sound often emphasize shiny digital magic at the expense of their mission, as was the case with the Evidence Vault app, which promised to record victims' reports of sexual assault and save them until the victims decide to report to the police. Though the site is offline as of this writing, when I tested it in 2016 it lacked basic protections like two-factor authentication or even a requirement for strong passwords to protect that very sensitive, personal data against theft. Security lapses like these leave the victims such services claim to serve vulnerable to a second victimization at the hands of their rapists or those who support rape.

Nor is every digital danger born of good intentions. You know what I'm talking about already, but yes, I have for years been on the receiving end of rape and death threats, ostentatious invasions of privacy, long treatises on my sexual desirability or lack thereof, digs about my mother, my desire to be raped, you name it. And I can tell you first-hand that the costs are enormous, whether they're measured in the price of high-tech security services or in insomnia, anxiety, terror, depression, exhaustion, self-censorship, and burnout. Not to mention the hit to my sex drive every time someone describes how they would rape me or how grotesque they find my body.

I am, of course, no anomaly. Women and girls are targeted on the Internet with shocking regularity, and sex is almost always the weapon. If you're a male journalist or expert, you can expect people to use the Internet to tell you you're stupid or that your argument is wrong. If you're a woman, expect commenters to assess whether or not they'd fuck you and dissenters to threaten sexual violence in elaborate detail. Some may even resort to doxxing (digging up and publicly releasing private contact information like a woman's home address and phone number), stalking, SWATting (calling in false police emergencies to a woman's address so that a SWAT team will show up at her house), and whatever other horrors they can dream up.

It's no accident that the inciting incident of GamerGate was a woman being accused of having sex in a way that a man disapproved of. It's no accident that when Emma Watson gave a feminist speech at the United Nations, the backlash consisted of a highly publicized threat to leak naked pictures of her. It's no accident that, when Ashley Judd tweeted about a college basketball game, she received rape threats, or that a college athlete used the word *slut* to attack trailblazing Little League pitcher Mo'Ne Davis. Sexual shame and fear are the primary tools of online harassment, exploiting the fauxpowerment gap to the maximum.

It's worth paying attention to the exact kinds of sexual threats women get online. As Chemaly points out, it's not just that most threats and abuse directed toward women leverage sexual stigma. Much of the abuse has a very specific eroticized theme: silencing women. "It's specifically about women shutting up. For example, dick pics with captions that read something like 'choke on my cock.' All kinds of images having to do with strangling, choking, gagging, putting things in women's mouths. I'm not even sure that the harassers understand what they're doing," she observes. One particularly gruesome story illustrates this dynamic: Grace Mann, an undergraduate and feminist activist at University of Mary Washington, was murdered by a former rugby player shortly after she had spoken out against a violently misogynist anthem performed by the rugby team. The murder weapon? A plastic bag shoved down her throat.

Sadly, the silencing is working, and not just on outspoken activists and public figures. Studies find that girls who play multiplayer games online don't use their microphones nearly as often as boys do, because when they do, when they speak up and their voices are recognizably female, they're targeted in-game with sexual harassment from other players. They are isolating themselves from the very real community that some of these games can provide, out of fear of sexualized violence.

More and more, sexualized attacks on women are normalized by the very architecture of the Web, automated through algorithms meant to make the Web better. One example is Wiki Detox, an algorithm built to learn what attacking and aggressive comments look like on Wikipedia, with the goal of making Wikipedia a less "toxic" space in which to participate. Trouble is, it's learning the wrong things. It codes the phrase "You're a dick" as maximally aggressive and maximally an attack, scoring 1 out of a possible 1 on both metrics. And, sure, there's never a nice reason to say that to someone. But type in "You should be raped" and it will tell you it's only 0.66 aggressive, and only 0.30 an attack. Try "abort yourself," as some charmer on Twitter just said to me while I was writing this, and you learn it's only 0.29 attacking and 0.18 aggressive.

One hopes and assumes that the makers of the algorithm don't think "You're a dick" is a more toxic thing to say to someone than "You should be raped" or "abort yourself." After all, the former is just a run-of-the-mill insult, whereas the latter are veiled threats of sexualized violence. But good intentions don't translate to outcomes without active intervention. The algorithm is learning what's "toxic" via human coders, using a website called CrowdFlower, which is known mostly in very nerdy tech circles. No data are available that I could find on the gender breakdown of their testers, but knowing what the gender break-down is in the tech industry, I have some guesses. Algorithms don't automatically produce a "neutral" result, because the culture is already not neutral. And so, if coders of algorithms want the algorithms to pro-duce truly balanced and just outcomes, they need to actively intervene to get the kind of input that will produce that result. "What we need is intersectional data," points out Chemaly. "It would make some sense to survey the people who are most likely to get the threat, and ask them to code the language."[3]

So, yes: the Internet is great for sexual liberation, and it's also hor-ribly oppressive. The key question is this: How do we curb bias and abuse without losing the freedom and connection? How do we drain the bathwater and save the baby?

It's a question I've been grappling with for years, and I know no one better to grapple with than Chemaly. I met her in 2012 when she asked me to lunch somewhat out of the blue, and I, having read an essay of hers about leaving the Catholic Church, was intrigued enough to say yes. She was glamorous and garrulous, curious and charming.

Born in the Bahamas to parents she characterizes as "obedient Cath-olics," she challenged them from early on, announcing her intention to become a priest (her mother punted to their priest to explain why she couldn't do that) and protesting the gendered division of house-hold chores, a move that, at age nine, succeeded in forcing her brother to do an equal part of the cleaning up after dinner.

She brought that sharp sense of gender justice with her to George-town, where, as an undergraduate, she quickly realized that women's voices and stories were sidelined. She set to rectify that by launching the school's first feminist magazine. But she didn't stop there—she fought for two years to get it institutionally funded (and thereby institu-tionally sanctioned), showing up in the president's office every month until she got her way. Male students protested, of course, claiming the magazine was discriminating against men. "One guy, when I said that we were starting a magazine focused on women," remembers Chem-aly, "he was like, are you going to have centerfolds? So . . . you know what I did that was really funny? On every page we had, this was our form of subversion." She leans over and draws a small circle on a nearby notepad, then puts a dot in the middle of it. A nipple. They placed a tiny one on the corner of each page of the magazine.[4]

After college she worked for a while in publishing, but when her growing family demanded a growing income, she switched to the business side, working for a newspaper conglomerate, where she happened upon a fascinating niche: "new media," aka, the Internet. She took to it like a duck to water, first reading the tea leaves to predict, in 1992, that newspaper classified ad revenue would be wiped out by this new technology ("The response that I got was, more or less, 'Isn't she cute?'"), and then spearheading the creation of the first-ever digital databases for business-to-business and business-to-subscriber marketing.

But one day late in 2010, her focus abruptly shifted back to gender. That was the day her oldest daughter, who was thirteen at the time, decided to take a step toward independence. "It was late evening, and she was in her soccer uniform and wanted to go get ice cream by herself. She just wanted to walk several blocks away to get ice cream," recalls Chemaly.

> I was caught off guard because this was the first time she really said, "It's getting dark but I want to go out by myself." She was really excited—she's a very adventurous person—and I excused myself and I went into the bathroom and had what I realized in retrospect was a full-blown triggering anxiety attack. In about 10 seconds I felt like I could see and hear every form of harassment I'd ever experienced. They just came flooding back one after another. And I was really filled with rage, because I thought, "Oh my god, this is the point at which she could start to turn in on herself, because she has to now adapt to the fact that she has to think about keeping herself safe, and not go certain places, and not do certain things and not go out at night, and all the lessons that come from the culture about girls staying safe." And I really rebelled against any of that.

She let her daughter go out for her treat, and then, with her husband's support, quit her job to return to writing and publishing. "It was the only thing I could think to do. I thought, 'I've lived with this silently my whole life and everybody else has too, and I'm not really sure why, and I'm not going to anymore.'"

Chemaly is a whirlwind. Her mind is always at work. She never seems afraid or hesitant. If I need to reach an executive at any of the major tech firms, I call her, because I know she has them on speed dial. When I mentioned her omnipotence, she told me her simple secret: "I force myself in, to be honest. I just pick up the phone and I call or I write a pointed email, or I make a request." Once, we found ourselves both presenting at a conference for college administrators grappling with sexual assault on their campuses. On the way out of a session, we happened to spot Anita Hill, the keynoter for that evening, walking by herself down a hall. Starstruck, I stopped and whispered to Chemaly, thinking we would just admire Hill from afar for a moment before going on with our day. Chemaly had other plans. She immediately strode forward and introduced herself and me, and for a few minutes, there we were, just chatting it up with one of the most iconic and impactful women of the twentieth century.

I wasn't really surprised. By then, Chemaly and I had been two-thirds of the team that won one of the biggest feminist digital victories of the decade. It all started when I was still the executive director of Women, Action, and the Media (WAM!), the nonprofit I founded to fight for gender justice in all media, both online and off. We were launching a new direct action project and looking for a worthy target for our first outing. Chemaly had written several pieces about Face-book's failure to address the rampant spread of imagery promoting violence against women on its site. There were pages with names like "Killing Bitches" (which featured a gun pointing at the viewer and comments from men describing how they'd like to kill women they know) and "Kicking a slut in the vagina and losing your foot inside" and with imagery like a woman falling down the stairs with the caption "Next time don't get pregnant" emblazoned over it or a woman giving a blowjob with the man's hand on the back of her head and a caption reading "What's the difference between spit and swallow? A few pounds of pressure on the back of the head." When the content was reported, Facebook would tell users it didn't violate its Terms of Service, calling it "controversial humor," even though the site already had a policy banning hate speech. So I reached out to Chemaly to see if she thought there was a way forward. She suggested we loop in Laura Bates, founder of the UK's Everyday Sexism project, who had also been attempting to make inroads with Facebook on the issue.

It was Laura who came up with the winning strategy. On a small scale, Everyday Sexism had already experimented with tweeting at advertisers whose ads appeared next to the violent images, and it'd had some encouraging responses. From an organizing perspective, it made perfect sense: if hundreds of thousands of women signing a petition wasn't enough to pressure Facebook to act, we clearly weren't the constituency Facebook cared about. Advertisers were. So we'd inspire ad buyers to apply the pressure for us. We set about defining the scope of our protest, writing a call to action, and quietly reaching out to an international coalition of women's groups to sign on before launch so that, from the moment we went live, we would have the power to engage women around the globe. We identified five key companies that seemed to care about appealing to their female customers and who advertised on Facebook on a large enough scale that the withdrawal of their ad dollars would get attention in the executive suites. We built web tools and wrote press releases. We searched and we scrolled until we had a grim library of violent images. (Sometimes that part of the work got so hard that we would have to take turns with it, allowing each of us a rotating break from absorbing the relentless violence and hate.) And then, finally, we were ready, and we launched. And it worked. Sixty thousand tweets, five thousand emails, and precisely one week later, Facebook agreed to change its policy. The hateful content started to come down almost immediately. We celebrated. The *New York Times* praised us in an editorial. Everyone I'd ever known reached out to say thanks or offer congrats. And then things got complicated.

A few weeks after our triumph, we started to get strange, hostile messages on WAM!'s Facebook page, people mad at us because Facebook had taken down their pages dedicated to sharing BDSM-themed images—pictures of women tied up, being whipped, and the like. The owners of the pages were told they were in violation of Facebook's new hate speech policy against content promoting violence against women. It was clear almost immediately what had happened. Facebook higher-ups had sent the new standard to their moderation team without nuance or thought, and their moderation team was applying it without context. It's a more common problem than most users know— Facebook outsources much of its frontline moderation to workers in countries where labor is cheap and, often, where men wildly outnumber women in the labor force and traditional gender norms are rigidly enforced. They have, on average, maybe thirty seconds to decide whether any particular piece of content reported to them falls afoul of Facebook's byzantine regulations. (The regulations users see are just the tip of the iceberg. Like many social media companies, Facebook doesn't publicize the minutiae of its content policies in order to keep bad actors from finding it too easy to color juuuuuust inside the lines.) The moderators were taking down anything that might be considered to promote violence against women, without considering important context, like consent.

We see the impact of this contextless approach everywhere in social media moderation: it's in Facebook's policies on nipples, which until Chemaly and other people's good work finally paid off, treated images of women breastfeeding as indistinguishable from still shots from porn. It's since carved out a breastfeeding exception, but still we constantly see banned images of women using toplessness as a means of political protest and art involving female nudity, while misogynist and sexualized images remain up as long as they don't show the dreaded nipple. Chemaly once intervened on behalf of a woman whose page of cervixes was taken down by Facebook moderators, and she had to explain that the page didn't violate the prohibition on depictions of genitals because genitals are on the outside of the body, and the cervix is not.

Twitter refuses to treat messages like "someone should rape you" and "I hope you choke to death on a dick" as threats of violence because such messages don't explicitly state the writer's actual intentions, even though the effect on the recipient—fear and silencing—is the same. And Twitter full-on permits doxxing as long as the information can be found "in the public domain," completely ignoring the wide gap between "my home address is listed in some obscure city office if you know where to look" and "my home address has been retweeted by hundreds of men, some of whom are presently sending me rape threats." YouTube goes so far as to permit "upskirt" videos—videos made by men nonconsensually filming up women's skirts—as long as they were shot and posted from places where such photography is legal, including many US states. The site profits from ads sold against these videos, and when the clips get enough views, the perpetrators get paid, too. All because it's "legal." And, more importantly, because the men who own and build these platforms don't often enough stop to consider experiences outside their own when deciding what should or shouldn't be permissible online.

That leads to situations like Jordan Belamire's in the fall of 2016. Invited by a friend to try out QuiVr, a new virtual reality game, she tried it first on a solo player setting, and then, delighted, switched to a setting in which she could interact with all other online gamers presently playing the game. Within three minutes, she was being groped and stalked by a man who simply heard her female voice and decided to attack her. She had no idea how to escape or report him.

That didn't have to happen, and it wouldn't have if the male game developers had made an effort to seek input from the many, many women in gaming who would have been happy to give it. "Online harassment of women and marginalized people in multiplayer gaming has been and continues to be a massive problem," wrote Anita Sarkeesian, founder of Feminist Frequency, a project that uses video to analyze modern media's relationship to societal issues such as gender, race, and sexuality (and survivor of a level of online harassment and abuse most of us can't even imagine). "That the newest tech in gaming was built without taking into consideration the fact that it could be used to harass and that anti-harassment functions weren't built into it from the start is a travesty. These conversations need to be a central part of the development process, period."

I've been in too many conference rooms and online conversations where the men who own these spaces, as well as many of the men who use them, like to wax eloquent about free speech and an ideal they call the "neutral platform," a fantasyland in which lack of intervention by platform owners results in a space where everyone, regardless of background, identity, or status, is equally heard. There is, they maintain, an inherent tension between free speech and "safety," and they only reluctantly and under great duress will impinge on the former in favor of the latter. Of course, what they mean when they position free speech and safety as opposites is that there's an inherent tension between men's free speech and women's safety. They're right about that. But their "neutral platform" only seems neutral to them because they're at the top of every social hierarchy. Women, people of color, trans people, queer people—we all know that our free speech is intrinsically bound up with our safety, that we can't exercise the one without the other. How "free" am I to speak, really, if users are free to shower me with baroque slurs and threats of violence every time I use my voice? If you're a woman on the Internet with opinions, your speech almost always comes at a cost.

Not that there's anything unique about men's dominance in the tech industry. Men dominate the top jobs in media, academia, law, corporations, and entertainment. It's just that the Internet happens at the intersection of all of those industries, creating what Chemaly describes as a "very safe space" for men. Human psychology doesn't help pierce that bubble. We tend to want to affiliate with people who feel familiar to us, people who remind us of us. Without a deliberate, accountable plan to resist that impulse, it creates a self-replicating echo chamber in which gatekeepers like Paul Graham, the head of Y Combinator, which has funded and incubated some of the most successful tech companies in the world, feel perfectly comfortable telling NPR that he can tell who would be a good founder because they have a look that's "the right kind of nerdy." It's how it's possible that the (male, of course) CEOs of Google, Apple, and Tesla followed almost no women whatsoever on Twitter[5] until a reporter from *The Guardian* shamed them into it.

The pressure to change this is increasing. Just last year, insiders told reporters at *Bloomberg* that Disney declined to buy out Twitter partly because of how poorly the platform addresses abuse.[6] But changing the power structures in Silicon Valley and incentivizing tech companies to stop abuse are just a start. Chemaly envisions a world in which the companies that profit from our digital lives don't just protect us from harm but use their tech to proactively make the world a better place for women and sexuality. She envisions a future version of YouTube that integrates ideas of consent at every level so that users have recourse if others use their image without permission and we all—but especially young users—learn what it's like to operate in a community that values each person's sovereignty. She thinks companies like Google should be donating ad credits to women who create videos that promote healthy ideas about sexuality. "Can we have a rape demythologizing series of videos produced by YouTube stars that then hits, I don't know, 20 million people in a day so that we can bypass all of the creepiness in schools that won't talk about it?" she muses. It's a rhetorical question, of course. With Chemaly, the answer to any question of possibility is always yes.

That's not to say that she's naive about what she's up against or what she can accomplish in the short term. "My goal is literally to just move things along a little bit," she confesses. "Like curling. I'm just like ch ch ch" (and here she makes a motion like a curler sweeping the ice in small frantic strokes in front of the curling stone). "I'm just pushing. I'm going as fast as I can."

She does a lot of her pushing in a traditionally female way: by building coalitions. She almost can't help but build them: the one that helped propel our #FBrape campaign to victory, the one she leads as head of the Women's Media Center's Speech Project, and the Speech and Safety Coalition she spearheaded and still corrals, a herd of activists and organizations, each with a different stake in reducing online misogyny, each with limited time and attention. In the group are anti-harassment activists, civil rights lawyers, domestic violence organizations, crusaders against revenge porn, and more. She forces us to communicate with each other, to build relationships, to be more than the sum of our parts. That's more than an operational method—it's who she is. When I asked her how she describes her job, this is what she told me: "I try and build networks of people who can leverage each other's expertise and provide support, and be more efficient in our advocacy work."

Those networks include anyone who will listen. Recently, Chemaly came up to Boston to speak to Women Explore, a local group that produces a series of daytime discussions on complex and provocative topics. The women there were the Cambridge analogue of the women I met in Minnesota with Sarah Deer: well educated, well intentioned, and almost uniformly white and above retirement age. I had spoken here some years previously and remembered them as a warm and curious group, though I was surprised Chemaly had been willing to spend an entire day flying up from DC and back again for what I knew to be a very small honorarium.

The woman who introduced Chemaly opened with a story about being a girl in elementary school encountering two boys who wanted to scare her by shoving a big bug in her face. Proudly, she described refusing to give them the satisfaction of a response. It was, she told us, the only time she'd ever been bullied. But now that we have the Internet, everything has changed. She then proceeded to describe the years-long hate campaign called GamerGate in such a strange and halting way that it felt like she had learned about it by reading a language she barely spoke, which is perhaps true, in a way.

I don't point this out to make fun, though I will confess that Chemaly and I had to studiously avoid eye contact while this was happening, lest we lost control over our suppressed giggles. But afterward over lunch, she and I agreed on something more important: as two women who spend most of our lives not just online but also thinking about what it means to be a woman online and what it could mean, it's important for us to remember how arcane and foreign these issues seem to most people. That's where Chemaly shines: from meetings with Facebook executives to luncheons with, well, well-meaning older white ladies in Cambridge, she always knows how to read an audience and connect. As she took the stage after that long and winding introduction, she gently told her own story about being targeted by boys in elementary school. In her case, she faced down an assault, not a bug.

The Internet didn't invent men's violence against women. It just gave them a new place to operate.

During the Q&A, several women expressed shock and overwhelm, as though we had sprung on them a particularly scary haunted house. One told me afterward that she didn't think she even understood the terminology. It's good that these women learned something from Chemaly, but I couldn't help but think about all the people who are similarly in the dark and whose ignorance influences our lives both online and off, like the police and the FBI, who routinely tell victims of online threats and abuse to just shut the computer off, as if Twitter is a frivolous game and not a part of how many of us do our jobs and a place where all of us should have the opportunity to have our voices heard. Their ignorance of how our new public squares work is actively denying women our right to experience both safety and free speech.

The last question asked that afternoon was perhaps both the simplest and hardest to answer. What, a woman asked, should tech leaders be doing to make platforms safer and freer for women? I thought Chemaly would talk about the need for women to achieve equity in corporate suites or share some of the future visions she's shared with me. I even thought she might borrow one of my favorite responses to this question: activists like Chemaly and me don't have to have all the answers to point out the need for solutions. The minds in Silicon Valley invented self-driving cars. Surely, if they were invested in women's online safety and freedom, they could invent solutions that far exceed what either of us could dream of.

But she didn't even say that. Instead, she said simply, "We don't have to fix the Internet. We have to fix the culture that expresses itself through the Internet." In other words: we can't unscrew the Internet without unscrewing the world. Let's get to work.

# HOW TO JOIN THE RESISTANCE

I N EARLY 2014, five years after the release of my first book, *Yes Means Yes*, the news broke about a new effort in California to pass what it was calling a "Yes Means Yes" law. The bill would require any college receiving state funds to use an affirmative consent standard in deciding sexual assault cases on campus. I was delighted, but cynical. "This is so awesome," I remember telling my boyfriend. "It'll never pass, but still. So awesome."

I'm glad the authors of the bill never asked me for my opinion. Yes Means Yes became law in California later that year. It's since become law in New York and has been introduced in numerous other states. California has even added similar provisions for high schools. And those laws don't just make a difference when someone commits a sexual assault. They require the schools covered by the law to teach affirmative consent as part of their social norms, making sex better and safer for everyone on campus. When I do new-student orientation talks on various college campuses, I always ask the students how many of them have heard the terms "yes means yes" or "affirmative consent." Usually a minority raise their hands. But when I ask that same question to incoming classes in New York, nearly every hand goes up. That's how culture changes.

The change makers I've introduced you to are just a small sample of the people I could have profiled. None of us working to unscrew the sexual culture possesses any special magic beyond our refusal to believe that change is impossible. It's the difference between saying "That's horrible" when you learn that your school system doesn't offer comprehensive sex education and "That's horrible. Let's make it better." That's the one weird trick behind what each of the pioneers you've met has done. They saw something in our sexual culture that needed healing, and they set about figuring out how they could help make that happen.

They are not, for the most part, grand visionaries, a fact I discovered when I asked them to share their grand visions. I originally imagined that this epilogue would be full of those visions, which I would assemble into a mosaic of a sexual utopia, detailing a world in which we're all equally free and equally sovereign, where sex is joy, or power, or play, or pleasure, but never a source of shame or fear or pain. But I can't make a liberation mosaic out of the awkward pauses and stumped facial expressions I actually received when I asked the question.

In part, that's because trying to describe a truly unscrewed sexual culture is like trying to prove a negative. It requires describing a lot of absences—no capitalist insecurity, no whore stigma, no pussy-grabbing POTUS. And because sexualities are as diverse as fingerprints, it's difficult to start detailing them without leaving someone out.

Too, it's difficult because many of the people doing the hard work of changing the institutions that create our sexual culture are the very people most harmed by them in the present tense. That makes it hard to think beyond the next move. When I asked Sarah Deer, the Mac-Arthur Genius who helped Native women and girls win the right to prosecute non-Native rapists, what her sexual utopia would look like, she told me this story instead:

> I remember several years back I was at some meeting of the feminist bigwigs in the world. . . . They were going around and having us do a visioning session of what justice means for women. And I was sitting with a few Native women, and we just looked at each other and had no idea.

Everybody else, all the other tables, could visualize some image of justice for women. And it was our little table of Native women that were going like, "You know, we got nothing." And that was really overwhelming and paralyzing. We don't even know how to talk about this. . . . We're so struggling with day to day sustenance and survival that we really are struggling to even think outside that box. But I think there are a few things that we do know. I think we know that particularly gender fluidity, LGBT, two spirit, what have you . . . we know that two-spirit people were celebrated and revered, and we know that there were same-sex couples. We know that women had more than one sexual partner. We know these things.

This is not to say that these leaders don't have vision. It's just that their visions are more specific, which I discovered when, eventually, I found my way to a more specific question. Instead of posing an open-ended query about their perfect future, I asked them to imagine I was a genie and could grant them three wishes that would make the sexual culture better for the people they work with. I may not be a real genie, but those were certainly the magic words. Bianca Palmisano told me she'd abolish managed care, institute single-payer health care in its place, and mandate that every medical provider participate in a culturally competent SAR. Soraya Chemaly wished for privacy and affirmative consent principles to be baked into the way every digital platform functions, and for the makers of algorithms to "use intersectional data, understand bias, and create methodologies and standards for offsetting bias in those systems." (In true Chemaly fashion, she also squeezed in a fourth wish: "If I could send them all to school to study feminism I would.") Matt Theodores would go for paid paternity leave, a rethinking-masculinities program for every new dad, and a way for the GDP to value work that produces care and nurture at least as highly as it values work that produces capital. For Cyndee Clay, it was decriminalization of sex work and drug use, diversion of the funds previously used to police those activities into services that actually, noncoercively help people who want to leave sex work or stop using, and a national conversation about sex work and stigma. Sarah Deer would wish for the repeal of all US laws that make it difficult for a tribal nation to take action in cases of violent crime, well-funded advocacy and shelter programs on reservations and in urban communities ("Without advocacy front and center," she says, "other reforms will fall flat"), and giving Native women the power to reform tribal laws to meet the needs of their communities, "with an eye for traditional values and tenets that keep women and children safe."

Each of these responses is individually instructive and interesting. But together they tell us something bigger: the road to change doesn't require a grand unified vision of the future. That way lies overwhelm and paralysis. It instead requires that each of us pick a subject we care about, figure out concrete ways to make it better, and get to work.

Here are some things I've learned about working for change:

- Always give someone the chance to do the right thing for the right reasons before you make the situation adversarial. Not only is it the right thing to do but also it gives you the moral high ground if things get contentious. When, as an undergraduate, I found out how badly rape cases were being handled by the campus judicial system, the first thing I did was to take the dean of students out for breakfast to talk over my concerns. It was only when she refused to take them seriously that I organized the student-led investigation and pressure campaign that eventually succeeded.

- No matter how powerful the person or institution that stands in the way of the change you seek, it has a vulnerability. Figure out what it is, and you can exploit it. When Soraya Chemaly, Laura Bates, and I took on Facebook, we won because we figured out that advertisers were the site's Achilles' heel. Whatever change you're working for, ask yourself: Who has the power to make that change? What do they care about? What are they motivated by? How can you use what they care about to make them care about you? If someone thrives on public adulation, can you promise (and deliver) great press if they work with you? If they care about celebrities, what famous people can you recruit to your side?

- If a goal feels overwhelming or unwinnable, try breaking it down into smaller steps. Maybe you don't know how to make your state implement comprehensive, pleasure-positive, age-appropriate K–12 sex ed. Start by taking a look at what's being taught in your school district. Can you organize to add affirmative consent to the curriculum or make sure the clitoris is taught?

- To that end, make sure you celebrate partial wins and baby steps in the right direction. Almost all change happens incrementally. If you wait to celebrate until everything is perfect, you'll get demoralized and burn out.

- If you don't feel like you're cut out to be an organizer, or your life isn't allowing you the time and resources to do the change work you want to do, that's okay. Leaders need followers! Organizers need people to organize! Find a group or even just a person who's doing work to change the sexual culture that you want to support, and ask them what they need. Maybe they'll ask you to donate, stuff envelopes, call your representatives, show up at rallies and town meetings, or do other behind-the-scenes work—it's not glamorous, but every little bit helps.

- If you prefer, start with identifying a talent or skill you want to share, and then figure out who needs it. Graphic design, copywriting, and computer skills are always useful, and lawyers and accountants are clutch, but don't stop there. If you're a crafter, you could sell thematic crafts to benefit a cause you support. If you're a baker, run a bake sale or bring goodies to the staff of your favorite local organization. Everyone has a role to play.

- Or just find ways to live your values in your day-to-day life. Donate and volunteer for politicians who aren't beholden to the

Religious Right. Hire a current or former sex worker for a job. Refuse to give money or attention to media that traffics in faux-powerment. Maybe even grab some friends and produce your own alternative media that depicts women with real sexual power. (That last one is key, because it's a lot easier to motivate people to work toward something they want than to keep folks energized to fight against something bad.)

In the days after Trump won the Electoral College, many of my friends and family shared a particular quote with each other on social media. It's from the legendary sci-fi pioneer Ursula Le Guin, from a speech she gave in acceptance of the National Book Foundation's 2014 Medal for Distinguished Contribution to American Letters. In it, she calls on everyone listening to refuse to participate in the increasing encroachment of commercialism on the art of writing, saying, "We live in capitalism. Its power seems inescapable. So did the divine right of kings. Any human power can be resisted and changed by human beings."

There's nothing immutable about the customs, beliefs, and institutions that shape our sexual culture. For proof, just look to other societies. You know about how differently sex ed is taught in the Netherlands, and how much healthier that nation's teens are about sex as a result. But did you know that in Quebec, most women keep their last names when they marry? Before European colonization, most Native American cultures accepted both homosexuality and promiscuity as normal, and individuals who practiced both or either lived freely without stigma. Similarly, the Mosuo people of southwestern China live in a matriarchal culture where women wield both political and sexual power and suffer no stigma if they choose to reject marriage and have multiple sexual partners and children with different fathers. Every society chooses its sexual culture, and the people in that society have the power to change it.

The key is to pick one small piece, to start somewhere, and to be willing to fail and learn and grow and keep trying new ideas. And when you feel overwhelmed or discouraged, which you most certainly will—which everyone you've met in this book feels more frequently than you imagine—I offer you the piece of wisdom that keeps me going, that has driven me since I was in high school to do what I could to try to repair the world. It is a Jewish teaching from the first century, written by Rabbi Tarfon, and it translates more or less to this:

*It is not yours to complete the work, neither is it yours to desist from it.*

Do what you can. Nothing more and nothing less. And we can all unscrew our sex lives together.

# ACKNOWLEDGMENTS

This project fought me every step of the way, but Anna Sproul-Latimer, the best literary agent a writer could have, never stopped believing in it (and me). Thanks, Anna, for pep talks, stiff drinks, inappropriate text messages, and for never ever going easy on me when you knew I could do better, no matter how much I cried. (Big thanks also to Amanda Hess, for introducing us.)

Much gratitude is due to the whole team at Seal Press, most especially my editor, Stephanie Knapp, for being patient and pushy in equal measure, and for polishing all my rough edges until the words shone. (She, too, provided excellent cocktails. This book was fueled by good booze.)

If anyone could have written this book other than me, at this point it's Jessica Critcher. Thanks for cheerfully and skillfully transcribing every last interview, assisting with research, and always keeping me encouraged about smashing the patriarchy.

Brianna Garcia was a stranger to me when she heard that I was utterly blocked in the aftermath of the 2016 election. Through gentle words and kind deeds, she reminded me that not only were people counting on me but I could count on them, too. I can never thank her enough.

My deepest gratitude goes out to everyone who shared their wisdom, experience, time, and insight with me for this book, with a special thanks to Anita Sarkeesian, Renee Bracey Sherman, Jiz Lee, Kate D'Adamo, Pamela Merritt, Erin Matson, Reverend Beverly Dale, Nate Glass, and all the other folks whose names didn't otherwise make it into these pages. Thanks also to Kelly Wooten, Jennifer Scott,

Gretchen Sisson, Lisa Wade, and Veronica Arreola, for all the clutch research help.

Thanks to Ann Friedman, for being one of my first readers and for having believed in my voice since the beginning. Thanks to Shana Katz Ross for coaching me through that initial writer's block with a firm hand and an adorable fox mug.

And something much greater than thanks goes to Colin, my partner and my social justice quartermaster, who fact-checked and brainstormed and cooked and cleaned and snuggled and listened and cheered and generally loved me through every moment of the work. I love you, and I'm so glad to be on your team.

# NOTES

## Introduction: We the Fauxpowered

1. D. A. Frederick, H. K. John, J. R. Garcia, and E. A. Lloyd, "Differences in Orgasm Frequency among Gay, Lesbian, Bisexual, and Heterosexual Men and Women in a U.S. National Sample," *Archives of Sexual Behavior*. Published electronically February 17, 2017. doi:10.1007/s10508-017-0939-z.

2. "A History of Federal Funding for Abstinence-Only-Until-Marriage Programs," Sexuality Information and Education Council of the United States, http://www.siecus.org/index.cfm?fuseaction=page.viewpage&pageid=1340&nodeid=1.

3. Nancy Ritter, *Down the Road: Testing Evidence in Sexual Assaults*, National Institute of Justice Special Report NCJ 249805 (Washington, DC: US Department of Justice, June 2016), https://www.ncjrs.gov/pdffiles1/nij/249805.pdf.

4. Men's rights activists, aka MRAs, are a loose conglomeration of misogynists who claim that women have all the power in society, feminism is evil, and men are the real oppressed class. But instead of working to improve men's lives in any way, they mostly focus on harassing and threatening women.

5. Sam Morgan, "Rape Threats Hell of Revenge Porn Victim," *The Sun*, August 27, 2014, updated April 6, 2016, https://www.thesun.co.uk/archives/news/1059014/rape-threats-hell-of-revenge-porn-victim/.

## Chapter One: This Is Not My Beautiful House

1. Leah M. Smith, Jay S. Kaufman, Erin C. Strumpf, and Linda E. Lévesque, "Effect of Human Papillomavirus (HPV) Vaccination on Clinical Indicators of Sexual Behaviour among Adolescent Girls: The Ontario Grade 8 HPV Vaccine Cohort Study," *Canadian Medical Association Journal* 187, no. 2 (2015): E74–E81. doi:10.1503/cmaj.140900.

2. John Patrick Diggins, *The Proud Decades: America in War and Peace, 1941–1960* (New York: W. W. Norton, 1989), 212.

3. Virginia Ironside, "'We Paid the Price for Free Love': The Flip Side of the Sexual Revolution," *Daily Mail*, January 18, 2011, http://www.dailymail .co.uk/home/you/article-1346813/The-flip-1960s-sexual-revolution-We-paid -price-free-love.html.

4. Ellen Willis, "Toward a Feminist Sexual Revolution," in *The Essential Ellen Willis*, ed. Nona Willis Aronowitz (Minneapolis: University of Minnesota Press, 2014), 14, 17.

5. Alix Kates Shulman, "Organs and Orgasms," in *A Marriage Agreement and Other Essays* (New York: Open Road Integrated Media, 2012), 24.

6. "Lavender Menace," *Wikipedia*, last modified March 11, 2017, https:// en.wikipedia.org/w/index.php?title=Lavender_Menace&oldid=769839753.

7. Helen Croydon, "What It's Really Like to Be a Playboy Cover Girl," *The Telegraph*, October 17, 2015, http://www.telegraph.co.uk/women/11935885 /What-its-really-like-to-be-a-Playboy-cover-girl.html.

8. Anthony Paik, Kenneth J. Sanchagrin, and Karen Heimer, "Broken Promises: Abstinence Pledging and Sexual and Reproductive Health," *Journal of Marriage and the Family* 78 (2016): 546–561. doi:10.1111/ jomf.12279.

9. William Saletan, *Bearing Right: How Conservatives Won the Abortion War* (Berkeley: University of California Press, 2003).

10. Loretta Ross, interview by Joyce Follet, November 3–5 and December 1–3, 2004, and February 4, 2005, Voices of Feminism Oral History Project, Sophia Smith Collection, Women's History Archives at Smith College, Northampton, MA, https://www.smith.edu/library/libs/ssc/vof/transcripts /Ross.pdf.

11. Asian Communities for Reproductive Justice, "What Is Reproductive Justice?," http://strongfamiliesmovement.org/what-is-reproductive-justice.

12. Loretta Ross, interview by Joyce Follet, Voices of Feminism Oral History Project, Sophia Smith Collection, Tape 15 of 23: Ross F 14_17 9 05, https://www.smith.edu/library/libs/ssc/vof/vof-narrators.html#Ross.

13. "Falwell Apologizes to Gays, Feminists, Lesbians," CNN.com, September 14, 2001, http://www.cnn.com/2001/US/09/14/Falwell.apology/.

14. For a great deep dive into this phenomenon, read Susan Faludi's book, *The Terror Dream*.

15. Jennifer Baumgardner, "Feminism Is a Failure, and Other Myths," Alternet, November 16, 2005, http://www.alternet.org/story/28237/feminism _is_a_failure%2C_and_other_myths.

16. Jessica Valenti, "The Power of Raunch," Feministing, September 19, 2005, http://feministing.com/2005/09/19/the_power_of_raunch/.

17. Jessica Valenti, interview with author, December 14, 2016.

18. Loretta Ross, interview by Joyce Follet, Voices of Feminism Oral History Project, Sophia Smith Collection, Tape 20 of 23: Ross F 18_20 9 05, 13:00.

19. Loretta Ross, interview with author, January 27, 2016.

20. Ibid.

21. Ibid.

22. Ibid.

## Chapter Two: What Women Want

1. *Cis* is short for *cisgender*. It describes anyone who still identifies with the gender they were assigned at birth.

2. H. A. Rupp and K. Wallen, "Sex Differences in Viewing Sexual Stimuli: An Eye-Tracking Study in Men and Women," *Hormones and Behavior* 51, no. 4 (2007): 524–533.

3. Unless otherwise noted, studies cited didn't specify if trans people were included as subjects, leaving yet another gap in knowledge to be filled with stereotypes and assumptions.

4. Barbara L. Fredrickson, Tomi-Ann Roberts, Stephanie M. Noll, Diane M. Quinn, and Jean M. Twenge, "That Swimsuit Becomes You: Sex Differences in Self-Objectification, Restrained Eating, and Math Performance," *Journalism of Personality and Social Psychology* 75 (1998): 269–284.

5. Maria G. Pacilli, Carlo Tomasetto, and Mara Cadinu, "Exposure to Sexualized Advertisements Disrupts Children's Math Performance by Reducing Working Memory," *Sex Roles* 74 (2016): 389–398. doi:10.1007/s11199-016-0581-6.

6. Henry E. Adams, Lester W. Wright, and Bethany A. Lohr, "Is Homophobia Associated with Homosexual Arousal?" *Journal of Abnormal Psychology* 105, no. 3 (August 1996): 440–445, http://dx.doi.org/10.1037/0021-843X.105.3.440.

7. S. J. Dawson, M. L. Sawatsky, and M. L. Lalumière, "Assessment of Introital Lubrication," *Archives of Sexual Behavior* 44 (2015): 1527.doi: 10.1007/s10508-015-0519-z.

8. Meredith Chivers, interview with author, June 9, 2016.

9. Liz Klinger, interview with author, May 28, 2015.

## Chapter Three: Fauxpowerment Will Be Televised

1. Anne T. Donahue, "Beyoncé, Nicki Minaj, Rihanna, and the Power of Going Pants-Free," *MTV News*, February 29, 2016, http://www.mtv.com/news/2746167/beyonce-nicki-minaj-rihanna-and-the-power-of-going-pants-free/.

2. Noah Berlatsky, "Beyoncé Doesn't Perform for the Male Gaze," *Pacific Standard*, October 7, 2014, https://psmag.com/beyonc%C3%A9-doesn-t-perform-for-the-male-gaze-3ec44f3fb568#.kioxwgwmr.

3. Caroline Heldman, *Hitting the Bullseye: Reel Girl Archers Inspire Real Girl Archers* (Los Angeles: Geena Davis Institute on Gender in Media, 2016), https://seejane.org/wp-content/uploads/hitting-the-bullseye-reel-girl-archers-inspire-real-girl-archers-full.pdf.

4. Paul Lamere, "Gender Specific Listening," Music Machinery, February 10, 2014, updated February 13, 2014, https://musicmachinery.com/2014/02/10/gender-specific-listening/.

5. "Destiny's Child," *Wikipedia*, last updated March 11, 2017, accessed March 19, 2017, https://en.wikipedia.org/w/index.php?title=Destiny%27s_Child&oldid=769694228.

6. "Top 50 Video Game Makers," IGN, accessed March 18, 2017, http://www.ign.com/lists/video-game-makers. (One of the ten, Maxis, was female led, but then it was acquired by EA, which is male led.)

7. Martha M. Lauzen, *The Celluloid Ceiling: Behind-the-Scenes Employment of Women on the Top 100, 250, and 500 Films of 2016* (San Diego: Center for the Study of Women in Television & Film, San Diego State University, 2017), http://womenintvfilm.sdsu.edu/files/2015_Celluloid_Ceiling_Report.pdf.

8. *Who Makes the News: United States of America Global Media Monitoring Project 2015 National Report* (Toronto: Global Media Monitoring Project and WACC, 2015), http://cdn.agilitycms.com/who-makes-the-news/Imported/reports_2015/national/USA.pdf.

9. VIDA, "The 2015 VIDA Count: The Year of Intersectional Thinking," VIDA: Women in Literary Arts, March 30, 2016, accessed March 18, 2017, http://www.vidaweb.org/the-2015-vida-count/#Highlights & Observations.

10. Stacy L. Smith, Marc Choueiti, and Katherine Pieper, *Gender Bias without Borders: An Investigation of Female Characters in Popular Films across 11 Countries* (Los Angeles: Geena Davis Institute on Gender in Media, 2014), http://seejane.org/wp-content/uploads/gender-bias-without-borders-executive-summary.pdf.

11. "Gender Representation in Video Games," *Wikipedia*, last updated March 15, 2017, accessed March 19, 2017, https://en.wikipedia.org/w/index.php?title=Gender_representation_in_video_games&oldid=770514883.

12. Walt Hickey, "The Dollar-and-Cents Case against Hollywood's Exclusion of Women," FiveThirtyEight, April 1, 2014, https://fivethirtyeight.com/features/the-dollar-and-cents-case-against-hollywoods-exclusion-of-women/.

13. Melissa Silverstein, interview with author, March 14, 2017.

14. Thelma Adams, "The Curious Case of the Missing Women in Film Criticism," *Variety*, December 29, 2015, http://variety.com/2015/film/spotlight/lack-of-women-film-criticism-1201667282/.

15. Walt Hickey, "Men Are Sabotaging the Online Reviews of TV Shows Aimed at Women," FiveThirtyEight, May 18, 2016, http://fivethirtyeight.com/features/men-are-sabotaging-the-online-reviews-of-tv-shows-aimed-at-women/.

16. "The 80 Best Books Every Man Should Read," *Esquire*, April 1, 2015, http://www.esquire.com/entertainment/books/g96/80-books/?.

17. Rebecca Solnit, "80 Books No Woman Should Read," LitHub, November 18, 2015, http://lithub.com/80-books-no-woman-should-read/.

18. "Worst TV Show of the Week," Parents Television Council, September 11, 2009, accessed March 18, 2017, http://www.parentstv.org/ptc/publications/bw/2009/0911worst.asp.

19. Christopher J. Ferguson, Rune K. L. Nielsen, and Patrick M. Markey, "Does Sexy Media Promote Teen Sex? A Meta-Analytic and Methodological Review," *Psychiatric Quarterly*. Published electronically June 29, 2016. doi:10.1007/s11126-016-9442-2.

20. Jean M. Twenge, Ryne A. Sherman, and Brooke E. Wells, "Sexual Inactivity during Young Adulthood Is More Common among U.S. Millennials and iGen: Age, Period, and Cohort Effects on Having No Sexual Partners After Age 18," *Archives of Sexual Behavior* 46, no. 2 (2017): 433. doi:10.1007/s10508-016-0798-z.

21. Tani Ikeda, interview with author, April 3, 2016.

## Chapter Four: Money Makes the Sex Go Round

1. Chyng Sun, Ana Bridges, Jennifer A. Johnson, and Matthew B. Ezzell, "Pornography and the Male Sexual Script: An Analysis of Consumption and Sexual Relations," *Archives of Sexual Behavior* 45, no. 4 (2016): 983–994. doi:10.1007/s10508-014-0391-2.

2. For more on the economics of MindGeek and the pornography industry, I recommend David Auerbach's "Vampire Porn" at Slate.com; the essay "'Ethical Porn' Starts When We Pay for It," available at jizlee.com; and Shira Tarrant's book *The Pornography Industry*.

3. Ingo Lütkebohle, Frank Hegel, Simon Schulz, Matthias Hackel, Britta Wrede, Sven Wachsmuth, and Gerhard Sagerer, "The Bielefeld Anthropomorphic Robot Head 'Flobi,'" *2010 IEEE International Conference on Robotics and Automation (ICRA)* (2010). doi:10.1109/ROBOT.2010.5509173.

NOTES

4. "Adult Products and Services," Facebook Advertising Policies, accessed March 18, 2017, https://www.facebook.com/policies/ads/prohibited_content /adult_products_or_services.

5. Mike Monteiro, "Facebook Is Still a Gun Marketplace," BoingBoing, July 12, 2016, http://boingboing.net/2016/07/12/facebook-is-still-a-gun-market.html.

6. Google Terms of Service, last modified April 14, 2014, accessed May 11, 2017, https://www.google.com/policies/terms/.

7. Andi Zeisler, "Worst Sales Pitch Ever: The Ad Industry's Shameless History of Using Feminism to Sell Products," *Salon*, July 21, 2014, http://www .salon.com/2014/7/21/worst_sales_pitch_ever_the_ad_industrys_shameless _history_of_using_feminism_to_sell_products/.

8. Drew Armstrong, "No Burning Desire for Valeant's Female Arousal Drug: Chart," Bloomberg, July 1, 2016, https://www.bloomberg.com/news /articles/2016-07-01/no-burning-desire-for-valeant-s-female-arousal-drug-chart.

9. Corey G. Johnson, "Female Inmates Sterilized in California Prisons Without Approval," Center for Investigative Reporting, July 7, 2013, http:// cironline.org/reports/female-inmates-sterilized-california-prisons-without -approval-4917.

10. Susan Basow and Alexandra Minieri, "'You Owe Me': Effects of Date Cost, Who Pays, Participant Gender, and Rape Myth Beliefs on Perceptions of Rape," *Journal of Interpersonal Violence* 26, no. 3 (2011): 497.

## Chapter Five: The Separation of Church and Sex

1. Diana Adams, interview with author, May 27, 2015.

2. David Jackson, "Trump Takes Aim at Clinton in Appeal to Evangelicals," *USA Today*, June 10, 2016, http://www.usatoday.com/story/news/politics /elections/2016/06/10/donald-trump-faith-freedom-coalition-hillary-clinton /85691020/.

3. Jeremy Scahill, "Mike Pence Will Be the Most Powerful Christian Supremacist in U.S. History," *The Intercept*, November 15, 2016, https://the intercept.com/2016/11/15/mike-pence-will-be-the-most-powerful-christian -supremacist-in-us-history/.

4. Benjamin Wermund, "Trump's Education Pick Says Reform Can 'Advance God's Kingdom,'" *Politico*, December 2, 2016, http://www.politico .com/story/2016/12/betsy-devos-education-trump-religion-232150.

5. Katie Sanders, "Did Hobby Lobby Once Provide the Birth Control Coverage It Sued the Obama Administration Over?" PunditFact, July 1, 2014, http://www.politifact.com/punditfact/statements/2014/jul/01/sally-kohn/did -hobby-lobby-once-provide-birth-control-coverag/.

6. "Anti-LGBT Religious Refusals Legislation across the Country: 2015 Bills," ACLU, accessed March 18, 2017, https://www.aclu.org/anti-lgbt-religious -refusals-legislation-across-country-2015-bills.

7. Daniel Cox and Robert P. Jones, "Majority of Americans Oppose Transgender Bathroom Restrictions," Public Religion Research Institute, March 10, 2017, http://www.prri.org/research/lgbt-transgender-bathroom-discrimination -religious-liberty/.

8. Ian Millhiser, "When 'Religious Liberty' Was Used to Justify Racism Instead of Homophobia," Think Progress, February 26, 2014, https://think progress.org/when-religious-liberty-was-used-to-justify-racism-instead-of -homophobia-67bc973c4042#.

9. Daniel Cox and Robert P. Jones, "47% of the Country Say Trump Has Violated the Constitution, but Few Support Impeachment," Public Religion Research Institute, February 24, 2017, http://www.prri.org/research/poll -trump-impeachment-constitution-partisanship-muslim-ban/.

10. Alyssa Offman, "The Satanic Temple Will Interrupt Planned Parenthood Protests in Classic Satanic Temple Fashion," *Detroit Metro Times*, April 23, 2016, http://www.metrotimes.com/news-hits/archives/2016/04/23 /the-satanic-temple-plans-to-interrupt-some-planned-parenthood-in-classic -satanic-temple-fashion.

11. Stephen Bates, "Outsourcing Justice? That's Obscene," *Washington Post*, July 15, 2007, http://www.washingtonpost.com/wp-dyn/content/article /2007/07/13/AR2007071301728.html.

12. Amber Phillips, "Porn Has Been Declared a 'Public Health Crisis' in Utah. Here's Why," *Washington Post*, April 12, 2016, https://www .washingtonpost.com/news/the-fix/wp/2016/04/22/anti-porn-advocates-are -changing-the-game-and-it-starts-with-utah-declaring-it-a-public-health-crisis /?utm_term=.725ef91d5f79.

13. Meaghan Winter, "What Some Pregnancy Centers Are Really Saying to Women with Unplanned Pregnancies," *Cosmopolitan*, July 14, 2015, http:// www.cosmopolitan.com/politics/news/a43101/pregnancy-centers-august -2015/.

14. Cherisse Scott, interview with author, December 7, 2016.

15. Cherisse Scott, interview with author, January 20, 2017.

16. John Gilmore, interview with author, March 10, 2017.

17. Callie Marie Rennison, "Privilege, among Rape Victims," *New York Times*, December 22, 2014, A27.

18. Cherisse Scott, interview with author, January 20, 2017.

## Chapter Six: Saving Ourselves from Rescue

1. Hanna Rosin, "Why Kids Sext," *The Atlantic*, November 2014, https://www.theatlantic.com/magazine/archive/2014/11/why-kids-sext/380798/?single_page=true.

2. Erica Goode, "Researchers See Decline in Child Sex Abuse Rate," *New York Times*, June 29, 2012, A13.

3. Sandra Song, "The Abject Dehumanization of Kim Kardashian," *Paper Magazine*, October 3, 2016, http://www.papermag.com/the-abject-dehumanization-of-kim-kardashian-2029087678.html.

4. Gersh Kuntsman, "Kim Kardashian's Paris Robbery Is Too Good to Be True," *New York Daily News*, October 4, 2016, http://www.nydailynews.com/entertainment/kim-kardashian-paris-robbery-good-true-article-1.2815747.

5. Diana Falzone, "Kim Kardashian's Robbery Story Raises Questions, Experts Say," Fox News, October 5, 2016, http://www.foxnews.com/entertainment/2016/10/05/kim-kardashian-robbery-story-raises-questions-experts-say.html.

6. Julia Brucculieri, "This Kim Kardashian Robbery Costume Is About as Misogynistic as It Gets," *Huffington Post*, October 11, 2016, http://www.huffingtonpost.com/entry/kim-kardashian-robbery-costume_us_57fce7b0e4b0b6a430356ced.

7. Rebecca L. Stotzer, "Violence against Transgender People: A Review of United States Data," *Aggression and Violent Behavior* 14 (2009): 170–179. doi:10.1016/j.avb.2009.01.006.

8. Tina Horn, interview with author, October 18, 2016.

9. Tierney McCafee, "Press Corps with Trump Now Needs Police Escort as Crowd Shouts 'Whores!'" *People Magazine*, October 14, 2016, http://people.com/politics/trump-crowds-attack-press-corps-rally-whores/.

10. Audacia Ray, interview with author, May 26, 2015.

11. Anne Elizabeth Moore, "Special Report: Money and Lies in Anti–Human Trafficking NGOs," Truthout, January 27, 2015, http://www.truth-out.org/news/item/28763-special-report-money-and-lies-in-anti-human-trafficking-ngos#.

12. Ariane Lange, "'8 Minutes' Wanted to Help a Certain Kind of Sex Worker, Sources Say," BuzzFeed, June 12, 2015, updated June 14, 2015, https://www.buzzfeed.com/arianelange/8-minutes-identities-resources?utm_term=.lk9EXAE63#.kfPLz5L6R.

13. Ariane Lange, "Sex Workers Say A&E Show Lied to Them About Providing Resources and Protecting Their Privacy," BuzzFeed, May 4, 2015, updated May 5, 2015, https://www.buzzfeed.com/arianelange/sex-workers

-say-ae-show-lied-to-them-about-providing-resourc?utm_term=.yxYp8Bp5Y#
.uy8L9MLjP.

14. Cyndee Clay, interview with author, October 16, 2016.

## Chapter Seven: Only Human

1. Joanna Walters, "An 11-Year-Old Reported Being Raped Twice, Wound Up with a Conviction," *Washington Post*, March 12, 2015, https://www.washingtonpost.com/lifestyle/magazine/a-seven-year-search-for-justice/2015/03/12/b1cccb30-abe9-11e4-abe8-e1ef60ca26de_story.html?utm_term=.15b2e76ba3b2.

2. Malika Saada Saar, Rebecca Epstein, Lindsay Rosenthal, and Yasmin Vafa, *The Sexual Abuse to Prison Pipeline: The Girls' Story* (Washington, DC: Human Rights Project for Girls, the Georgetown Law Center on Poverty and Inequality, and Ms. Foundation for Women, 2015), http://rights4girls.org/wp-content/uploads/r4g/2015/02/2015_COP_sexual-abuse_layout_web-1.pdf.

3. Jennifer Katz, Christine Merrilees, Jill C. Hoxmeier, and Marisa Motisi, "White Female Bystanders' Responses to a Black Woman at Risk for Incapacitated Sexual Assault," *Psychology of Women Quarterly*, February 10, 2017. doi:10.1177/0361684316689367.

4. Lasana T. Harris and Susan T. Fiske, "Social Groups That Elicit Disgust Are Differentially Processed in mPFC," *Social Cognitive and Affective Neuroscience* 2, no. 1 (2007): 45–51. doi:10.1093/scan/nsl037.

5. Tonya Garcia, "David Letterman's Rebuttal to Bill O'Reilly's Beyoncé Criticism: What About Miley Cyrus and Justin Bieber?" MadameNoire, March 17, 2014, http://madamenoire.com/410769/david-lettermans-rebuttal-bill-oreillys-beyonce-criticism-miley-cyrus-justin-bieber/.

6. Madeleine Davies, "Bill O'Reilly Thinks Beyoncé Is Bad for Teenage Girls," Jezebel.com, March 11, 2014, http://jezebel.com/bill-oreilly-is-the-latest-to-take-issue-with-beyonce-1541381749.

7. Amanda Marcotte, "Bill O'Reilly Blames Beyoncé for Everything," Slate.com, April 28, 2014, http://www.slate.com/blogs/xx_factor/2014/04/28/bill_o_reilly_to_beyonc_out_of_wedlock_teen_pregnancy_is_all_your_fault.html.

8. Tamara Winfrey Harris, *The Sisters Are Alright: Challenging the Broken Narrative of Black Women in America* (Oakland, CA: Berrett-Koehler, 2015), 8.

9. Urbane Professional, comment on Brittney Cooper, "Single, Saved and Sexin'," Crunk Feminist Collective, February 11, 2011 (8:12 A.M.), accessed

March 19, 2017, https://crunkfeministcollective.wordpress.com/2011/02/03
/single-saved-and-sexin-the-gospel-of-gettin-your-freak-on/#comment-2107.

10. eve, comment on "Thread: Single, Saved, and Sexin?" Holy Culture,
February 11, 2011 (11:38 A.M.), accessed March 19, 2017, http://forum.holy
culture.net/showthread.php?49846-Single-Saved-and-Sexin.

11. Winfrey Harris, *Sisters Are Alright*, 15.

12. Brittney Cooper, "Disrespectability Politics: On Jay-Z's Bitch,
Beyoncé's 'Fly' Ass, and Black Girl Blue," Crunk Feminist Collective, January 19, 2012, https://crunkfeministcollective.wordpress.com/2012/01/19
/disrespectability-politics-on-jay-zs-bitch-beyonces-fly-ass-and-black-girl-blue/.

13. Hallie Levine, "The Vulnerable Group Sex Ed Completely Ignores—
& Why That's So Dangerous," Refinery 29, December 1, 2016, http://www
.refinery29.com/2016/12/131205/intellectual-disabilities-sexual-assault
-statistics-sex-education.

14. Heather Corinna, interview with author, May 16, 2016.

15. "A Survey of LGBT Americans," Pew Research Center, June 13, 2013,
http://www.pewsocialtrends.org/2013/06/13/a-survey-of-lgbt-americans/.

16. *Health Disparities among Bisexual People* (Washington, DC: Human
Rights Campaign, September 2015), http://hrc-assets.s3-website-us-east-1
.amazonaws.com//files/assets/resources/HRC-BiHealthBrief.pdf.

17. "Jian Ghomeshi Verdict: Read Justice Horkins's Full Decision in the
Sexual Assault and Choking Trial," *National Post*, March 24, 2016, http://
news.nationalpost.com/news/canada/jian-ghomeshi-verdict-read-justice
-horkinss-full-decision-in-the-sexual-assault-and-choking-trial.

18. Jaclyn Friedman, "What We Talk about When We Talk about
Rape," *The American Prospect*, December 9, 2010, http://prospect.org/article
/what-we-talk-about-when-we-talk-about-rape-0.

19. David Lisak and Paul M. Miller, "Repeat Rape and Multiple Offend-
ing among Undetected Rapists," *Violence and Victims* 17, no. 1 (2002): 73–84.

20. M. C. Black, K. C. Basile, M. J. Breiding, S. G. Smith, M. L. Walters,
M. T. Merrick, J. Chen, and M. R. Stevens, *The National Intimate Partner
and Sexual Violence Survey (NISVS): 2010 Summary Report* (Atlanta, GA:
National Center for Injury Prevention and Control, Centers for Disease
Control and Prevention, 2011).

21. Newton D. Mereness, ed., *Travels in the American Colonies* (New
York: Macmillan, 1916).

22. Antonio J. Waring, ed., *Laws of the Creek Nation* (Athens: University
of Georgia Press, 1960), 24.

23. Sarah Deer, *The Beginning and End of Rape* (Minneapolis: University
of Minnesota Press, 2015), chap. 3, page 6.

24. Ibid., chap. 5, page 18.

25. Scott Keyes, "Top GOP Senator: Native American Juries Are Incapable of Trying White People Fairly," ThinkProgress, February 21, 2013, https:// thinkprogress.org/top-gop-senator-native-american-juries-are-incapable-of -trying-white-people-fairly-c399c20454cd#.p1gen0lgt.

26. Amnesty International, *Maze of Injustice: The Failure to Protect Indigenous Women from Sexual Violence in the USA* (New York: Amnesty International, 2007), http://www.amnestyusa.org/pdfs/mazeofinjustice.pdf.

27. Deer, *Beginning and End of Rape*, chap. 8, page 18.

28. *Free to Be You and Me* is a record album, with accompanying illustrated book (and subsequently a television special), released in 1972. It featured witty songs and skits, sung by celebrities of the day, all with the basic message that gender stereotypes are bunk and that boys and girls can both be and do however they please. It was enormously popular, and for many Gen Xers like Deer and myself, quite formative.

29. Deer, *Beginning and End of Rape*, chap. 8, page 30.

## Chapter Eight: How to Build a Better Man

1. Soraya Chemaly, "Why Are We Deliberately Keeping Boys Ignorant About Sexism?" Role Reboot, September 6, 2016, http://www.role reboot.org/culture-and-politics/details/2016-09-deliberately-keeping-boys -ignorant-sexism/.

2. Dave Hon, "Why I'll Never Date a Feminist," *News-Press Now,* September 7, 2016, http://www.newspressnow.com/josephine/why-i-ll-never -date-a-feminist/article_c694161d-7e44-5237-9452-4465e82670e0.html.

3. Catey Hill, "Why Men Are Threatened by Smart Women," Market Watch, October 25, 2015, http://www.marketwatch.com/story/why-smart -women-may-threaten-your-manhood-2015-10-16.

4. *The Shriver Report Snapshot: An Insight into the 21st Century Man: Groundbreaking New Survey Cracks Old Stereotypes of Masculinity* (Shriver Media, April 24, 2015), http://www.shrivermedia.com/wp-content /uploads/2016/05/FINAL-Shriver-Report-Snapshot-Press-Release.pdf.

5. Dillon Cheverere, "ΦKT Member from Georgia Tech Sends Rapiest Email Ever—'Let Them Grind against Your Dick,'" Total Frat Move, October 7, 2013, http://totalfratmove.com/%CE%A6kt-member-from-georgia-tech -sends-rapiest-email-ever/.

6. Danielle DeCourcey, "This Photo Is Raising a Debate About Toxic Masculinity," attn:, September 8, 2016, http://www.attn.com/stories/11249 /men-facebook-are-uncomfortable-father-and-son-photo.

7. Alex Krasodomski-Jones, "New Demos Study Reveals Scale of Social Media Misogyny," Centre for the Analysis of Social Media at Demos, May 2016, https://www.demos.co.uk/press-release/staggering-scale-of-social-media-misogyny-mapped-in-new-demos-study/.

8. James Dunn, "Playboy Model Who Mocked Pensioner's Body at the Gym Is Set to Face Charges After Police Finally Succeed in Tracking Down the Victim," *Daily Mail*, September 5, 2016, http://www.daily mail.co.uk/news/article-3774287/Playboy-model-mocked-pensioner-s-body-gym-set-face-charges-police-finally-succeed-tracking-victim.html?ito=social-facebook.

9. Clover Hope, "Classmate Expelled for Vaping Says *Dora the Explorer* Actress Called Her a 'Pussy,'" Jezebel, July 14, 2016, http://jezebel.com/classmate-expelled-for-vaping-says-dora-the-explorer-ac-1783686108.

10. Y. Joel Wong, Moon-Ho Ringo Ho, Shu-Yi Wang, and I. S. Keino Miller, "Meta-Analyses of the Relationship between Conformity to Masculine Norms and Mental Health–Related Outcomes," *Journal of Counseling Psychology* 64, no. 1 (January 2017): 80–93.

11. Karen B. K. Chan, "The New Sex Education: Lessons from Masculinity," Sexology International, https://sexologyinternational.com/the-new-sex-education-lessons-from-masculinity/.

12. Lizzy Acker, "Oregon High School Athletes Rep Feminism in the Locker Room," *Oregon Live*, October 14, 2016, http://www.oregonlive.com/trending/2016/10/oregon_high_school_athletes_re.html.

13. Anna Speigel, "DC Is Getting an All-Male Burlesque Brunch," *Washingtonian*, August 26, 2016, https://www.washingtonian.com/2016/08/26/dc-is-getting-an-all-male-burlesque-brunch/.

14. Jennifer Keller, Benjamin O. Mboya, Jake Sinclair, Oscar W. Githua, Munyae Mulinge, Lou Bergholz, Lee Paiva, Neville H. Golden, and Cynthia Kapphahn, "A 6-Week School Curriculum Improves Boys' Attitudes and Behaviors Related to Gender-Based Violence in Kenya," *Journal of Interpersonal Violence* 32, no. 4 (June 2015): 535–557.

15. The Cut, "An Exhaustive List of the Allegations Women Have Made Against Donald Trump," *New York Magazine*, October 27, 2016, http://nymag.com/thecut/2016/10/all-the-women-accusing-trump-of-rape-sexual-assault.html.

16. Gabriel Sherman, "The Revenge of Roger's Angels," *New York Magazine*, September 2, 2016, http://nymag.com/daily/intelligencer/2016/09/how-fox-news-women-took-down-roger-ailes.html.

17. David Reby, Florence Levréro, Erik Gustafsson, and Nicolas Mathevon, "Sex Stereotypes Influence Adults' Perception of Babies' Cries,"

*BMC Psychology.* Published electronically April 14, 2016. doi:10.1186/s40359 -016-0123-6.

18. Niobe Way, Jessica Cressen, Samuel Bodian, Justin Preston, Joseph Nelson, and Diane Hughes, "'It Might Be Nice to Be a Girl . . . Then You Wouldn't Have to Be Emotionless': Boys' Resistance to Norms of Masculinity during Adolescence," *Psychology of Men & Masculinity* 15, no. 3 (2014): 241.

19. D. L. Espelage, S. Low, J. R. Polanin, and E. C. Brown, "The Impact of a Middle School Program to Reduce Aggression, Victimization, and Sexual Violence," *Journal of Adolescent Health* 53, no. 2 (2013): 180–186.

## Chapter Nine: Students of Desire

1. Richard Campbell, *Structure Fires in Educational Properties* (Quincy, MA: National Fire Protection Association, January 2016), http:// www.nfpa.org/news-and-research/fire-statistics-and-reports/fire-statistics /fires-by-property-type/educational/structure-fires-in-educational-properties.

2. Lawrence A. Greenfeld, *Sex Offenses and Offenders* (Washington, DC: Department of Justice, Office of Justice Programs, Bureau of Justice Statistics, February 1997), https://bjs.gov/content/pub/pdf/SOO.PDF.

3. "Sex and HIV Education," Guttmacher Institute, updated April 1, 2017, accessed March 19, 2017, https://www.guttmacher.org/sites/default/files/pdfs /spibs/spib_SE.pdf.

4. "Template:Sex Education Disputes 2016," *Ballotpedia*, accessed March 19, 2017, https://ballotpedia.org/Template:Sex_education_disputes_2016.

5. Amanda Bohman, "School Board Nixes Three Sites for Sex Ed Classes," *Daily News-Miner*, October 19, 2016, http://www.newsminer.com/news /education/school-board-nixes-three-sites-for-sex-ed-classes/article_24868842 -95d5-11e6-b847-dff93b6c2619.html.

6. Zewditu Demissie, Nancy D. Brener, Tim McManus, Shari L. Shanklin, Joseph Hawkins, and Laura Kann, *School Health Profiles 2014* (Atlanta: US Department of Health and Human Services, Centers for Disease Control and Prevention, 2015), accessed March 19, 2017, http://www.cdc.gov /healthyyouth/data/profiles/pdf/2014/2014_profiles_report.pdf.

7. Heather R. Hlavka, "Normalizing Sexual Violence," *Gender & Society* 28, no. 3 (2014): 337–358.

8. Katie J. M. Baker, "Sent Home from Middle School After Reporting a Rape," BuzzFeed, March 14, 2016, https://www.buzzfeed.com/katiejmbaker /sent-home-from-middle-school-after-reporting-a-rape?utm_term=.fw Qr0zy9p#.yn9lOmx2X.

9. Gabby Bess, "Teen Says She Was Sexually Assaulted in School—Then Suspended for Being 'Lewd,'" *Broadly*, June 13, 2016, https://broadly .vice.com/en_us/article/teen-says-she-was-sexually-assaulted-in-schoolthen -suspended-for-being-lewd.

10. Sandy Banks, "Teacher's Protest of Tasteless T-Shirt Creates a Teachable Moment," *Los Angeles Times*, September 8, 2014, http://www.latimes.com /local/la-me-0909-banks-sexist-shirts-20140909-column.html.

11. National Women's Law Center, *Let Her Learn: A Toolkit to Stop School Push Out for Girls of Color* (Washington, DC: National Women's Law Center, 2016), https://nwlc.org/wp-content/uploads/2016/11/final_nwlc _NOVO2016Toolkit.pdf.

12. Title IX of the Education Amendments of 1972 is best known for mandating equal funding and support for men's and women's sports but actually mandates that all educational institutions that receive federal funding provide equal educational opportunity to everyone, regardless of gender.

13. Kathleen A. Bogle, *Hooking Up: Sex, Dating, and Relationships on Campus* (New York: New York University Press, 2008).

14. Lisa Wade, *American Hookup: The New Culture of Sex on Campus* (New York: W.W. Norton, 2017).

15. Edward O. Laumann, *The Social Organization of Sexuality: Sexual Practices in the United States* (Chicago: University of Chicago Press, December 15, 2000).

16. Wade, *American Hookup*, 167.

17. "Sexual Assault on Campus," Center for Public Integrity, accessed March 19, 2017, https://www.publicintegrity.org/accountability/education/ sexual-assault-campus.

18. Allie Bidwell, "College Sexual Violence Complaints Up 1,000 Percent in 5 Years," *U.S. News & World Report*, May 15, 2015, http://www.usnews.com /news/blogs/data-mine/2015/05/05/college-title-ix-sexual-violence-complaints -increase-more-than-1-000-percent-in-5-years.

19. Katie J. M. Baker, "Meet the Sexual Assault Adviser Top U.S. Colleges Have on Speed Dial," BuzzFeed, July 28, 2014, accessed March 19, 2017, https://www.buzzfeed.com/katiejmbaker/meet-the-sexual-assault-adviser-top -us-colleges-have-on-spee?utm_term=.nq5aN2eJ4#.hu5roZV7n.

20. N. Bedera and K. Nordmeyer, "'Never Go Out Alone': An Analysis of College Rape Prevention Tips," *Sexuality & Culture* 19 (2015): 533. doi:10.1007/s12119-015-9274-5.

21. C. Ramsey Fahs, "Sexual Assault Report Lambasts Final Clubs," *The Harvard Crimson*, March 9, 2016, http://www.thecrimson.com/article /2016/3/9/report-lambasts-final-clubs/.

22. Justin Wm. Moyer, "Secretive Harvard Club Breaks Silence to Say That Admitting Women Could Increase Sexual Misconduct," *Washington Post*, April 13, 2016, https://www.washingtonpost.com/news/morning-mix/wp/2016/04/13/secretive-harvard-club-breaks-225-years-of-silence-to-say-that-admitting-women-could-increase-sexual-misconduct/.

23. Sarah DeGue, Linda Anne Valle, Melissa K. Holt, Greta M. Massetti, Jennifer L. Matjasko, and Andra Teten Tharp, "A Systematic Review of Primary Prevention Strategies for Sexual Violence Perpetration," *Aggression and Violent Behavior* 19, no. 4 (July–August 2014): 346–362. http://dx.doi.org/10.1016/j.avb.2014.05.004.

24. Ann L. Coker, Heather M. Bush, Patricia G. Cook-Craig, Sarah A. DeGue, Emily R. Clear, Candace J. Brancato, Bonnie S. Fisher, and Eileen A. Recktenwald, "RCT Testing Bystander Effectiveness to Reduce Violence," *American Journal of Preventive Medicine*, March 06, 2017. doi:http://dx.doi.org/10.1016/j.amepre.2017.01.020.

25. Alyson Currey, interview with author, November 14, 2016.

26. Carole Miller, interview with author, November 14, 2016.

27. Tasha Elizarde, "The Power of Understanding Your Body," MTV News, September 13, 2016, http://www.mtv.com/news/2931188/the-power-of-understanding-your-body/.

## Chapter Ten: The Professionals

1. Melissa Gira Grant, "The NYPD Arrests Women for Who They Are and Where They Go—Now They're Fighting Back," *Village Voice*, November 22, 2016, http://www.villagevoice.com/news/the-nypd-arrests-women-for-who-they-are-and-where-they-go-now-theyre-fighting-back-9372920.

2. Carl Hessler Jr., "Bill Cosby Claims Blindness Hinders Defense of Sex Charges," *Montgomery News*, November 3, 2016, http://www.montgomerynews.com/timeschronicle/news/bill-cosby-claims-blindness-hinders-defense-of-sex-charges/article_0810f810-3076-5054-b4e2-6857582f21b0.html; "Fremont Teacher Arrested for Having Sex with Student," KTVU.com, December 1, 2016, http://www.ktvu.com/news/220856642-story.

3. Bianca I. Laureano, "What Do We Expect from a Sexual Attitudes Reassessment Workshop," *Rewire*, September 15, 2010, https://rewire.news/article/2010/09/15/what-expect/.

4. Aida Manduley, interview with author, November 22, 2016.

5. Bianca Palmisano, interview with author, October 25, 2016.

6. Diane E. Hoffmann and Anita J. Tarzian, "The Girl Who Cried Pain: A Bias Against Women in the Treatment of Pain," *Journal of Law, Medicine & Ethics* 29 (2001): 13–27.

7. Olivia Goldhill, "Period Pain Can Be 'Almost as Bad as a Heart Attack.' Why Aren't We Researching How to Treat It?" *Quartz*, February 15, 2016, https://qz.com/611774/period-pain-can-be-as-bad-as-a-heart-attack-so-why -arent-we-researching-how-to-treat-it/.

8. Allyson Herbst, "This Is the Kind of Sexism Women Who Want to Be Doctors Deal with in Med School," *Washington Post*, October 4, 2016, https:// www.washingtonpost.com/posteverything/wp/2016/10/04/this-is-the-kind-of -sexism-women-who-want-to-be-doctors-deal-with-in-med-school/?utm_term =.1c579fbd6314.

9. Lori A. J. Scott-Sheldon and Blair T. Johnson, "Eroticizing Creates Safer Sex: A Research Synthesis," *Journal of Primary Prevention* 27, no. 6 (November 2006): 619–640.

10. Diana Adams, interview with author, May 27, 2015.

## Chapter Eleven: Our Internet, Ourselves

1. Soraya Chemaly, interview with author, October 27, 2016.

2. Andrea Pino, interview with author, November 6, 2016.

3. Soraya Chemaly, interview with author, October 27, 2016.

4. Ibid.

5. Julia Carrie Wong, "From Elon Musk to Tim Cook, Tech Leaders Hardly Follow Women on Twitter," *The Guardian*, October 4, 2016, https:// www.theguardian.com/technology/2016/oct/04/twitter-women-gender-elon -musk-tim-cook?CMP=share_btn_tw.

6. Alex Sherman, Christopher Palmeri, and Sarah Frier, "Disney Dropped Twitter Pursuit Partly over Image," *Bloomberg Technology*, October 17, 2016, https://www.bloomberg.com/news/articles/2016-10-17/disney -said-to-have-dropped-twitter-pursuit-partly-over-image.

# INDEX

on college campuses, 196–197,
200–201
programs for preventing, 200
Roger Ailes, 171–172
training media for proper
reporting, 207–208
transforming into social activism,
112–113
Trump administration's view of,
125
Trump's verbal attacks on women,
122–123
See also campus assaults; rape
Sexual Attitude Reassessment (SAR),
210–211
sexual concordance, 46–48, 50–51
sexual desire and pleasure
decline in younger generations,
68
educating medical professionals
about, 216
responsive and spontaneous
arousal, 44
sex education programs' failure to
teach, 194–195
sexual concordance, 46–51
the hookup culture and,
193–194
treating women as individuals,
51–52
what women want, 44–46
women's difficulty accessing,
87–88
sexual freedom
Ariel Levy conflating
fauxpowerment and real power,
33
male exploitation and cooptation
of women's, 31–32
the myth of, 1–2

sexual harassment
Clarence Thomas's Supreme
Court nomination, 28–30
multiplayer games, 226, 232
online community, 232–234
parental concerns for young girls,
228–229
sexual predators, 195–196
sexual revolution
background and elements of,
16–18
commodification of, 22–23
Hugh Hefner coopting, 19–22
Playboy empire exploiting,
20–21
removing the reason to say 'no' to
sex, 18–19
teen pregnancy, 25
sexuality of homeless women,
142–144
sexualization of girls, 68–69,
120–121
sexually-transmitted diseases, 18, 25
shame
dress codes for girls, 190–191
escorting and, 5–6
See also slut shaming; victim
blaming
shelter system, LGBT youth and, 94
shootings, gender statistics on,
162–163
Shulman, Alix Kates, 19
silencing women, 225–226
Sister Reach, 112–116
*The Sisters Are All Right:
Challenging the Broken
Narrative of Black Women in
America* (Winfrey Harris), 140
SisterSong collective, 35
slavery, 137–138

*Thelma and Louise* (film), 13
Theodores, Matthew, 176, 182, 239
Third Wave Direct Action
    Corporation, 30
Third Wave feminism, 30–31
Thomas, Clarence, 28
Thunder Mountain High School,
    Juneau, Alaska, 183, 187,
    201–204
"Tik Tok" (Ke$ha), 193
Till, Emmett, 124
Tinder, 222
toxic masculinity
    consequences to men, 166–168
    emanating from women, 166
    girls excusing rape behavior,
        180–181
    hostile sexism and, 173–174
    instilling a healthy mindset in
        children, 175–182
    people shoring up, 172
    pro-sex feminists and, 24
    rapists' unwillingness to change
        behavior, 173
    replicating itself, 163–166
    Trump embodying, 170
    *See also* masculinity
Trainor, Meghan, 4
trans individuals
    dehumanizing experiences,
        138–139
    sexual professionals and,
        205–206
    *See also* LGBT individuals
TrenchcoatX, 81–82
Tribal Law and Order Act (2010),
    151
Trump, Donald
    Affordable Care Act, 214–215
    misogynist epithets, 162

attack on foreign nationals, 124
benevolent sexism as response to,
    174
embodying toxic masculinity,
    170
evangelical Christians backing,
    101
humiliating women, 122–123
religious stance, 100
reproductive justice movement,
    39
resistance to, 242
Turner, Brock, 175, 196
Twitter, 123, 165, 231–233

University of Virginia, 207

vagina, structure and function of,
    53–54
*Vagina: A New Biography* (Wolf), 4
vaginismus, 52
Valenti, Jessica, 33–34, 36
values: media gatekeepers, 67–68
Viagra, 87–88
victim blaming
    campus rape, 189–190, 199
    dehumanization of Black women,
        139–141
    girls excusing rape behavior,
        180–181
    Jian Ghomeshi litigation,
        146–147
    policing women's sexuality,
        117–120
    sex workers as victims, 129–130
    sexting, 119–121
    sexual assault, 69, 122
    toxic masculinity, 163–164
    *See also* slut shaming
*Village Voice*, 206